THE
PUMA
YEARS

THE PUMA YEARS

A MEMOIR

YEARS

LAURA COLEMAN

Little
a

"She Unnames Them" by Ursula K. Le Guin was published in the
January 21, 1985, print edition of the *New Yorker* magazine.

Published by Little A, New York
www.apub.com

Amazon, the Amazon logo, and Little A are trademarks of Amazon.com, Inc., or its affiliates.

ISBN-13: 9781542022194 (hardcover)
ISBN-10: 1542022193 (hardcover)
ISBN-13: 9781542022187 (paperback)
ISBN-10: 1542022185 (paperback)

Cover design and illustration by Micaela Alcaino

Interior map by Mapping Specialists, Ltd.

Unless otherwise noted, all photos and illustrations are courtesy of the author.

Printed in the United States of America

First edition

For anyone who has ever loved the parque.
And for Wayra.

None were left now to unname, and yet how close
I felt to them when I saw one of them swim or fly
or trot or crawl across my way or over my skin, or
stalk me in the night, or go along beside me for a
while in the day. They seemed far closer than when
their names had stood between myself and them
like a clear barrier: so close that my fear of them
and their fear of me became one same fear. And
the attraction that many of us felt, the desire to
feel or rub or caress one another's scales or skin or
feathers or fur, taste one another's blood or flesh,
keep one another warm—that attraction was now
all one with the fear, and the hunter could not be
told from the hunted, nor the eater from the food.

—Ursula K. Le Guin, "She Unnames Them"

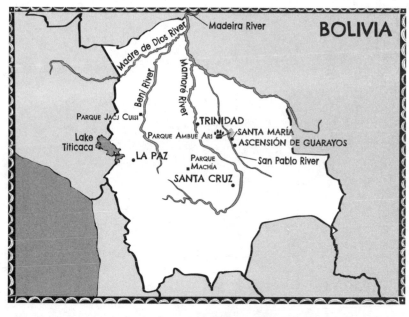

BOLIVIA

Madeira River
Madre de Dios River
Beni River
Mamoré River
Parque Jacj Cuisi
Lake Titicaca
Parque Ambue Ari
TRINIDAD
SANTA MARÍA
ASCENSIÓN DE GUARAYOS
LA PAZ
Parque Machía
San Pablo River
SANTA CRUZ

VENEZUELA
GUYANA
SURINAME
FRENCH GUIANA
COLOMBIA
ECUADOR
Amazon River
PERU
BRAZIL
BOLIVIA

Amazon rainforest
Forest fires 2019 (approximation)

AUTHOR'S NOTE

Pumas are known by many names. Perhaps because they once ranged across the full expanse of the Americas, from Canada to the edges of Tierra del Fuego. Florida panther, cougar, mountain lion, catamount, painter, mountain screamer, red tiger, cuguacuarana, ghost cat . . . It is alleged that they have over eighty recorded names, more than any other animal. But for me, in Bolivia, I knew them simply as "puma" (pronounced *poo-ma*).

Most of the names in this book have been changed. Some of the characters are composites, and some timelines and events have been altered to fit within a reasonably sized book, although most are as I remember them. The organisation and the place, I have not changed. Comunidad Inti Wara Yassi is a Bolivian NGO, dedicated to offering victims of wildlife trafficking a second opportunity in life. The sanctuary is Ambue Ari. Both are kept alive by people with more strength than it's possible to put into words.

PART ONE

It is 2007 and I'm twenty-four years old. I am not small, although not really large either. About five foot seven, with a crooked nose, boobs that give me backache and feet that flap. I am a bit lost, for no reason I understand. I've been single most of my life. I eat and smoke when I'm nervous, and I'm nervous a lot. My parents are psychologists. I have a sister and two brothers, all very successful. I'm from England and I'm an art history graduate who doesn't know that monkeys can make jokes or be depressed. I don't know what a puma looks like.

"Gringa. ¡Aquí!"

We've been rumbling along in a rickety bus for I don't know how long, five hours perhaps.

I rub my sleeve against the cracked window and peer through a streak in the condensation. I see only jungle.

"¿En serio?" I can't keep the fear out of my voice.

"¡Sí! El parque."

The woman next to me hauls her child off my lap, and a man—already climbing over the rows of seats, over other squashed passengers, chickens, babies, some kind of exotic bird and sacks of rice—lays claim to my precious inches of space. Then I'm standing by myself on an empty, straight road in the middle of the Bolivian Amazon, watching the bus lights fade. There's a soft haze that makes the thin, broken tarmac float like water. Tall grasses and trees, green, purple, orange and gold, overhang the banks. There are leaves of every shade until everything seems to melt into a looming vastness. It smells hot, as if the air is too tight, and I struggle to breathe. The sky is blue but the edges are already turning reddish gold. It'll be night soon. From inside the bus, I'd thought there would be a resounding silence out here, but I was wrong. The jungle hums, speaking no language I've heard before.

I slap at a mosquito on my neck and my hand comes back bloody. Another buzzes around my ear. I wave my arms, whimpering, spinning on the spot. The jungle is everywhere and, as I turn and see a monkey sitting on a signpost, I leap back with a yelp. He's the size of a small child, hunched, with thick ginger fur. The signpost clearly says NO MONKEYS ON THE ROAD! in bright-red letters. He just stares at me. *Yeah, so. What are you going to do about it?* I'm not going to do anything. It's about to get dark and I'm on my own in the jungle. I feel faint. Then I hear something else over the jungle hum. It's a terrible rumbling, and a huge black pig suddenly catapults out of the undergrowth. She raises her head—a red bra clasped between her teeth—and locks eyes with me. I'm about to turn and run when a man bursts out after her, pulling sticks from his hair.

"Panchita!"

The pig spins and hurtles away. I hear the echo of her hooves until the green haze sucks her up and she is gone.

There's a forest—not even a forest, a small, scraggly wood—where I grew up. Once when I was eight, I tried to spend the night in it. My dad walked me there and left me, as requested. Later I found out that he didn't leave at all, he settled himself around the corner with a packet of biscuits and a flask of hot tea. But I'd curled up in my sleeping bag with the alien scent of mud and moss in my nose, the hot thrill of fear coursing through my blood. I lasted ten minutes before I ran back home crying, my sleeping bag trailing under my arm, firm in the belief that the trees that crackled and brushed above my head were full of monsters.

"¡Bienvenidos!" The man in front of me grins cheerfully. "Agustino. Soy el veterinario aquí." He looks me up and down as if he's not at all surprised to see me here on this road with this monkey, the acrid scent of a disappearing pig still in the air. As if random foreigners turn up here all the time to be greeted by such creatures. I don't. I don't turn up in places like this.

Backpacking in Bolivia for three months was meant to give me the perspective I needed after quitting the latest in a long string of jobs. I felt like I'd been given a map of what my life should be, but I was off course. Too many jobs I'd quit, hoping each one would point me to the path of success. This last one, marketing at a high-profile travel company, had been the final straw. Backpacking would sort me out, surely. I planned to return transformed, like a millennial Elizabeth Gilbert, a person who rides roller coasters with arms in the air, makes good decisions, goes on dates with abandon, and knows what she wants to do with her life. A person who loves office parties, who doesn't binge peanut butter at midnight on the floor of the kitchen and then can't leave the house because she can't find anything to wear that doesn't make her look fat. Who turns up on the side of the road in a random place and doesn't worry about it. Who can be a girlfriend and will at some point be a wife, a mother, and a successful career woman. Everything that I am not, but think I want to be.

But it's two months into my trip, and I'm tired of the shared dorm rooms that stink of beer and cold vomit. I'm still shy of the fellow backpackers who try to make friends and I struggle with the contrived tourist sites that sell llama steaks for more than the cost of a flight. It was at one of these that I overheard someone saying that if you went north, you could hitch a ride on a local boat off the path of the Lonely Planet. You could swing in a hammock, watch pink river dolphins and drink coconut milk. That sounded nice, I thought. So north I went and spent two weeks sitting on a muddy riverbank. Waiting for a boat that never came. Sunburnt, lonely, bloated from all the empanadas, washed out by the rains, I finally left to find an internet café where I could change my flight. I was giving up. I wanted to go home. But it was in that internet café, where—over cold pizza, sweaty beer and a pack of cigarettes—I picked up a flyer for a Bolivian animal welfare charity with a cheerful-looking monkey on the front. It said they took volunteers. So for no reason other than a desperate lack of purpose, and my inner voice goading me not to give up quite yet, here I am. I don't even know what this place is, other than that there are monkeys and they're supposed to look cheerful.

This monkey does not look cheerful. He's crawling towards us, grabbing Agustino's trousers and pulling himself up by the seams until he's cradled morosely in the man's arms. I'd thought the vet was around my age but now I'm not sure. He's got lines around his eyes, which are dark brown and gentle, and black hair that is wild and unkempt. He's short, a little overweight, with a round face that I can't help but like. He reaches inside his jacket and pulls out a piece of cheese. The monkey howls with delight, grabs the cheese and stuffs it into his mouth. Agustino looks at me sheepishly. He kisses the top of the monkey's furry head. "Coco not meant to have cheese, but only thing that get him off road. It is too dangerous for him here. Too many cars."

I gaze back and forth down the empty road, and nod weakly. The threat of too many cars seems ridiculous. We are at the end of the universe, and even the tiny, local bus that I arrived on is a distant memory.

"Come!" Agustino sets off at a quick trot, swerving onto a thin, winding path. Coco climbs up to hang tightly around Agustino's shoulders. As he bobs up and down, small hairy fingers gripping Agustino's collar, he blows a long, loud, and deeply depressed raspberry.

"Yeah," I mutter under my breath, "you and me both."

It's heavy and humid, the air hazy as we vanish, just like the pig did, under the canopy. I trot to catch up, my rucksack slamming against my shoulder blades. I repeatedly brush my hands across my face as *things* buzz up my nose, into my mouth and my ears. Branches, sharp and insistent, catch my hair, bloody my skin. The track is dark. I can hear not just the pitch of mosquitoes but birds too, bugs and crickets, something ominously large in the undergrowth. The noises close in and I can smell dirt, damp, rot.

We walk maybe five minutes, although it feels like much more, before Agustino finally stops and turns.

"Welcome to el parque!"

We've come out on the edge of a clearing, surrounded by huts and dilapidated buildings. A few people mill about, some locals, some foreigners, a splatter of mud, clothes and gumboots thick with dirt. Agustino starts waving his arms and calling, high-pitched and cheerful, "Samita!"

A girl peels off from the others and starts towards us. She, also, is carrying a monkey. He is a twin to Coco, although where Coco has an impressive red beard, this one has no beard at all, as if it's been chopped off around his chin. As soon as the girl is close enough, Coco launches off Agustino. Somehow the girl manages to catch him in her stride and, as the two monkeys jostle jealously for space, grunting angrily at each other, she doesn't break pace. She just leans forwards, holding out her hand.

"I'm Samantha. Sammie."

The smell coming off her is phenomenal.

I'm making a broad assessment. My situation is alarming. The monkeys are wondrous, but . . . there's an overwhelming smell, a bit like a wet T-shirt that's been wrapped in fish and left to fester in forty-degree heat. And there are other animals, too. The monstrous pig is spread-eagled across the mud, snoring, oblivious to the people having to step over her. I know it's the same pig because the lacy bra is next to her like bounty. There's a racoon-type creature making a loud, aggressive beeping noise, his tail at a right angle to the ground, working hard to dig underneath the door of one of the buildings. It's also the way the jungle just hangs over everything, shutting out any semblance of light or space. I haven't come far from the road. The sky was turning red there, now I cannot see the sky. The air is dark and dusky—as if I could brush my arm through it and it might move like smoke.

"I . . . uh . . . ," I mumble.

Sammie raises her eyebrows. She's a foreigner, like me—American, I think. She's about my age. She's short and a little stout. I think she might be pretty. It's hard to tell. The mud is everywhere, caked into her thick clumps of hair, her clothes, her skin. There's a rusty, wicked-looking machete hanging from her belt. She rubs sweat off her forehead with her stale, wet sleeve and laughs. She's got a manic laugh. It reverberates off the trees, making her seem bigger than she is.

"Don't worry," she tells me.

"I'm not worried," I say quickly. It's a lie. I'm very worried.

"Do you have a headlamp?" she says over her shoulder as she starts to walk, beckoning for me to follow. "We've got no electricity, no hot water."

What do these people do, I wonder frantically, without electricity and hot water?

The two monkeys are clinging to her neck, and they are eyeing me dubiously.

"La Paz'll be your dorm," she says, helping me put down my ruck-sack by a long brick building that might have been, at some point, white. There are four doors, peeling with old green paint, and hung with signs. SANTA CRUZ. LA PAZ. BENI. POTOSÍ.

"La Paz is a nice one," she continues as I rummage for my torch. "Only three people in there at the moment. Showers." She points to a wooden shack just visible under the trees. "Flushing toilets, but don't use them if you know what's good for you." She makes air quotes around the word *flushing*, and Coco grunts as if in agreement. She looks down at him affectionately. I wonder how long she's been here. Years? It said two weeks was the minimum on the flyer . . .

"We call this the patio." She optimistically indicates the clearing, which is more of a muddy sort of crossroads, the pathways lined with loose brickwork. In the centre are a few sad-looking benches and a lopsided standing tap. Sammie points off to the side. "Comedor, where we eat." A rectangular wooden construction, with no walls, just green netting, presumably to keep out the bugs. Candles have been lit inside, spreading dancing shadows across the ground.

"Behind the dorms is Agustino's clinic," Sammie continues. "If you get injured, go there."

"To the *vet*?"

"Agustino's a whizz with a scalpel." Sammie laughs, loudly. I flinch. Just one night, I say to myself. I just need to survive one night. I can leave in the morning.

"If I shouldn't use the flushing toilet . . . where should I . . . um . . ." I trail off, blushing red as the monkeys' fur.

She turns and points off into the darkness. "Long drop." Then, leaning against the wall for balance, she casually lifts one of her gum-boots, tilts it upside down, and a long stream of brown water pours out onto the ground. I stare at it, horrified.

She winks impishly. "Swamp."

My mouth falls open. "Swamp?"

Then, with a wave, she just wanders off. The monkeys turn their heads to watch me, their eyes shining in the now near-pitch darkness. The gloom is so thick it's like I've been swallowed. For a moment, I stand alone in the screaming darkness. In the mass of whirrs and pulses and beats, I cannot quite work out what to do. Then my stomach makes an unpleasant lurch and, with little option, I set off recklessly down the path-not-really-a-path that Sammie indicated, a slightly less-dark space between other dark spaces in the trees. My torch beam hits branches, making them shine white like ribs, like dead bodies stacked and slotted on top of each other.

Within a few minutes, I'm surrounded on all sides by thick foliage. The "path" is a dead end, the long drop a shed at the end of it. I drag open the rickety door, my heart thudding, pull down my jeans and hover over the cracked seat of what is less toilet, more infinity hole. The smell is so bad I gag. There's a noisy plop as what I expunge hits something soupy, far below. My knees hit the back of the door and I read the message that's been scrawled on it. *El lugar perfecto para meditar, pensar, soñar, amar, compartir, escuchar, hablar y estar.* This is the perfect place to meditate, think, dream, love, share, listen, talk and be. I snort. Someone has a sense of humour. I think my relationship with insects is pretty normal. I don't like them. I once locked my bedroom door and slept on the sofa for a week because a house spider crawled across my pillow. But now on the edge of this seat is a mass of grey cobwebs. Lines of termites etch the walls. I turn, not meaning to, but I can't stop myself. I look down the hole. There's movement. Writhing. Shit and maggots. I scream. A spider the size of a teacup is crawling lazily up the seat, black with yellow fangs.

I'm out the door, my jeans not even done up. When I get back to the patio, thankfully there's no one there to watch me pant, folded over painfully as I nurse a stitch in my side. It brings back memories of school, when we'd be made to run desperate laps around the block, high-vis vests shining stark against the wintry evenings. It was an ambitious all-girls school, and these runs were a chance for us to assess who was at the highest level of Darwinian survival of the fittest—training for later, when we'd compete again as lawyers, doctors, city folk, commuters with soft hands and softer briefcases. Even then, I knew this type of competition might not be for me. I kept on trying though, going round and round, my face the colour of a tomato and stitches searing up my side, as girls giggled and the cold English damp got into my bones.

Catching my breath, I gaze into the bright candlelight of the comedor. People are laughing, eating dinner. The smell of fried garlic makes my mouth water, but I'm exhausted, sweaty and my hair . . . I don't even want to think about what my hair looks like.

I find the door to La Paz. There are candle stubs on the floor. When I light one, eerie shadows flutter across the cobwebbed brick. I don't know what time it is, probably not much later than seven. The dorm holds three bunks, six beds in all, with just one tiny window at the back. There's stuff everywhere: rucksacks, shoes, old boots, ropes between the beds acting as washing lines. Wet clothes draped along them, giving the impression of a mouldy, damp cave. I inspect an empty top bunk and find that the mattress is hay, hard and unforgiving, sheathed in plastic. Well, that's not going to be sweaty at all, I think with a desperate laugh. There's no sheet but there is a mosquito net that even with a cursory glance reveals rips and bloodstains. The implications of this are too horrific. I launch myself up fully clothed. Then, even though it's too early and I'm so hot I could puke and I haven't brushed my teeth, I just pull my sleeping bag over my head, close my eyes and pray that no one—and no thing—notices me.

When I wake up, something is roaring. There's a lion in my room. I jolt upright, hitting my head on the beams. Light is creeping through the green window netting. Where am I? What the . . .

There's a monkey by my feet. It's not a lion. I'm light-headed with a moment's relief, then I realise: there's a *monkey* by my feet. On my sleeping bag! He's the one without the beard, and he still doesn't look happy, not happy at all! I edge away as quickly as I can until I'm smushed against the wall. I don't want to touch anything. Not the monkey, nor the mosquito net, the cobwebbed brick, the shiny rock-hard, lumpy mattress that's slick with my sweat, probably seething with bed bugs,

fleas. The monkey pauses. His brown eyes are full—pity, anger, misery
. . . I can't tell. He takes another breath, puffs out his chest and lets loose
another gigantic howl. I put my hands over my ears.

"Don't worry. It's just his morning ritual. He likes to meet the new
girls."

A head pops up. Bushy curls, a strawberry-blond beard, rugby player's neck. The face is startlingly pale, covered in freckles. Grey-blue eyes.
English with a Mancunian accent. He reaches out to give the monkey
a stroke, smiling. The skin around his eyes crinkles.

"Hola Faustino," he whispers.

"He should *not* be *in here*!"

We all jump. I peer through my net. In the middle of the room, a
girl has her hands on her hips. Dark curls cascade from the top of her
head, and her face is scarlet.

"Thomas!" She glares at the guy. "Get that monkey out of here. Damn
it Tom." She points her finger accusingly at all of us, as if for some reason
this is my fault too. The monkey just sticks his tongue out at her. She lets
out a loud exclamation of disgust, then runs over to a backpack leaning
against the wall and starts rummaging aggressively. Her accent is thick,
Eastern European, I think. "If he's been through my things again—"

"He hasn't, Katarina. He's not a thief, are you Foz?"

The monkey looks at Tom pathetically. Then he crawls into Tom's
arms, and they both shoot the girl baleful looks as they leave the room,
the door rattling as it closes behind them.

"Where *is* it?" Clothes are flying now.

"What have you lost?" I peek out from under my net.

The girl peers up at me, still scowling. "Oh, you're alive. We weren't
sure." I blush as she goes back to the pile of clothes. "My bra. He's taken
my fucking bra again."

"There was a pig yesterday. It had a bra. A red one." I laugh, suddenly aware of how stupid this sounds. But I want her to forgive me for
the monkey intrusion. Her large brown eyes expand.

"*Panchita?*"

And before I can say anything else, she's hurtling out the door. Her accusatory yells spread across the patio. I lie back down, looking up into the rafters. I hope I haven't made a massive mistake. The last thing I want to do is piss off that pig.

I stand on the patio. It's barely six thirty and I'm surrounded by a hive of activity. I wish fervently that, instead of spending my youth day-dreaming and smoking behind the gym, I'd actually learnt something useful, like woodwork or how to scale trees with just my wits. Everyone here looks seamless, like they've been in the jungle their whole lives. I stare at them all, awed. There are a mixture of ages and nationalities, more Bolivians than foreigners, and children too—I see at least five. One chubby-cheeked boy who looks no more than eleven is carrying the racoon creature in his arms—Teanji, I've heard someone call him. The racoon, not the boy. They are having some kind of conversation, conducted in beeps.

In the daylight, I cannot help but notice that camp looks worse than it did last night. Strange, busy animals wander around. Squirrels, guinea-pig-rats with spots arranged in lines, like racing stripes, that pig again—although I'm not sure anymore if it is a pig . . . It's more of a massive tropical pig-boar hybrid. There are roughly maintained trails that lead off into the forest, and I feel a sort of pressing at the back of my neck where the trees lean in. Old tools, planks and rusty fencing are knotted among mud, loose bricks, decaying leaves, crumbling cement, and puddles. It looks as if there's been some attempt to make the place cheery—the dorm building was once decorated with bright pictures of jungle creatures, but now it's more peeling paint and cobwebs than toucans and parrots. When I look closely, I see thousands of tiny pink eggs nestled in the grout. I give an involuntary shudder, trying not to imagine what kinds of heartbeats are gestating in those eggs. Everything smells overwhelmingly of wet earth and rotting fruit.

"Laura?"

I turn. A woman is approaching. She's Bolivian, short with a round face framed with thickly plaited black hair, reaching almost to her waist. She walks with a slouch and there are exhaustion lines around her dark eyes. She wears jeans, gumboots, a thick shirt and a battered old cowboy hat. She's carrying a backpack, from which hangs a machete, ropes, carabiners, buckets. The way she walks is an attack, swinging her arms as if she's pushing the air out of the way. I feel as if I have to step backwards to give her room. And I do, backing up against the door of La Paz. But then she's there, next to me, and she's smiling. When she smiles, the lines on her face smooth, her skin gleams and suddenly I want to step forwards, not back.

"Vamos," she says briskly.

She's already walking and I'm behind her, following through the netted door of the comedor, my hand opening as she passes me a steaming mug of coffee, my body folding obediently onto a bench, which wobbles. I have to grip the table for balance. She sits across from me and places her hands palm down on the cracked wood between us. Her hands are criss-crossed with scars.

The room is . . . quaint. There are three long tables, capable of taking perhaps thirty people at a squeeze, although now it's only us. The walls are brick until they just stop, at about waist height, replaced by that green netting. The floor is compacted dirt, the roof is made of panels of sheet metal. It feels as if we aren't really in a room at all. The two red monkeys are sitting on a low overhanging vine just outside, eyeballing me hard. Coco and Faustino.

I look down at my coffee, wrapping my fingers around the heat of the old plastic mug. I don't drink coffee. It makes my atoms rattle. But I hold on to my coffee as if my life depends on it, because I know what this is. I know what this smells like. This is normal.

"¿Hablas español?" The woman's voice is low, as if she's pitching to someone else, someone I can't see. I think she's probably in her thirties. Late thirties, perhaps.

I grimace, making a so-so sign with my hand. "Más o menos."

She nods. "Entonces mi nombre es Mila." She switches to heavily accented English. "I am in charge of this parque, with our vet, Agustino. You've met him, I think?"

I nod rapidly.

"We look after wild animals rescued from the illegal pet trade. Monos, aves, chanchos, tapires, gatos—"

"Gatos?" I stop her. Cats? I wonder if there are any dogs too. This cheers me up. I like dogs. But as I look around outside, having forgotten the word in Spanish, all I see are those monkeys. Some people have brightly coloured birds on their shoulders. I start when I see a boy with what seems to be a baby anaconda around his neck.

"Sí. We have sixteen cats. Jaguars, ocelots. And pumas."

I stare at her dumbly. Right. Not house cats, then.

"I have a puma you can work with."

"A *puma*?"

She nods. "But if you want this, you must commit to a month. Minimum thirty days, for work with a puma." Then she hesitates, staring at me hard. I pull at my collar anxiously, looking down at her scarred hands. "If not, you may stay shorter. Two weeks. Work with birds, monkeys."

I barely hear anything after the word *puma,* though. I'm not quite sure what a puma is. I think it must be large, wild and powerful. Goose bumps come up on my arms, despite the heat. The hard flecks around Mila's irises are like the swirls in a tiger's eye. I'm not sure if I'm the sort of person she wants working with something large and wild and powerful. I've got weak ankles. Maybe I should just be getting my stuff. Maybe I should hail down a bus, or call a taxi? Can I, call a taxi?

Her eyes rake over me.

"This puma is called Wayra."

I press hard on the edges of my mug. When I don't manage to say anything, it looks like she's about to stand up. She's realised that yes, actually this girl isn't right for this.

I look around desperately. My eyes land on the monkeys. Could I, be right for this? The one without the beard, the one that was in my bed, has The Bra. He's clutching it in one hand, hairy fingers wrapped around the straps. My mouth opens and closes. The thief! Slyly, he raises it to his nose and takes a long, deep sniff before pushing it at Coco, who stares, askance. Faustino grunts, forcing Coco to pick it up. Coco scales the roof, shoving The Bra into a hole in the wall before sliding back down, guilt written all over his face.

A *puma*. Me.

I find that I'm nodding, a little dazed. It's the exhaustion, the heat, those damned monkeys . . . But Mila's smile, when she looks back at me and sees me nodding, is incandescent.

One of my happiest memories is curling up with my sister on our parents' bed and tracing the golden vines across the cover of Mum's old, weighty copy of *The Lord of the Rings*. The darkness would be close outside the curtains, but we were safe. One night, Mum would read to us, the next, Dad would take over as the hobbits made their slow, tantalising, terrifying progress across Middle-earth. And later, as I grew up, I continued to inhale fantasy, sci-fi . . . I couldn't get enough of dark forests, deep oceans and howling mountain peaks. But a big part of the fun was knowing that I was safe at home.

I sit there, nodding and smiling like a fool to Mila across the table—desperate to please. And I think about what I'll be going home to in a month. All those crushing jobs I've quit. The first wedding invites have started arriving, from all the girls I was asked to compete with at school. I'm not even dating unless you count the "friends" I've been hooking up with, once in a blue moon, drunkenly and in secret. Is it me who wants to keep it a secret, or them? I'm not even sure. Was it at school where I learnt my go-to survival technique?

Smile when you get your arse pinched, your breasts poked, your fat laughed at. Sometimes it feels as if I've been smiling for so long, I do it in my sleep. Oh, person I thought was my boyfriend—you've been dating someone else for the last month? Not a problem. Smile. Parents—you're getting a divorce? That's a curveball. Not to worry though, if you're unhappy. Smile. Boss is a wanker. Smile. And now, it seems I've managed to smile and nod my way into potentially being mauled by a puma.

Breakfast passes in a blur of more coffee and bread rolls. People gradually filter into the comedor from outside, looking work-worn and extremely cheerful. There's rat poo in the bag the bread arrives in, though, as well as armies of big black cockroaches. I attempt to eat anyway, as the others do, but as I bite down on my piece of stale bread, it's hard to retain composure when a family of red ants explodes over my tongue. Sammie tells me in passing, with minimal concern, that it's "just protein." The result of trying to store bread in the jungle, I suppose . . . Food is fair game for everyone.

I'm back on the road now. It seems to stretch and stretch into an eternity of nothing but jungle. It's the cover of a cheap sci-fi novel where you just know everyone is doomed. The sky is no longer red or gold. It is bright, bright blue. The girl in front of me is rocking back on the heels of her boots. Jane. She's brought me out here, in her oversized dungarees and a jaunty straw hat. Oscar is next to her, wearing a grin as jaunty as her hat. He's tall like a giraffe, spectacularly handsome with a beard and pungent American accent. Jane is petite, an Australian with black curls and a button nose that makes me think they should be in some glossy magazine, Jane balancing on Oscar's shoulders, a beautiful circus double act that has gone terribly wrong, and they've both lost their minds.

Things are moving very fast.

Mila had smiled so beautifully. She'd taken my hand, taken me to find old work clothes and boots, led me to Agustino so I could pay him. I'd handed over less than $200, which he'd promised would cover everything from food to accommodation for thirty days. And *Puma* was still imaginary, mythic.

But now . . .

"You walk jaguars and pumas? Outside of their cages? On *ropes*?" I'm trying to look like I'm taking this in my stride. Like this sort of thing happens to me every day.

Oscar nods cheerfully.

"And that's what we're going to do right now?" I look between the two of them, and I know my voice is spiking.

Jane's eyes are green flashes in the dazzling sunlight, bouncing off the tarmac with a slap. "Yup."

I take a hefty drag of my cigarette. It's not even nine, and it must be topping thirty-five degrees. The forest looms menacingly on both sides, glutinous and heavy. There's an inch of sweat surrounding my body like the water layer in a wet suit. I shake my head, looking back at the hopeful faces of Jane and Oscar, at a forest that is a green I only ever imagined in my dreams.

I think of all the times my parents lectured me about giving up. I wonder what they would say about this, and I chuckle. *Give up! Give up right now!*

I attempt a brave smile.

"Let's go meet Wayra then."

Jane walks at a quick pace down the road, as if worried that if she doesn't move fast enough, I will change my mind. She's right. I'm trotting to keep up. Oscar meanders happily along behind, pointing at what he tells me are wild capuchin monkeys. They're swinging along the edge of the road, chirping. Every now and then one makes a leap and misses, crashing into the bushes to sounds of derision from their peers. My heart goes out to them, and the first couple of times I gasp, straining my eyes to see if they're OK, but they quickly bounce back as if their bones are made of rubber. Oscar has told me he's been here five weeks. I have no idea how long Jane's been here. Longer than Oscar, I think. She's unconcerned by the monkeys and I stick close to her.

"Wayra's a wild animal," she tells me over her shoulder. "We get her out of her cage so she can have some freedom, stretch her legs, get a little bit of that feeling she might have had if she'd been left to live as she should have, in the wild."

I nod rapidly. What I've understood: we're working with rescued animals. Animals that have been taken out of the jungle illegally, sold as pets on the black market or housed in circuses and zoos, never to be released again. I'd probably feel more sad about this if there wasn't just one huge question tearing around my brain.

"Is it not dangerous?" I whisper.

Jane doesn't answer me at first, but she does stop walking. The green in her eyes turns bronze.

"Maybe it is," she finally says. "But we each have to decide whether we think these animals are worth it." There's tension in the way she looks at me, her shoulders up near her ears. Then she points to the left, where two tall trunks, their branches gnarled as witches' faces, are set a little forwards from the rest. They're angled towards the sun, giving their bodies a sheen like silk. "Just look for those two," she says, as if they're the ones who get to decide who goes in and who doesn't. "We go in here." Then she pauses, her shoulders relaxing. "Come on." She smiles. "She'll be waiting."

I stumble between the witches and into darkness. My feet hit uneven dirt and the smell of dew clogs my nose. I claw at the grass but it's wild, high above my head, the edges razor-sharp. I can barely see more than a few feet in front of me. The jungle has two seasons, wet and dry. I've arrived in April, at the end of wet season. The jungle is rarely more beautiful than it is now, after five months of rain. Soon it will dry and the earth will parch, the mud crack and the leaves crumble. Right now though? It's just staggering. Somehow, it's a green made up of every single colour.

I swing my head, taking a number of too-quick breaths. There's no sky, just towering trees plastered with leaves as broad as wizards' cloaks. There are trees that are so big they are giants, their heads swollen, skin peeling in rivers of bronze, their bodies armoured with thorns. Birds. Somewhere to my left there's a woodpecker, a macaw too perhaps. High above there are monkeys, howlers the same as Coco and Faustino, their screams reverberating. There are curtains of bamboo that look like they belong in medieval torture chambers. Everywhere there are mosses, lichens, cascades of acid-green ferns, lianas like ropes, rainbows of fungus, aliens blooming blue, purple, sunflower yellow. Trees strangle other trees. Ants make moats. They carry leaves many times their body size, carcasses, dead things, seeds, flowers. Ants smaller than a freckle, bigger than my thumb, strawberry red, shiny black. Ants with pincers to stitch wounds. Beetles, their shells polished crystals, toads the size of tennis balls, termite nests like beach balls. Petals are splashes of yellow, copper, cobalt blue, ultramarine. There's a tree with buttresses so large I could walk between them, standing up, and no one would find me. It's covered with mushrooms the colour of poison, of primordial worlds.

I cast one long look behind me at the place where my brain tells me the road still is, and then I start to walk. It's a fairy tale. The trail weaves, the ground flat until it isn't, twisting sharply over a little hillock, and then I can see no more. A carpet of moss is on the ground and white blossoms shine in scarce patches of sunlight. We go in I don't know what direction, only knowing that we are getting further and further from safety. We walk for ten minutes, twenty, I'm not sure. Whiffs of scent slam into me, choking me, before they fade, replaced by others, sweeter, thicker, heavier. It hurts to breathe. To think. The greens grow darker, the smells more sickly, rotten, the trail more overgrown, the sky nothing more than a memory.

"Every day I think it's a dream," Jane murmurs.

I'm caught on yet another overhanging bit of bamboo, a snarling vine of thorns. It is a dream, I think as I untangle myself. I don't think I've ever been in a place that has its own heartbeat. Millions of heartbeats. I picture people on the Tube, jostling for space on the London Underground that smells of sweat and humans. There are more than a million heartbeats there but they're all the same. They're all like mine. Here, nothing is like mine.

Jane stops. "We're almost there."

We're standing in the shadow of a strangler fig. The trunk is wrapped in parasitic limbs, vines as intricate as hair that's been braided, over and over, until it's more braid than it is vine, continuing until it's lost in an endless canopy.

Abruptly my fear of everything around me is supplanted with something deeper. Another fear, sharper, more concentrated. And yet, something else too. Curiosity. Anticipation. It tingles up my spine.

A sign has been nailed to the bark. It's old and rotten but I can still read what it says: HOLA WAYRA PRINCESA.

Jane's voice is high and clear. "¡Hola, Wayra!"

I stare at her. She seems to have grown five inches.

"Hola, sweet pea!" Oscar hollers.

"You say hello too," Jane tells me. "So you don't scare her."

I nod, gulping. "¡Hola, Wayra!"

I don't know what I expect to see as the trail curves. But Jane's eyes, which can't seem to decide whether they're green or brown, are flooded with a kind of rapture.

"My love! Princesa. ¿Cómo estás?" It is almost a poem.

We drop down a steep bank. The dirt is sandy and my feet scrabble for purchase. There's another little mound and then another strangled tree, bark red as the leaves of maples. Oscar helps me over a rotten log. I smell something fruity, and then suddenly, even though I'm expecting it, we're at the top of a rise, overlooking a large clearing. About the size of two tennis courts, end to end. It's edged by swathes of a singular plant that's as tall as I am and has leaves like lacquered paddles, viridian green on top, lime where the sun catches it. Above is the blue of the sky, which shocks me. I'm almost surprised it's still there. But I don't look at it for long, because less than ten steps away is the cage.

Nestled against the bottom of the rise, it's probably about ten metres by twelve, a little longer on the front than on the sides. It takes up about a third of the clearing. It's roofed in a low triangular tent and a knotted tree is the central support, standing tall as a maypole, poking out through the apex. The floor of the cage is mud, the colour of burnt butter. There are a few interconnected wooden platforms, some high, some low. A few cut logs, some leafy shrubs and palm leaves. A raised house in the back, shaded by a blue tarpaulin. A tall, box-like protruding door on the front left. Patches of light dapple the ground but most of it, unlike the rest of the clearing, is still in shade.

She's hard to see at first, so similar in colour to the shadows. But then her long tail whips.

"Hola, Wayra," I whisper.

The only parts of her that stand out are her eyes, which are as green as the tops of those paddle-shaped plants, and her nose, pink as the tip of a sunset. She looks at us for a long, silent moment. So long that I start to think she might not move at all, and when she does finally leap from the top of a platform, landing so gracefully it's almost like she's not moved, I step back with respect.

She prowls towards us and I'm staring, so overwhelmed, that when Jane slides both her arms carefully through the fence, I almost yelp. I take another quick step backwards. What is she *thinking*? There's no doctor for fifty miles! I'll have to carry her back through the jungle and watch a vet stitch her skin back together. I think all this in the second it takes for Wayra to cross the cage. Then she's licking. Actually licking Jane. And Jane's face is transcendent. She's rolled up her sleeves and the puma is pressed up against her hands.

I know what she is, now. I've always called it a mountain lion. Other terminologies surface too, from the hidden spaces of my brain. Cougar, panther . . . I don't know. I didn't realise these were all the same thing. I think about saying this out loud but decide not to. I can hear the licks, a sound harsh as rough sandpaper.

"How was your night?" Jane murmurs, reaching under Wayra's chin to scratch her neck. The puma raises her throat, angling her face—all sharp-edged bones and soft colours—to the sky, squeezing up her eyes. She seems . . . calm. She's skinny, lithe. Maybe I'm not going to get mauled by her after all. The edges of her spine are defined. The muscles along her back, shoulders, thighs too. She's the colour of a lead-grey sky. Then I blink and she's not, she's the colour of tawny ochre. She's smaller than I imagined. Perhaps the size of a large dog, only slightly bigger than my mum's German shepherd.

I take an involuntary step forwards. But as I do, she whirls. Her eyes widen, suddenly going black as her pupils expand, and her ears flatten as she pins me with a look as if to say: *WHAT. THE. FUCK. ARE. YOU?* Then she opens her jaws and hisses. I feel a rush of fear and bile so sharp it's like I've been kicked in the face. It's physical. So violent, so savage, so utterly unquestionable that I almost, horrifyingly, burst into tears.

Wayra sprints away, jumps up onto her highest platform—at least a metre above my head—and glares. Then she starts to angrily lick her paws, her claws flicked out.

"It means 'wind,'" Jane says with a luminous smile, pulling her arms out of the cage and standing up. "Isn't she gorgeous?"

When I look at Jane, uncomprehending, she cocks her head to one side.

"Her name. It's Quechua."

"Don't worry," Oscar says, patting me on the back, jaunty grin still in place. "She just takes time to warm up. She's a puma."

I watch a red ant carrying a dead ant over my boot. I've been a receptionist, an envelope stuffer, a barmaid, a philosophy student, an English student, an art student, a cleaner, a cold caller, a fuel-pump operator, a marketing specialist . . . and none of these things have prepared me for this. In another life, maybe Jane, Oscar and I would have been friends. Maybe we could have met on a bus to Patagonia or something and we would have hit it off over empanadas and badly dubbed kung-fu movies. But right now, I can't even look at them. Out of the corner of my eye, I'm aware that Wayra is watching me but pretending she's not, tail hanging half in, half out of her mouth. Jane pulls a key from around her neck and slots it into a big padlock on the door. I feel muddled. I think the floor is moving.

"Are you about to open that door?"

"Yes."

"And . . ." I don't know what to say. "What will happen then?"

She beckons me over. When I don't move, she smiles, eyes glistening a bit. Her cheeks have paled, freckles darkening like a galaxy inverted. I want to trust her. I really do. But she's holding the key to the cage of a puma who's just hissed at me like she wants me dead! Suddenly the full, ridiculous reality floods in. I almost laugh as Jane holds up a rope. It may have been red at some point but now it's an old, faded pink. It's hanging off a cable which stretches at head height from one corner of the cage, right by the door, all the way to the other end of the clearing, where it's tied around a big silver-barked tree. I'm frowning at this, unsure of the purpose, when I hear a low, evil growl. I spin and jump back about two metres. My hand flies to my heart. Wayra has materialised in the doorway. Her ears are back against her head so far that it looks as if she doesn't even have ears, like a very angry seal. I school my face under control as Jane reaches in and puts her arm in front of Wayra's nose. A sacrificial offering. Wayra ignores it.

"Try not to make any sudden movements, OK?" Jane says. "She doesn't like to be startled."

She doesn't like to be startled? What about me? I take a number of breaths, swallowing the fear that I know is coming off me in waves. I stay very, very still. Jane threads the rope through the door. On one end is a carabiner, the kind that climbers use to scale cliffs. And Wayra is wearing a black collar (like night, like the colour of her eyes right now), through which there is a shining silver loop. Ready to be clipped on.

"You see the size of her cage?" Oscar asks, edging up to stand next to me, his sweaty, hairy arm pressing into mine. I'm grateful for it. I lean imperceptibly against him. "In the wild she'd roam over eighty square miles. Her world has shrunk to just this because a human wanted a puma for a pet."

"So we're going to put her on that rope?" I whisper, not wanting to point out the irony.

Oscar inclines his head, ignoring my wry tone. "Only if she wants us to."

Wayra has stopped growling. She's lain down and is pressing her neck up against the fence. I'm ashamed that in that moment, I do hope she might not want to. But Jane is already slipping the carabiner through the loop on Wayra's collar. As it snaps shut, Oscar pulls open the door. There's a long moment of silence. Wayra plants her front paws on the earth. Then—she's away! Out of the cage. The rope moves along the cable, "the runner" Oscar has called it, with a noise like a zip wire. She flies. When she reaches the other end, I think she'll just keep going. But in the gloom of the silver tree, its branches curving—tall as a sentinel—she spins. Its shadows fall across her back, turning her silver too. Her ears prick, the tips black to match the end of her tail. And there's no fence, no walls between us. The speed with which she crossed the clearing was inconceivable. She's only what . . . thirty metres away from me? She could cover that in seconds. My heart is so terrifyingly loud, it's making it hard to hear anything else. Yesterday I was in a city. There were buildings there, light switches and doctors. Things that I understand. Now I'm standing in the jungle with a puma!

Jane whispers, "The runner is here so she can have space outside the cage, without being attached to us."

I do not move and I do not speak. Wayra's head is cocked to one side. Her mouth is open and she's growling, low in her belly. Her teeth are gleaming, sending my heart into my bowels. One of her front canines is cracked and jagged. She raises one paw. There is no reason I have to think this, nothing in my experience whatsoever, but I know she is judging me. Weighing me up. My fear won't stay down where it belongs. It's wafting off me, strong as old fish, as cheese that's been left at the bottom of the cupboard, a dog when she's rolled in shit. There's so much adrenaline, someone's stabbing my chest with hot needles. She's a million shades of grey and brown, pewter and black. What am I *doing* here? Don't move. Don't run. Don't . . .

"Come on, let's go!" Jane grabs my hand and suddenly we're moving. I let out a kind of gurgle, which I mean to be some kind of question, but it gets lost between brain and tongue. Wayra has turned disdainfully and is walking away. I don't have time to be relieved because Jane's fingers are digging into my arm. Wayra's tail is swishing and there's a dark-tawny line down her back, cut through with stark, geometric shadows. She's still growling.

"When she wants to walk, off the runner," Jane tells me as we move forwards way too fast, "someone always goes in front. She needs someone to protect her."

Protect her? *She* needs protecting? She's confidently heading out of the clearing.

"We have to hurry," Jane mutters. "Está bien, chica. Está bien." I'm confused whether she's reassuring me or Wayra. But I concentrate on her voice. Australian. If I close my eyes, maybe I'll wake up in Sydney. She moves me forwards. With each step, I am not in Sydney. I'm closer to Wayra. Wayra looks back over her shoulder, shooting me a look of absolute disgust. My hands are shaking so I cover them with my sleeves. I focus on the mottled leaf litter, crunching too loudly. The leaves melt into the mulch of the roots, then up into the ocean colours of the canopy. Down again. I can smell flowers mixed with the acrid scent of cat pee. There's tension on Wayra's rope, she's reached as far as she can get and her growl has got louder, an engine now, coming from inside her belly. It was an illusion before: her size, thinking she wasn't big. She's huge. Her back is as tall as my upper thigh and her paws are plates.

Jane grabs my hand. "Go!"

Oscar transfers Wayra's rope to a belt at his waist. There's a trail leading past the tree and Wayra's blocking the way but Jane doesn't hesitate. She keeps walking as if she'll just push past, taking me with her. Jane is so close my nostrils flare with the sour scent of her sweat. One moment, I'm staring at a rumbling puma, thinking there is nothing in this world that would make me go past her. The next, it's done and I'm looking back, faintly touching my thigh where her fur has brushed my side. Then we're running. I'm running. I see a flash of blue sky, a blur of green, but mostly all I can think about is Jane's grip on my arm. Moving, not stopping and not breaking an ankle, *running*. Blood rushes to my ears and my lungs feel as if they're about to pop. I can't hear Wayra but I can hear Oscar and he's behind me, crashing down the trail. Somewhere, between me and him, is her.

I stumble when we reach a junction made of bamboo and those paddle plants. I think my face is on fire. I think I'm on fire. I've never run like this in my life. I turn back, elated, my head so light I think it might burst right off my neck.

"Is she . . ." I pant, pulling my arm away and trying desperately to see past the junction, but I can't see anything, just a brace of bushes and tangled red and blue vines, like the veins around a heart. I can hear the slowed thump of Oscar's feet. "Is she chasing us?"

Jane's cheeks are so flushed the blood has sucked up all her freckles. "No! She just wants to run too!"

I hear a rustle. A paw, a pink nose, pricked ears. She pads round the junction, casting one sharp look in our direction, cursory rather than predatory. Some fear, the top layer, blows away. She's not chasing us. I'm in the jungle with a puma and she's not chasing me!

She's stopped, looking upwards. Oscar stops too, a few metres behind. There's a squirrel above Wayra's head. He's an English squirrel on speed. His fur is the colour of a traffic cone, and his tail looks as if he's spent the last week at the salon, getting it blow-dried. He's in one of the stalks of bamboo, a brown nut clasped tightly in his paws. He knows. He's got a wide-eyed look that I recognise. Absolute terror and yet, hope. Hope that if he just stays very, very still, no one will notice him. But the tip of Wayra's tail is jerking like a house cat's. I know what this means. This is when your feather, or sparkly little fish toy, or sock, or whatever you've got is about to get royally fucked up. I gaze helplessly at the squirrel, trying to transmit mind-to-mind: RUN! A drop of drool falls to the ground. Wayra's face, the way it's angled upwards makes her eyes seem bigger, like an animal who's been living in the dark. Her eyes have had to grow, suddenly, to take all this in. The white fur around her chin stands out like snow. Her face is almost all green. I realise she hadn't looked small in the cage, she'd looked squashed. And now, outside, she's expanded to fill what she should have been filling all along.

I think with a sickening jolt: if I'd changed my flight, I'd be on my way back to England right now. And in a few weeks, I'd probably be back in an office. I'd be staring at tabs open on my computer screen. Facebook, BBC news, travel sites where I browsed places I yearned to visit, job sites where I looked at jobs I yearned to apply for. Then, when I couldn't look at these anymore, when I felt as if my brain had spiralled, gone into a dark place it couldn't crawl its way out of, I'd stare through the window at the only things I could see. Pale clouds and concrete.

She moves so suddenly that I'm caught, distracted, sluggish like I'm back at my computer screen. Jane has to steady me, and then she's pulling me forwards as Wayra, having leapt four feet off the ground into a branch above the squirrel, hampered only slightly by the rope and the six-foot-five American holding it, pitches forwards. The squirrel's bolted but Wayra doesn't care. She lunges and it's all I can do to keep in front of her. The trail is something she devours. Monkeys to chase here, massive rats—the size of small dogs—there, a tree to scratch, a pile of leaves to roll in, a herd of wild pigs, a shiny armadillo that's snuffling so close to my boot we all almost trip over it, a group of the orange racoonish things—tejones, Jane tells me, or *coati* in English—about fifty of them, leaping from tree to tree as if they're monkeys and beeping madly.

I have no idea where we are, how long we're going to be walking for, what time of day it is even, but all I care about is staying in front, staying with Jane. Finally, when I don't think I can run or walk any longer, Wayra's energy changes. I'd thought she was having a good time. But now she growls at the tejones, swishing her tail, and leaves them behind. She gets grumpy. Really grumpy. She starts hissing at Oscar, slamming her paws down as if suddenly, now, for no reason whatsoever, she hates this jungle. And she hates us for bringing her here, she hates Oscar for being attached to her. The sun powers down on our heads. I try to pull forwards to get away but Jane drags me back, until we're so close I can hear the pad of her paws, the rush of her breath. I can smell her musty fur, feel her eyes boring into my back.

"It's OK, princess," Jane murmurs. "Don't be scared."

For a second, I think she's talking to me. When I realise that she isn't, she's talking to Wayra, I just gape. The last thing Wayra looks is scared. But Jane is crouching down, getting closer, seeming to have no fear at all. Wayra is looking all around. We're in an overgrown spot, a sort of junction, the paths hidden by a curtain of creepers. Jane and I have taken the left path, the less overgrown one, but Wayra is flashing looks of disgust at the other, as if she can't decide. Then she turns around, takes a step towards Oscar. I can see only her back, her bristling tail, the tense snake of her spine. And Oscar is flinching and inching away.

Wayra spits at him, putting her paw on the rope and snarling.

"You're OK, love," Jane murmurs, laughing softly. She has lost her mind. But she just continues to murmur, and smile, and murmur, as if everything is fine. As if there isn't a puma snarling at a guy who is attached to her on a rope. "Princess, you know you can choose whichever path you want."

I hold my breath. Wayra turns back. She looks at Jane, kneeling on the ground. And, just with a sort of questioning look in her eyes, she lets out a long, explosive sigh, looks once more down the overgrown trail and chooses the path we are on. Jane grins, standing up quickly. She grabs my arm again and nudges me forwards. Minutes later we're emerging into a sort of clearing. The sunlight trickles and then suddenly, floods. The bottoms of giant leaves, spreading in multilayered fans, are dark. Like a greenhouse, the light refracts double, triple. The gaps are stars, white and far away.

I can't appreciate it. I can't even see it. I've still got the echo of Wayra's growl in my ears. My thighs are shaking. I've got a banging headache between my eyes. I must have sweated out all the water in my body and then some. My face must have tripled in size. I'm aflame with bites. Wayra, though, she just gazes around. Happy again, unconcerned.

She yawns while I'm drowning in the bloated whine of mosquitoes and the memory of her unfathomable shit-fit.

Grass lines the path. She looks one way, then the other. She yawns again. Furrows up her forehead. There's a bush of yellow flowers. One of the blossoms has somehow got stuck to her nose. She looks at the sky, at a sunny patch on the edge of the grass. Another turn, another yawn. The blossom falls. Then she flops into the grass. She takes her left paw in her mouth and begins to clean away the mud.

"Well, that's it." Oscar laughs.

Jane stretches her arms above her head and sits on the ground, careful so as not to make any unwarranted noise. Wayra, watching out of the corner of her eye, waits until Jane leans against a broad shady palm tree before going back to her paws.

"It's OK to sit?" I whisper, my knees almost buckling. We were on the road only a few hours ago, a lifetime, before my heart and voice and world pitched, before Jane and Oscar walked me along the baked tarmac and told me that we were about to walk a puma. Jane has rested her head against her palm tree and closed her eyes. Oscar's on a log and is staring dreamily into the trees.

"It's fine." Jane's eyes stay closed. "She doesn't mind. It's better for her, if we're relaxed."

I look at Wayra. She's gazing hard at each of her paws.

Puma. The word is weighty. I'm breaking the rules. I wrestle with a voice that tells me I shouldn't be here. None of us should be here! This isn't a fairy story. This is real! Wayra crosses her paws, rests her chin on them and delicately squeezes her eyes shut. The lines across her face and eyes are stark, charcoal and grey. I see little other than colours. Her belly and chin white, the end of her tail and tips of her ears black, her nose pink. There's a neon-green caterpillar, thick as my thumb and covered in spikes, crawling past her paw. Mosquitoes swirl around her ears, cheeks, the same mosquitoes that are attacking my hands and face, my

eyebrows, the side of my jaw. Blood swells their stomachs, mine and
hers, maybe both.

I rub my sweat-clumped hair. Across the ground, dark, earthy
mounds rise up, hinting at massive colonies seething just below our
feet. I touch my face. I feel clammy, hot and feverish. The sun is making kaleidoscope patterns, brown and gold and yellow, in the dust.
I am exhausted, raw and terrified. I think, I'm not going to survive
this month. But then that other feeling I had earlier, the deeper, more
compelling one, floods over me again. Curiosity. Anticipation. *Hope.*

Suddenly I sigh too, then I'm sitting down next to Jane. She turns
her head and opens one eye. And grins.

When it gets dark, when we've taken Wayra back to her cage and we've
come back to camp, when I've braved the freezing shower and eaten
sweaty soup, squashed onto tables with sweatier people, I take the trail
out to the road again. I'm looking for silence, for space to think, and
the only place where there's any space at all is this road. I haven't seen a
single car. I walk by myself down the cracked tarmac, still baking from
the day's sun. It burns the soles of my sandals. The leaves on either side
of me seem to flutter, silhouettes on strings. I turn, looking up. The
Milky Way stretches in a parallel copy of this road. A highway. Huge,
silvery, breath-taking. I've never seen so many stars. When I reach my
hands up, slightly dazed, a star shoots off like I've knocked it. I gasp
a little, pulling my hands away. An owl calls, then falls silent. A dog
barks. This makes me think there must be other humans, somewhere.

Wayra stayed where she was until the sun started to set. We missed
lunch. She slept on and off, groomed herself, turned onto her side,
ignored us mostly. She'd growl though, if we coughed or spoke too
loudly. Or worse, she'd hiss, like she was a hair's breadth away from
attacking. Why she didn't, I don't know. She could have done. And

just the possibility was enough to keep my nerves impossibly frayed. I concentrated on holding my questions to a minimum but towards the end, when my stomach was eating itself with hunger, I was finding it hard. Would we be out all night? How could we possibly convince her to get back to the cage? The forest had hushed, edged with the grainy golds of dusk. And then, right then, everything changed. Suddenly she *wanted* to go back. The cage was no more than five minutes from where we'd been sitting—we'd been walking in circles, Jane told me, rather than further and further away from anything, as my brain had tricked me into believing. And Wayra hurried back to that small, cramped cage like a magnet finding her way home, just in time for dinner.

Home. The only home I know is my mum's house, the one by that scraggly wood. It's where I still go when I'm sad, or lost. It's where I went when I quit my last job in London. It's a converted farmhouse, white with a red-tiled roof. I was born in my sister's room, next door to my dad's childhood bedroom. Dad moved back there when he married my mum. After they divorced and he moved out, my mum wanted to stay. She rescued Fletcher, a massive, confused dog. And she's happy, I think. Just her and Fletch. All year round, the garden is wild with colour. It was planted by my grandmother Sonya. The yellow of daffodils in spring, seas of bluebells, pink with roses and the red of maples in summer, carpets of scarlet and orange as the oak leaves fall, white with winter frosts. Now I think the house smells like my mum, of old cushions and freshly watered plants. She's probably asleep there now, Fletcher snoring downstairs unless he's awake, eyes wide at nothing.

Over two generations, that house, I think, has felt like a refuge. A long time ago, my dad's family—who were Jewish—left their homes in Germany, Russia, and Poland, to come to England. On the other side, my mum is Czech. Her parents escaped from Czechoslovakia after the war. However safe our house now feels, has been made to feel, I know that a home, however stable you think it is, can come crashing down. I learnt that, a little bit, when my parents split up. And I do think the world I was born into does its best, in its built-up, walled-up way, to fool the "lucky ones" into believing that we're strong enough to last forever. That we're invincible.

I think of Wayra. She must have had a proper home once upon a time. I've been wondering about this all day, as I lay in the dirt and now as I look up at the stark, unfamiliar marks of the Southern Cross. How did she come to be here? What happened to her family? Her mum? Her home?

I'm at the place where the two witches stand, just off the road, their bark bone-white in the moonlight. I almost mutter something, I don't know what. An incantation, a prayer. Something like: "Don't let me die" or "Just let me get out of here safely without being mauled or bitten or poisoned by a spider on the toilet seat." I laugh, feeling foolish, before rubbing my eyes, trying not to scratch the constellations of swollen bites, and turning around, away from the path that I know leads to Wayra. I'm about to start walking back—there's a candle burning now by the entrance to camp, its flame stuttering like a blinking eye—and as I do, I whisper, "Please, just don't let me quit this."

I stand a moment, unable to move. There's a resounding silence, filled with the voices of what I think are frogs, mating in the verge, and the hum of the jungle, which is something that never, ever seems to stop.

Just before you turn off the road to go into camp, there's a smokers' hut. It's called the fumador and inside are two hammocks strung between the beams. The roof is thatched and there are no walls, just spaces that look out on one side to the road and on the other to the jungle, which is so close the palm leaves poke through to tickle your face. Tom, Faustino's friend, is passed out in one of the hammocks. He's snoring loudly. In the other is another guy, complete with ubiquitous beard.

He's handsome, if you ignore the filth, and wiry. The end of his cigarette flares as he turns his head. His brownish-blond hair is too long. His beard almost reaches his chest and he's got cutting blue eyes. He's not wearing a shirt and sweat gleams in the hollow of his stomach.

"Hey," I murmur, raising my hand.

"Hey." He's Australian.

I turn down the path and almost step on a monkey.

"Oh shit!" I swerve just in time. He's hunched in the middle of the darkness, his tail wrapped around himself. When I curse he just looks up at me, eyes desperately sad. The sound of frogs echoes, so loudly I can almost hear the flap of their throats. A thousand tinkling water glasses, bouncing up and around and back again.

The hammock creaks. "Coco?"

The monkey fixes his eyes on the ground. It must be Coco. I don't want either of them to think I'm afraid, so I reach my arms down in what I hope is an emulation of what I've seen others do, but Coco quickly pulls his lips back, showing impressively sharp canines, and crawls away, getting even closer to the road. There is a weary sigh, and bare feet slap against wood. The guy steps out of the fumador, crouches down and Coco immediately crawls into his arms. The monkey rests his head in the crook of the guy's shoulder and when he straightens, Coco held protectively against his chest, they both gaze miserably at the NO MONKEYS sign.

"I made that last week," he tells me. "Trying to stop him from killing himself."

I cannot think what to say to this. "Maybe he enjoys the irony," I try to joke.

He chuckles, as if surprised. "That's funny."

I blush.

"I'm Harry."

"Laura."

"I know. You want to take Coco back in?"

I stare at Harry, the planes of his face harsh in the flickering candle-light, then at Coco, then back at him. Harry strokes the top of Coco's head.

"He only bites people he doesn't like."

I'm not sure how to take this, so I continue to hesitate but Harry just steps towards me, grinning.

"Here." He smells of old smoke laced with salt. Stale sweat. Mould. He's not that much taller than me and as our shoulders touch, I feel a sudden weight as Coco climbs onto me, wrapping his tail around my neck. I wasn't expecting him to be so heavy and instinctively reach up to balance him. Little leathery hands clutch my fingers and wet lips touch my cheek. I gulp, not quite able to swallow. Coco grunts and his breath tickles my neck. I can't move.

Harry rubs his beard. "You good?"

"Yes, fine!" I'm holding a monkey. I cannot believe it! I desperately try to crane my neck to see Coco's face but just succeed in getting a mouthful of damp fur.

"He loves girls." Harry stares tiredly towards camp, the branches of tall trees dangling over the path. "I was just going to have another cigarette. Do you mind taking him?"

I don't mind, even though his tail is almost cutting off my wind-pipe. And I see, having now flicked on my head torch, that Harry's still dressed for work. Wet, slimy jeans drag around his ankles. His feet are caked with sloppy black mud and a pair of discarded gumboots are lying by the hammock. It's past nine. I wonder if he's just got back in from whatever animal he works with.

"Where should I put him?"

"In Santa Cruz."

"The dorm?"

"Yeah, next door to La Paz. Coco and Foz sleep in there."

"In Santa Cruz?" I repeat stupidly.

Harry nods, running his hand through his hair before turning back to the fumador. "They used to live in a hotel. They were beaten. Made to smoke cigarettes and drink alcohol," he says over his shoulder. "They watched TV all day. They're old, and every time they go into the jungle or into a cage, they're so terrified they start to shake, beat themselves, shit themselves . . ." He shrugs. "The government dumped them here, no money, no help, nothing. So we let them sleep in the dorms if they want. It seems to make them happy." He hesitates, then corrects himself. "Happier."

I stare at him. I don't know what else to say, so I just make to move towards the path. This is just one more traumatic, insane, wondrous thing that's happened to me today, so I let it fall onto the top of the list, along with "walked a puma" and "shared my shower with a tarantula the size of a dinner plate." I shine my head torch firmly at the obstacles around my feet and try not to think about all the ways this seemingly simple task that Harry has given me could go wrong.

"How did it go with Wayra?"

I turn back. He's standing a little lopsided, his head cocked, his hands deep in the pockets of his jeans. His beard curls around at the edges of his lips, the straggly ends long enough for him to suck, which he does now, absentmindedly.

"Great!" I reply, smile plastered on.

Harry raises his eyebrows and looks like he might query it, but then Tom emits a particularly loud snore and Harry just nods as if he has remembered that he's too tired to care.

Candlelight shines out of the comedor and across the ground, making the patio into a criss-cross of stark black shapes. The forest canopy hangs solid, like a roof. I look up and don't see the sky or the stars—they are like memories, I can only feel the edges of them. Fractured moonlight makes figures around my feet, turning the dusty earth on the patio pale. Tall trees surround us, stretching high into the darkness. Coco and I hover there, peering inside the comedor. His chin, heavy and surprisingly sharp, rests on the top of my head. The teenagers are hunched over something, their homework perhaps. I've been told they are from here, there's a village nearby, and Mila and Agustino take in kids every now and then. When their families aren't able to look after them. The money volunteers pay goes towards looking after not only animals but also these kids—buying them schoolbooks, clothes, food. A temporary—or permanent—home. Osito ("little bear") is the youngest. He's speaking disjointed English now, Sammie gently correcting him as she sits next to him on one of the benches. Someone, another tall American called Bobby, is playing the guitar. Agustino holds up the soup ladle, asking if anyone wants more food.

I give Coco a tentative stroke. I'm nervous that he'll bite me, despite—or because of—what Harry has said, but he just leans into my hand. His fur is puffed out, moist with sweat. He's a tiny red yeti with clutching fingers. His skin feels smooth as cured leather. But thin too. Around the edges of his joints, across his distended stomach, it feels fragile, as if by pressing too hard, I'll break through to his bones. In those places, he feels like silk. All I can hear is his breathing and the steady beat, beat, beat of our hearts.

"Is this OK?"

Coco leans his cheek against mine. He has soft, tickly whiskers. When I push open the door to Santa Cruz, he grips the frame and swings himself inside, as if he has done this a thousand times before, using his tail to wrap around a rope that hangs across the room. Faustino is cross-legged on one of the top bunks, gazing down at us reproachfully. When Coco lands next to him, Faustino pushes him away. Then he holds out his arms to me.

Me? I look around but there is no one else here. I take one disbelieving step and then I'm pressed against the bunk. Faustino's against my chest, and he's carefully taking my hands and wrapping them around his back. He's smaller than Coco, and his bones are hunched like an old man's. I press my hands into his crinkled fur, and he gives a low, contented grunt. Coco glares at us both, putting his chin in his hands gloomily. Faustino then pulls down my shirt and tries to lick my breasts.

"Careful!"

I jump back as the door bangs and Sammie and Jane come in.

"Faustino likes boobs. Filthy old man."

"You want to watch your ears too. And the sweaty bit under your armpit. Right Fozzy?"

Faustino wraps his tail around his body as if he's deeply wounded. But as I quickly close my shirt, buttoning the collar up to my neck, he watches, disappointed, like I've taken away something precious. I glare at him.

This room is the same as La Paz, only there's old monkey shit on the floor and fresh shit on someone's bed.

"You really sleep in here?"

Sammie laughs. "It's the best room."

My expression curdles. It doesn't look sanitary. Sammie laughs again, wrapping her arms around Coco.

"Was he on the road?"

I nod. Coco's eyes flick away. Sammie holds him a little tighter.

"You're going to get hit by a car," she whispers.

"Suicidal monkey." Jane leans back tiredly against one of the bunks. "Just what we need."

Coco continues to look down at his toes. There is mud caked under one of his nails and he picks it off slowly, then puts it in his mouth.

"You can't . . ." I hesitate, not sure how to phrase this. "Put them in a huge enclosure, rather than . . ." I look around uselessly and trail off. "Or release them?"

Jane laughs bitterly. "We've got no money for a huge enclosure. No people to build it. New animals turn up all the time and each one needs a home. Right now, this feels like the best we can do." She stares at Faustino, who sticks his tongue out at her. "They'll never be able to be released. They don't know how to be monkeys, and we don't have the resources to teach them." Then she turns to look at me. "Wayra will never be released either. None of the cats will."

I stare at a dried-up pile of poo behind the door. I can't look away. Its edges are starting to crust over, turning the same earthy colour as the compacted dirt floor. In some places, I'm not sure what is floor and what is faeces. Wayra seemed so wild. Surely if they just opened the cage door . . .

"Where did she come from?" I finally ask.

Jane shrugs, turning around and digging her chin into the edge of the bunk. Faustino crawls over to her and lays one long arm across her shoulders. She reaches round, holding his hand in hers. "She was taken from her mum as a cub," she says eventually, her voice dull, as if she's told this story many times. Too many times. I wonder then how many volunteers like me she's had to train. "Hunters would have shot her mum and smuggled her into the city to be sold on the black market. A street artist bought her, kept her in a little box in a loud, dusty place, and made her perform tricks. Baby Wayra. I just . . ." Jane visibly grits her teeth. "In the wild, she would have stayed with her mum until she was two. Instead she was kept on a chain, whipped and malnourished. Taught nothing about how to protect herself. It was only when she grew too aggressive that she was dumped here. She was ten months old."

I stare at Jane. I ask, my voice catching, "How old is she now?"

"Almost four."

There's a long silence as I think about this. I'm trying to think of something to say, but all I can do is imagine the puma that I saw today small and scared in a little box. I've been to zoos before. I don't remember worrying about it. Worrying where the animals came from. But now I do worry. I start to feel sick. Jane turns back around with a sigh and looks at me.

"You did well today."

I did *well*? Where was she, in some parallel universe? She smiles, the hazel in her eyes catching the candle that she's balanced on the end of the bed.

"You seemed calm, at least," she says.

I don't tell her how much of a lie this is. I look down. There are blisters bubbling around the tops and edges of my toes, which have been getting bigger as the day has worn on. Now they look less like toes and more like pasty, overinflated buoyancy devices.

"Oscar really needs to leave," she continues. "He's got a job lined up at home. We've been trying to find someone to replace him but . . . Wayra's not the easiest cat." Sammie snorts, and Jane shoots her a glare. "She needs people who understand her. The other cats . . . most are really happy here. She's not. She's . . ."

"Special." Sammie grins.

The door bangs and Harry comes in. "Yeah." He laughs. "Real special." He's still barefoot, spreading a line of mud and water across the ground.

Jane glares at him. Then she leans towards me, saying quietly but not quietly enough for the others not to hear. "Wayra hates Harry."

Harry rolls his eyes. As he starts to pull off his trousers, he mutters under his breath, like a curse. "Wayra volunteers." Then he glances at me. "Careful you don't go crazy like this one."

Jane picks up an old boot and throws it at him. He's too fast and the boot misses, hitting the wall with a dull thud. There's silence for a moment, and then Coco and Faustino explode. Harry lets out a muffled curse as both monkeys leap onto his back, grunts of righteous indignation filling the little room. I fling myself out of the way and am about to yell for help when I realise that Harry is laughing. Sammie leaps in too and one of the monkeys goes for her, pulling her ponytail before jumping onto someone's mosquito net like a trampoline, swinging off into the rafters and howling. Soon they are all careening around the room, pulling down nets, pulling hair, pulling beards, throwing missiles with their teeth bared.

I rush for the door, managing to leave before I get squashed or bitten or slapped around the face. But when I'm safe, I stand for a while on the doorstep, listening to the grunts, the crashes and the laughter. When I was three, a friend of my mum's, training to be a psychologist, needed an observation subject. She picked me, and much later I read the file she'd made. I'd been the shy child who'd played on her own, not quite understanding why everyone else was so loud. And even now, when I'm on the back foot, it's my default position. I'd come travelling on my own, not because I thought I was brave but because sometimes—right or wrong—it feels safer to play on my own. But as I listen now, on the other side of this door, I think their game sounds wonderful. I'm too tired, too physically shattered, too itchy and my blisters too painful. The idea of going back in seems as remote as peeling off my own skin, but even so—I stay. Just listening. And when the tiredness finally gets me and I stumble back to my own dorm, to my own bed where there are no monkeys and no shit on the floor, I fall asleep to the sounds of their laughter.

The next morning, I'm told that everyone works for an hour before breakfast, before going out to our assigned animals. For me, that's Wayra. But right now, it's still only six thirty, and I have work to do. My first task involves caring for one of the groups of animals that live around camp. There are birds in the aviary, for example, and more jungle pigs like Panchita—*peccaries*, I've been told they're called, *chanchos* here in Bolivia. There are two baby chanchos who live in an enclosure behind the comedor. Then there are the howler monkeys, Coco and Faustino, and Teanji the tejón . . .

I'm placed with a shiny-bald French drill sergeant called Gustave and six South American ostriches. Gustave calls them *pìos*, which is what Mila and Agustino call them, he tells me. In English, they're *rheas*, in Spanish, *ñandú*. Their actual names, though, are Matt, Damon, Ben, Affleck, Patrick and Petunia. Petunia, the largest and most intimidating, despite my attempts to ingratiate myself, quickly develops a dislike for me and follows me wherever I go, trying to peck the buttons off my shirt. Their breakfast is a vat of vegetables, which I have to grate meticulously in a cockroach-and-mosquito-infested shack Gustave calls the animal kitchen. The grater is rusty and soon there's more blood and knuckle skin in the carrots than actual carrot.

"It's a good thing," I say, trying to laugh, "you told me that pìos eat meat as well as carrots."

Gustave's face stays completely immobile. I quickly stop laughing.

He shows me how to run the gauntlet with the food, dodging giant dinosaur birds while protecting my eyes and my buttons. They have wings like sails and curl their long necks backwards, like coiling rattlesnakes, before hissing in my face. My borrowed gumboots have holes in them, soaking my socks within seconds, and Petunia's shit is beetroot purple, liquid as bad cow pats. The enclosure is enormous, large enough so that when I am inside it, I can't see any of the edges and I get lost, panicking because I have Matt or Damon on my heels and I can't find my way out. The birds in the aviary next door seem to find this hilariously funny. One macaw, Big Red, cackles with laughter, and his sidekick, a little blue parrot, screams, "Don't do that!" whenever my boots gets stuck in the mud. Which they do, a lot, because it's ankle deep and sucks and burps like the Bog of Eternal Stench. I can't believe how many different shades of mud there are. It blows my mind as I stare at the ground, trying to shovel poo, but the spade Gustave has given me is broken, cracked with no handle.

"Will I . . . ," I ask Gustave tentatively as I hang it up in the tool shed, a building almost as useless as the spade itself, barely a lean-to with sad, rusty equipment that—like everything—has seen better days. "Be working with the pìos for my whole month?"

He laughs for the first time, spreading his lips widely to show strong, white teeth. The top of his head gleams in the morning sun. "You no like pìos?"

Then he just wanders off, whistling infuriatingly, pointing me in the direction of a chalkboard, which, I'm told, is where I'll find my second task, a caretaking job that rotates daily. *Laura and Bobby: baños.* I read this with a sinking, sick feeling akin to how I felt this morning when I put on my left boot and my toes met something soft and squishy: a scaly toad the size of two fists.

Bobby is the guitar player. I've heard him waxing lyrical about this place so much that I've already taken to avoiding him, his guitar, his corkscrew-curly ferally wild hair and the T-shirt he's been wearing since I arrived—by the smell of it that he's been wearing since last Christmas—which says brightly: "SMILE!"

"Yeah," he drawls, holding a bucket of shit-covered toilet paper and leaning against the wall in the fashion of someone who has all the time in the world to chat, while I am desperate to get these baños cleaned as quickly as possible so that I can Just. Sit. Down. "I work with Rupi." I haven't asked. I don't care who he works with. "He's a jaguar. Jaguarupi." Bobby laughs, puffing out his chest as if I should be impressed. I am, kind of, but I'll never admit it. I stare at the lumpy pile of poo I'm scraping off the floor. Coco watches with concern from up in the rafters. I think—I hope—that it's his but I can't be sure.

"Rupi's my best friend."

I nod politely. The poo oozes a little as I try to pick it up.

Bobby's eyes focus somewhere in the middle distance. "I love him."

"Mm-hmm."

"I don't know who I was before I came here." He hesitates, then laughs out loud again, so loudly Coco jumps. Bobby starts to wheeze and slaps his thigh. "I mean, I was a carpenter. Working for 'the man,' you know." He laughs again. "But like . . . you know. Now I can't imagine a life without Rupi."

"Right." The poo is nearly off. I smile and nod.

"It's just his energy. He's a jaguar, but he's patient. He could kill us. He weighs ninety kilos!" Again, laughter. Slapping his thigh. "But he doesn't. He's so happy to let us walk with him. Proud almost, you know. Dignified. Have they told you he grew up in camp?"

I look up. "In *camp*?"

"In camp." He grins. "There wasn't anything here then. The dorms were the first things they built when Nena and Juan Carlos bought this land. They're the guys who founded this whole thing. In the nineties, with two rescued spider monkeys, two capuchins and a squirrel monkey, they started their first parque in the cloud forest near Cochabamba. It was the first-ever sanctuary for wild animals in Bolivia. Then in 2002, they raised the money to buy this land. There were only a few volunteers then. And López, the kid who walks around in sunglasses . . ."

I nod. I've seen López—he's about sixteen—sitting on the camp motorbike, wearing cool black sunglasses, his arms crossed imposingly over his wiry chest. Mila told me he used to live on the other side of the country, but when his dad died, he had to move away to live with his sister and find a job. He needed to support his mum. It was when he was looking for work that he met Nena and Juan Carlos. He was eleven. They gave him books and helped him go to school. Eventually, he started living here, and learned how to work with the animals.

"Well," Bobby continues. "Rupi was one of the first cats to come. He and López grew up together, roaming free with Panchita. That was before there was the money to build enclosures. Everybody just wanted to rescue animals, you know, and give them a happy life?" He puts a lot of emphasis on this last word, swinging the toilet paper bucket much too close to my face. "Imagine it!" Bobby sighs dramatically, leaning back against the wall. "A baby jaguar, a kleptomaniac pig and an eleven-year-old. Best friends."

I can't imagine it. It's a true fairy story.

"Does he remember him? Rupi?" I ask quietly.

Bobby grins. "I didn't know jaguars could smile, before I saw Rupi and López together."

When I was eleven, we had a class guinea pig called Agatha. I was terrified of her. She peed on me and bit me, and I dreaded the days when Mrs. Connell would carelessly drop her into my lap. I didn't even consider that Agatha probably feared those forced, chilling encounters just as much as I did. Slowly, I chuck the poo into the bushes and watch as it settles, smeared, across the heart of a pretty pink flower. Vaguely, I wonder what would've happened to me, if I'd been brought here at the age of eleven and been faced with a jaguar. But then I look up into the blinding blue sky and I just think tiredly, trying to wipe beads of shit off my hand: Only twenty-nine more days to go.

After breakfast, back at Wayra's cage, I'm too hot, too tired, too bitten and too sore to do anything other than what Jane tells me to do.

"Rub patuju over your face."

She points at the hard paddle-shaped leaves around the clearing.

OK.

"It'll make her like you."

I do it. She probably could have told me to take off all my clothes and rub myself in peanut butter, and I would have done that too. The patuju sticks to my clammy skin, stinking of me. When I poke the leaves through the fence, though, in some bizarre parody of a mating ritual, Wayra hisses from up on her high platform, her "throne," and I drop the leaves, pulling my hand out with a yelp.

When I glare at Jane, she just shrugs.

The days find a rhythm, a pattern that I hate but also cling to. I wake in a pool of sweat. My back aches and I get perpetual tension headaches from grinding my teeth through short snatches of sleep. I pull on the same rank clothes. I grate. I clean poo. I sweep whatever I'm told to sweep, then eat breakfast alone while listening to Mila reel off daily anuncios, mostly toilet and/or faeces related. Don't let Faustino steal people's underwear and then bury it behind the baños, don't let Coco spy on people in the baños, don't leave the door to the baños open or you'll find Panchita bathing in shit and Faustino eating soap with a beard of white bubbles.

I'm dizzy with exhaustion on the walks out to Wayra. Every trail, every step, every turn of my head is a new experience that I'm so unused to, my senses so unprepared, that part of me just wants to curl up and never open my eyes again. The other part never wants to shut them.

I watch Jane or Oscar clip Wayra on, I wait for her to lie down in some arbitrary spot that makes no sense to me, I flinch at her unpredictable, totally unfathomable growls and find myself losing my mind with I don't know what—anticipation, awe, respect—when she's silent. I spend five, six, seven, eight hours whilst she sleeps being bitten by ants, poisonous caterpillars, mosquitoes, horse-flies the size of acorns. I pray that Wayra doesn't notice me, particularly when I have to creep away to shit in the dirt, my stomach a seething mess of anxiety, bacteria and water, and then I leave at the end of the day disappointed that she hasn't noticed me. I shower with water so cold it burns. I watch my blisters swell, then pop in a mess of blood and pus. I hobble down the road and watch the stars fly. Fireworks that have lost their colours, let off ten thousand million miles away. I crawl into bed, trying and failing to find a comfortable dip among the lumps. I listen to rats getting up to important, busy work. I consider packing my things but just the idea of this is too exhausting. And so I escape into an old, mouldy copy of *The Lord of the Rings*, which I have found like a gift underneath one of the tables in the comedor.

Jane has said Wayra needs time to trust people, but from where I stand, Wayra doesn't care one way or the other whether I'm there or not.

Sometimes she gets swept up with her walks, sometimes running like that first day for a few moments, or for a few minutes, but mostly she's just pissed off. She's pissed off in the cage and she's pissed off outside of it. She's pissed off when she's eating, she's pissed off when she's licking. She's even, sometimes, pissed off when she's sleeping. And I'm nothing, just a tiny dot stuck amongst other dots, trying to breathe in a place that makes no sense, that lets eleven-year-olds hang out with jaguars, that lets people like me hang out with pumas, pigs hang out with monkeys, birds hang out with tejones, in a forest that has no end, until of course it does end, when it reaches some village, or town, or city, then the mountains, the Andes on one edge, the salt deserts on another, and I suppose the ocean after that, then the stars.

I've been in the parque five days and the only thing that's keeping me standing is the guarantee of a half-day off, just a half-day, once a week on a Saturday afternoon, but it's a magical, wonderful-sounding thing. On top of that, I've been promised that on Sunday, I'll be assigned another pre-breakfast animal task. No more pìos! See ya, Petunia! I have no more buttons left and I'm having to tie my shirts closed with string.

It's Friday, work has finished and I'm on my customary trip to the long drop. Shadows criss-cross the ground and Sammie is chatting with Harry, leaning against one of the shower blocks. Harry's carrying a candle, wrapped in nothing but a towel, oblivious to the mosquitoes hungry for his blood in the early evening.

There's a social hierarchy in the parque, and it didn't take me long to figure it out. The staff are all Bolivian: Mila, Agustino, the cook—Doña Lucia (who travels in every day by motorbike)—and the kids (youngest to oldest: Osito, Juana, Germáncito, Mariela and López). During mealtimes, they locate themselves on the front table in the comedor. They chat in rapid Spanish, or Quechua, and are generally very intimidating.

Then there are the long-term volunteers. Equally intimidating. If they're not with the staff, riffing in fluent Spanish, then they're sitting at the long table at the back of the comedor, closest to the rats. They're foreigners who've been here longer than a few months. Sammie and Harry are long-termers, as are Bobby, Tom and Jane. They shower on average once a week, have an unhealthy pallor and sleep in the monkey room. They wear permanent manic, exhausted, blissful expressions, as if they're ready to pick up a machete and race off into the jungle at any moment, and they'll talk to you about "their cat" until your ears fall off.

Anyone who isn't staff or a long-termer falls by default into the final group. The short-termers. People who still walk around wide-eyed, who find it weird that there are monkeys grooming themselves using the wing mirrors on the motorbike, who reminisce about hot showers and still use soap. Me. I'm a short-termer. And I cannot comprehend what it would take to be anything but that.

As I approach the trail to the long drop, I keep my gaze averted. But at the last minute, my eyes flick up, meeting Harry's. I regret it instantly. Katarina, who sleeps in the bunk below mine, who's been here about three weeks, who's from Serbia but lives in London, and who's engaged in an ongoing, savage war with Panchita, whispers gossip up through the slats in the bed frame as the candles flicker. She's told me about Harry. About the short-termers he sleeps with like it's a merry-go-round. And she's advised me not to touch him with a barge pole.

I trip on a loose brick, almost falling head first into Teanji, who's rooting around in a pile of laundry that has—by some misfortune—been pulled off the line and trampled by some large compost-covered four-legged beast. Teanji beeps in alarm, his stripy orange tail rising off the ground, and scurries away.

"Sorry!" I mutter, righting myself, my face hot.

"Frodo," Sammie calls. Her hair is wrestled back with a jaguar-print headband and she's fanning herself with the lid of a fruit bucket. Frodo? The word bounces off the overhanging trees, which give the little clearing the pervasive scent of rotting citrus. She beckons me over, the gesture sending out a long shadow. I hesitate, fearing a joke at my expense. I'm validated when she laughs. When I glance at Harry, my heart sinks further. He's trying not to laugh.

"Sorry." Sammie grins cheekily. "But, you know. You're always reading *The Lord of the Rings*. And that is what you look like."

"Like a hobbit?" I exclaim.

"No!" She has the decency to look embarrassed. "But just . . . like you're miserable. As if you're walking up a fire-spewing mountain and you don't know if you're going to make it." She shrugs, waving her hand. "Don't worry. It gets easier. Are you coming to the village? It's Oscar's last night."

My face is the colour of pìo poo. I quickly make an excuse and scurry away. It's only when I'm on my own in the long drop that my breathing steadies. Here! *Ridiculous.* I cannot believe I've started to sit in this long drop longer than I need to, because it's here that I feel safest. With the worms and maggots and the moths that are folded like origami!

My hands shake as I run them through my greasy hair. My normal ways of coping—making sure I look nice, I'm smiling, I fit in, I'm *fine*—are crumbling around my blistered, dirty fingers. The spider, the yellow-and-black one that made me scream on my first night, hangs from a huge web in the rafters. I've named him Hagrid. He watches me now, his dark eyes thoughtful. I can't seem to make my smile work. Can he see all the way into the dark place in my stomach, where all *the bad stuff* gets hidden? On the surface, it's all: Tea and a Jaffa Cake, please, how's the weather? But inside, I'm climbing fucking Mount Doom. Can Wayra see that too? Is that why she doesn't want to be around me? The realisation of this is so upsetting that I start to cry.

The world outside the long drop holds its breath and I try to cover my mouth, muffling the sound. Unlike any place I've ever been in, despite all the noise, all the other creatures, the trees, plants, fungi, rocks and earth that stretch for miles, the jungle really seems to listen to everything. I've never felt so vulnerable. It won't stop listening, and I don't know how to tell it that I hate it.

I make it to the road just as a big group starts to leave—nineteen of us, more volunteers have turned up, two more this morning. It's dark and I'm glad of it. There are no mirrors, so I can't see how red my eyes are, but I fall in beside Katarina and try to make the smile that I give her genuine. There's a full moon and the road is washed with silver, the trees made magical by fireflies. There is a loud singing, so loud I think it can't possibly be the frogs, but when I turn to Katarina to ask, she just nods an affirmative. I wish I knew what they were doing, what it meant that they're singing so loudly.

We start to walk.

"How far is this village, then?" I hear one of the new volunteers ask. There's suspicion dripped into every word. He feels familiar, like so many boys I went to college with. Lads playing rugby and driving their dads' cars. I would never have been friends with him. He's tall with baby-blue eyes that I can tell he's relied on since he learnt to walk. The way he looks around him suggests that he would be much more at home in some party hostel, like the ones I stayed in and hated. But seeing him here, now . . . his familiarity is worryingly reassuring. I think he introduced himself as Bryan. The other is Paddy. Toothpaste-model handsome, with a tan that's near orange and dimples deep enough to put a finger in. He's jumping around with enthusiasm, rolling his eyes at his miserable friend.

"Bry, don't whine!" He chuckles. "It's probably not that far."

"It's an hour-and-a-half walk," Katarina corrects tersely.

Paddy, Bryan and I stop short.

"An hour and a . . . *what now*?" Bryan splutters.

"Surely there are . . ." Paddy pauses. "Buses?"

Katarina snorts. "Twice a day, if you're really lucky. You might be able to hitch but . . ." She looks pointedly at the empty road. "I don't like your chances. Not at this time of night."

"Oh." Paddy nods, assimilating this information. Then his smile returns with a vengeance. "Well. An hour and a half isn't that far!"

"To get a beer?" Bryan gazes desperately at Katarina, but she's wandered off after the others, migrating away in a cloud of fireflies, torchlights bouncing. The road isn't empty. Not by half. Bryan seems to realise this now, and flinches. There are too many things out here, things you can and can't see, things you can and can't hear, an uncountable number, huddled around this one stretch of tarmac. "There's really no cars?" he whispers weakly, the dark jungle hanging over him.

I shrug. "This is my first time too."

Unimpressed, he gazes at me. "How long have you been here?"

"Almost a week." *Almost a week?* It's nothing and an eternity. A shooting star sails across the sky, the points of the Southern Cross edging over the tops of the trees, which are so black they look almost blue.

"Wow," Paddy marvels. "I assumed everyone had been here years. You look so efficient."

"Not me!"

"Yeah. I saw you cleaning the kitchen. You looked like you knew exactly what you were doing."

I stare at him. After I'd taken the compost bucket out, I'd flailed around in the darkness for at least twenty minutes trying to find the pigs' enclosure. I'd come back covered in muck and on the very edge of a serious mental breakdown. I think back to my first few days, when everyone had looked the same and I knew nobody's names. Every single person had indeed seemed like they'd lived here years. This rocks me.

Now I know, of course they hadn't. Maybe they'd all just been stumbling about in the darkness, just like me.

"This place sucks," Bryan mutters.

"It's not that bad!" I blurt out.

"Not that bad? Have you seen the dorm they've put us in? Six people in that thing? *Six?* And six plus what? I know this is an animal sanctuary but I don't have any desire to provide sanctuary to rats, thank you very much."

I grin. They've been put in La Paz with me.

"Give it a few days, Bry. Then decide whether to pack it in or not." Paddy looks at me hopefully. "It gets better, right?"

I hesitate. "Have they given you a cat yet?"

"Yeah." Bryan narrows his eyes. "I got some jaguar. Rupi?"

"And I got Yuma. I think she's a puma."

I don't know Rupi or Yuma. But I know Bobby now, a little. I feel oddly defensive of him and the cat that he loves beyond reason. And Tom, the quietest of the long-term volunteers, has told me about Yuma, once when he came home late one night covered in mud and scratches, his face gleaming. He told me as he lay in the hammock taking off his boots that she's sort of like Wayra. Wild. Confused. A bit crazy.

"Well," I say slowly, "once you've signed up for a month and you've started with your cat, it's hard to leave after that."

They both stare at me. The tarmac has a strong smell, like roasted meat and hot tar. The road is so straight, it's as if it's been dropped from the sky.

"Why?"

"I . . ." I trail off. I don't know why. It's just a cat, if they want to leave, why can't they? That's what I'd have said a few days ago. "It's something about trust," I mumble.

Paddy nods sagely. "Who's your cat?"

"Wayra," I answer too quickly. My cat. I picture her sharp cheekbones, angled away from me. When she looks upwards, at the clouds or at a troop of capuchins in the trees, the shape of her face changes. I'd noticed that my first day, but every day it seems to get starker, as if she's getting less and less real, as if she's going to metamorphize and fly off into the sky. I swallow painfully, my throat dry. "She's not," I clarify, "mine. She's no one's." And I surprise myself by laughing, thinking about how she sat in a patch of sticky mud today and when she realised, she snarled at it as if it had placed itself there on purpose just to torment her. She spent the next two hours angrily cleaning herself. When we laughed, she pinned us with a glowering death stare, as if we were all in cahoots.

Bryan looks at me strangely. "What's she like?"

My face falls. She hasn't hissed at me as savagely as that first day, but she has very obviously made the decision to ignore my presence. Although when she's trying to sleep, which she does for hours on end, she grumbles every time I move, breathe, make a noise. I ache to scratch the reams of mosquito bites I've incurred waiting for her to get up. I shake my head over how Oscar and Jane scuttle after her, attending to her every whim, and how she gives them nothing back apart from a few irate licks at the start of each day.

I sigh. "She can be a bit of a bitch really."

The village—Santa María—appears on first encounter to be little different from any of the other villages I've seen across Bolivia through the windows of buses. There is a row of huts flooded by a sorry trail of overhanging street lamps that flicker pale orange, struggling to keep themselves alive. It's in a sort of basin, sheltered by towering rocks that are so big they seem to have breath of their own. Dirt tracks peel off left and right, where I assume homes lie under the cover of darkness. Some of the huts on the main drag are shops, with fruits and vegetables stacked in wheelbarrows, manned by women in wide velvet skirts, long plaits hanging down their backs, babies on their hips. Some are little eating places with wooden tables where men sit and eat fried chicken, gesticulating with beer cans. Television sets blare out action movies that crinkle painfully at the edges. The dusty verge is littered with rubbish. Bones, plastic bags, broken bottles. Chickens get under our tired feet. Street dogs sleep uncaring in the road.

Katarina guides us towards a thatched building, lit by harsh electricity and the metallic hum of eighties music. She nods towards the walls, covered with posters of semi-naked ladies.

"Welcome to Porn Bar," she says wryly as she opens a fridge and pulls out a handful of beers. I stare at the one she hands me, not caring that it's warm, not caring that it smells faintly of urine. I cradle it as if it's made of moon dust. In front of me are shelves stacked with crumpled cigarette packets, potato chips and old, dusty spirits, the labels faded. Through a doorway I see a patio. There's a mattress on the floor, piled with the crumpled bodies of sleeping children. When the woman I've seen around camp comes out of the back, Katarina grins, hugging her. "Doña Lucia!"

The woman smiles shyly, adding up our purchases and putting the bolivianos we give her into a rickety old cash register. She has a tattoo that says "AMOR" across the knuckles of one hand. The fact that her bar is covered in porn seems incongruous. She's about forty, I think, with a warm, pretty face. A boy of about six is clutching her legs. He's holding a puppy, eyes barely open.

"She runs this place as well as cooking for us," Katarina whispers to me. I look around for a husband but I can't see any evidence of one. Later Katarina points him out to me, snoring, blind drunk in a hammock in front of the TV.

I lean back against a wall and take a sip of my beer.

Paddy's eyes are wide. "What do you make of this, then?"

I look around. The local men staring at us from one corner of the bar as if we're a zoo attraction? The edged, orange darkness outside?

The rocky hills that have risen out of nowhere, the flickering lights, the whirring hum of the generator. The screaming children climbing on Bobby's shoulders as Jane guards a box of puppies. The street dogs, two of them on the pool table being fed fried chicken bones by Harry and Tom. Doña Lucia patiently trying to shake awake her husband, the babies asleep in the back, the eighties CD that plays over and over on repeat, the cool dirt under my toes where I kick off my sandals, the heady taste of this cigarette, the moon looming above everything, the feeling of being in the middle of a wilderness that stretches for miles and miles, the knowledge that out there, not too far away, are wild jaguars and pumas and monkeys. Hunters too. I stare into Paddy's handsomely glowing face. He is from Peterborough. In Bolivian terms, where journeys can stretch over days, Peterborough is a short train ride from my home.

"I think it's very strange," I say, one of the few honest things I've said since I've arrived.

Paddy nods, holding up a bottle of cheap rum. "I do too. Want to get drunk?"

I wake up in the mud somewhere behind the comedor, bright sun scalding my eyeballs. Panchita's hairy snout is in my face, and Harry is next to me, not wearing very much at all. I'm naked and covered in dirt. The immediate "oh fuck" feeling hits me hard. I push Panchita away. She snorts as if she's finding this extremely amusing and can't wait to tell absolutely everyone what she's seen. I put my hands over my eyes and start to scrabble desperately for my clothes.

"You keep your mouth shut, Panchi," I hiss, whimpering as the night begins to come back. I remember rum. I remember dancing. Dancing on the pool table. Dancing on the pool table with Paddy, Jane,

Agustino, Tom, then, finally . . . Harry. I remember hitching back in the rickety heights of a cattle truck, oh gods. I remember . . .

Harry lies on his back, watching me scrabble, and grins. "That was fun."

"Um-hmm," I say, pulling on my jeans. Shit. *Shit.* I've been bitten to hell and cannot even begin to wonder at the horror of what might have crawled over me during the night. Let alone . . . Harry . . .

"You OK?"

I watch a line of ants bigger than my thumb passing inches from his leg. He seems not to care.

"I'm fine."

"Frodo, you don't look fine."

"I'm fine!" I snap. There's something deeply humiliating about being called a hobbit by someone who's just seen you naked. When I sneak a look at Harry's face, though, I think he didn't mean to offend me. I like his eyes and the way his smile crinkles behind his ridiculous beard. I look away, cursing myself. I've been told this guy has relationships with girls he can guarantee will be gone in a few weeks. Worse, he has sex and then doesn't talk to the person afterwards.

My mum sometimes tells me with a laugh that I have a fear of commitment. It's a fair call. It might be true. I've been single for a long time. Four years. Five. I don't really like to think about it to be honest. I've had only one relationship and it ended terribly. I'm just . . . I don't know. Not that interested? I'm sure I'll be fine. No need to panic, Mum . . . I don't need to go to therapy yet.

But Harry. Wow. I can only imagine the field day my mum would have with him. I look at him out of the corner of my eye as he scratches Panchita adoringly around her middle. I'm ashamed at the lump that comes up in my throat. He's had sex with me now. I suppose I fit his pattern. I'm a short-termer. I'm fleeting. I don't matter. I wander around with an expression like a hobbit out of Mordor. It feels the same as when Wayra stepped scathingly over my sweaty leaf without even a backward glance.

I'm counting down the days until I'll be able to shower with hot water again. Sit on a chair with a cushion. Be able to stand still for more than a second without being bitten . . . But there's something about the way Harry is sharing a kiss with a pig bigger than he is, as a wild capuchin monkey looks on from a branch above, casually eating mango, and the way the sun gleams through a crack and makes the mud golden . . . something that makes a part of me open a little inside. Something yearning. Something I hadn't even known was there.

But then I shake myself. By all accounts this guy is a massive jerk. And the pig is covered in old porridge and shit. And Wayra . . . Wayra is just an angry bully. I say this firmly to myself as I speed off, back to my dorm, leaving Harry and Panchita to wallow together to their hearts' content.

Oscar leaves before breakfast. I watch the bus pull away. I feel emotional, confused. I put it down to hormones, an outrageous hangover and a lack of vitamins. Mila cried. She clung to Oscar as if she couldn't bear to let go. But then the bus left, and it's—I don't know—it's as if Oscar never existed. Mila cleans up her face, and then she's giggling with Tom about something one of the cats has done. One moment Oscar is there, tall, laughing, and the next he and his bags are gone. The road is empty, and where for a moment it smelt of exhaust fumes, metal and burnt tyres, now it just smells like the jungle again.

Ten minutes later I catch Sammie vomiting behind the pig enclosure, the two babies, Panapana and Panini, watching with beady-eyed wonder from the caves they've made out of our old dinners. Agustino and Paddy pass out side by side over breakfast with their faces in the peanut butter, and Mila storms around them with an anger that seems electric in its ferocity. I only have to survive till lunchtime, I think giddily as I flinch away from her, trying to act very, very small. People whisper around me about *town*. A mythical place where there's internet, ice cream, pizza and electricity—maybe even air conditioning—and it's only an hour away by bus!

Surrounded on the way to the long drop by muffling thickets of bamboo, strangler figs out of nightmares and knotted clumps of vines, I dream of it, and other human things, so hard, I almost succumb to dizziness and have to sit down on the ground. Unfortunately Mila finds me and tells me, stony-faced, that we'll be doing construction all morning.

"¡Todavía están todos borrachos!" she exclaims, eyes flaring. You're all still drunk. "¡No puedes caminar con gatos! Puedes sudar el ron," she snorts. You can sweat out the rum, she says, thrusting a machete in my direction and sending me off towards the aviary, with an instruction to cut down foliage for the birds. On the way, I pass Agustino, nursing his head miserably on the patio bench. He gives me a rueful grin.

I stare at the rusty blade in my hand. Once I reach the aviary, I set out into the surrounding jungle following the sweat-drenched clumps of volunteers and begin to swing my machete wildly. It's the first time I've ever wielded a machete, and the excitement lasts a few quick minutes before it hits me what a bad idea this is. A worse idea than sending me out to walk a puma? It's impossible to keep track of all the other hungover volunteers, also madly wielding blades—probably too blunt to mistakenly remove someone's appendage, but I cannot be certain. Spines of bamboo darken my vision, trying to take out my eyes. Packs of mosquitoes steal my blood quicker than I can swipe them away. Innocuous, thin beige trees are infested to the core with ants. If you touch them, which I invariably do, it feels like you're being burnt by a thousand cigarettes. When I accidently hit one with my machete, fire ants swarm over me in vicious anger and I scream, thinking someone has thrown boiling tar across my scalp. It is Harry—why it has to be Harry, I don't know—who helps me get them off and tries at the same time not to laugh too hard.

This landscape spreads across the borders of countries. What is even more staggering is that if I put down my machete and walked in any direction, even though I'd be less than a mile from the road, I'd be disorientated. Lost. I might as well be halfway to Brazil for all I could do about it.

"Is that a . . ." Paddy, who is also on machete detail, points suddenly at my arm.

"Oh fuck!" I yell. "Get it off!"

Paddy is too busy shaking his own clothing and squealing.

"It's just a tick." Sammie passes by with a guy from Holland, known for telling such filthy stories that she's nicknamed him Dirty Dutch.

I stare at the thing deeply buried in my upper arm. "What do I do?"

"Twist and pull." Sammie puts down her side of the dead tree they're carrying and wipes the back of her arm across her dripping forehead. "We're coming into dry season. A million ticks. Horse-flies the size of wasps. Wasps the size of birds. We never catch a break here, whatever the time of year. You need to check yourself every night."

I continue to stare at the place where the tick's head is in my flesh.

"And when she says check." Dirty Dutch grins, nudging Sammie. "She means really *check*."

Paddy and I look between the two of them.

"What do you mean?" Paddy ventures nervously.

"Dirty Dutch and I have developed a tick X-rated system. Do you want to hear it?"

An itch blooms at the base of my spine. Paddy goes pale.

"There's X, double X, and the worst is triple X. It's—"

"No!" I put my hands over my ears.

"Single X is on the outers of your private parts. Double X is—"

"No!" Paddy shouts. "No, no!" Then he pauses, his eyes wide as if watching a car crash he cannot look away from. "Have either of you had a triple X?"

Sammie laughs. "You don't want to know. Always check, that's my advice."

"And if you can't get down there," Dirty Dutch says gleefully, "or *in* there, or whatever, get someone else to check for you!"

I shower for a long time. I scour my body, and when I finally put clothes back on, I start to sweat again immediately. I don't mind. I don't have to go into the jungle. I'm mere moments away from the internet and anything that isn't soup or rice on top of pasta on top of potatoes. Maybe I'll eat something green! It's gloriously hot. As Paddy and I lazily swing in one of the hammocks, we talk about ice cream. Dairy is one of my life's great joys, unconscious as I am of the mind-numbing impacts of intensive cattle farming. On this day, ice cream still sounds like paradise.

Nearly everyone is out here, trying to conjure cars out of nothing so they can hitch rather than wait for a bus that may never come. I smile blissfully, not really caring. I'm light-headed, just so happy I don't have to do any work, until I notice Harry watching me, a crooked smile on his lips. I glare at him.

"Hey, this is the first time I've seen you smile," he says, taking a slow drag on his cigarette. "Like properly."

I glare even harder, making Paddy laugh. "Apart from when she's got a bottle of rum in her hands." Paddy winks, grinning his Cheshire Cat grin. Harry, however, just rubs his beard thoughtfully, still looking at me, then gives an almost imperceptible shrug before turning away to talk to Bobby, who's laughing wildly about something on the other side of the fumador. I look away too, swallowing what? Disappointment, embarrassment . . . Then Paddy elbows me gently in the ribs and whispers, "I hear there's a lady in town who makes banana milkshakes. With ice!"

I'm smiling at him gratefully, shaking my head to shake Harry out of it, when someone yells: "Bus!"

Paddy almost tips me out of the hammock in his haste to get onto the tarmac. A small, local bus trundles towards us, and the road is so straight that I don't know how long it takes, five minutes perhaps, before the bus actually catches up with the noise of its engine and is rolling to a stop in front of us.

It's just at that moment that I turn. My foot is on the first step, Paddy jostling behind me.

"Jane?" I murmur.

Jane is walking up the track onto the road. She's dressed as she dresses every day, in her too-big Wayra dungarees and straw hat. She's carrying a book, Wayra's water jug and an egg.

"Is she going to Wayra?" I say to Harry, who is next to me, although I don't wait for him to answer. "Are you going to Wayra?" I back off the step and let Paddy and the others in the queue behind me go first.

"Yeah."

"But it's Saturday," I say stupidly.

Jane just shrugs. "I prefer to spend it with Wayra."

"Lau, what are you doing?" Paddy shouts out of the window.

I open my mouth to say I'm coming, but nothing comes out. Jane is already starting to walk in Wayra's direction and I take a few steps after her. "Will you walk her?"

She turns around. "No. We'll just stay in the clearing, on the runner. We'll hang out." She hesitates, breaking into a hopeful smile. "Want to come?"

"Laura!" Paddy yells. "Come on!"

The driver has started the engine. I'm frozen. Ice cream! I look back at Paddy desperately. I look at Jane, and then I look down the road towards where Wayra is. The bus is starting to move, everyone else is on now. I see Harry through the open door.

Jane starts to walk again, turning away. "You better hurry. The bus is leaving."

"I . . ." I close my eyes. Bus. Town. Internet. Harry . . .

"Give me five minutes!" I shout, and I'm sprinting back down the path into camp.

Wayra is sunning herself on her throne. Jane and I sit cross-legged on either side of the doorway, the cloudless sky punishing and the compacted earth cruelly hard on my bones. I've been watching a particularly flamboyant beetle trying to bury itself for the last half hour while trying to identify why exactly I am here. When we arrived Wayra looked at us, eyes narrowed, then back up the trail as if to say: *So, where the hell is Oscar?* Since then she stubbornly hasn't moved. She's in a sunny patch in her cage and shows no interest in coming down.

"Maybe she knows it's Saturday," I say miserably, looking up at the sky, which is as blue as forget-me-nots. I cannot believe I've given up an afternoon of freedom for this.

Jane turns a page of her book. "It's just good to be here."

I stare at Wayra, who has her eyes firmly closed, so firmly closed it makes me think that it is for our benefit. "She doesn't care."

Jane just raises her eyebrows and says nothing.

I sigh, lean my head back against the cage, and return to the beetle. I can just hear the croak of a toucan somewhere to my left. Above that is the high-pitched whistle of some creature I don't know, a truculent line of ca-caws, the throaty conversation of a pair of macaws. Lower down is the thud of a woodpecker's beak. I think the tree is hollow, the way the noise sounds empty. Settling between this is the hiss of crickets, the whine of mosquitoes that grows higher as I grow still and they grow bolder, gyrating nearer to my ears. There is the motor of a hummingbird's wings, the rustle of leaves, the muted squeal of toads, the crunch of sticks as something burrows in the undergrowth. I think with panic that these noises will be lodged in my brain forever and I'll never be free of them, but the more I think this, the more I listen. And as I listen, with the heat cushioning my body against the cool mud and the cold metal of the cage, my mind drifts. I become dreamy, the sounds less fractious. The hummingbird's whirl relaxes, the rustling deepens, the crickets lower, the toads sink, the woodpecker slows, the macaws start to speak somewhere else.

Time just passes.

Silence. Suddenly I look down at my wrist and realise I don't have my watch. For a moment I feel panicky, but then I realise too that I don't need it. It doesn't matter. I close my eyes and let the river of jungle wash over me. I think, at some point, I fall asleep.

"Laura!"

"What?" I mumble, turning my neck with a painful groan and opening my eyes. "Oh fuck!" I hiss, jerking backwards. Wayra is inches away, staring at me with apparent interest. My head has somehow migrated, my cheek now sandwiched against the fencing. I move back quickly, rubbing the indentation in my face. "I'm sorry, princess," I murmur, unconsciously using her nickname. "Lo siento."

Wayra sniffs. Her posture is impeccable, a long line of darkness stretching from the top of her head down the graceful arch of her neck all the way to the curved end of her tail. Around the edge of her pupils is a line of amber, sharp as an old layer in a fossil. The sun falls across her fur. Jane is already threading the rope through the door, but as Wayra saunters over to lie down, Jane hesitates.

"Do you want to do it?"

"Me?" I squeak.

Jane nods, holding the rope out to me.

I stare at it in my hands, as if I don't quite understand how it has got there. It's about the width of two thumbs, the edges frayed. As I run my fingers across it, it feels soft. As if it's been held by many different people before me. Wayra stares at me, waiting.

I nod.

"Put your arm in."

I close my eyes, take a deep breath and try to recapture the sounds that lulled me to sleep. I let them wash over me again, the toads and their songs, the toucans with their chatter, the heavy thunk of the woodpecker's beak. I let the shadows of the palms sit across my shoulder blades and the heaviness of the air lie over my hands. I grit my teeth over my fear. Then I crouch down and slide my arm through the bars. Wayra continues to lie very still, her eyes dramatically lined with black as if she's on her way to a stage play. I am just able to keep my hands steady. Her ears are ever so slightly back.

The first time she licks me, I don't know what to do.

"She's licking me!" I hiss.

Jane laughs, crouched on the other side of the door, hugging her knees.

"Don't get too excited. It's mostly for the salt."

But Wayra haughtily butts my arm with her forehead, turning it over so that she can lick the other side. It's almost—almost—possible to forget that she's in a cage and I am not. It feels as if it should be the other way around. The jungle out here with her, us in there. It cloaks her bottle-green. Her tongue is rough, ripping. It hurts more than I thought it would, but I don't want her to stop. She's making a low noise and it sounds to my desperate, exhausted ears like acceptance. She's leaning over my arms, head down, one relaxed paw balanced up on the edge of the fence, licking, licking, licking. My skin is turning raw and the rest of me feels nothing, it's only this small spot of skin that she's touching. That's the only part of me that exists. Everything else, the missed bus, the possibilities of town, my whole existence before this, fades. She's spirited me away to a place where cages aren't real. I can't believe this is the same cat that hissed at me on my first day. She looks the same but she's not. Everything is different. My head is full and I'm smiling so widely that I think for a ridiculous moment I might burst into tears again. What's happening to me?

"Thank you, Wayra."

She gives a little sniff as if to tell me not to make a big deal about it. My hands are shaking now and I fumble with the carabiner. She isn't looking, but her ears are turned towards me and her eyes are starting to narrow. She can smell the sudden surge of alarm that makes my head hot then blisteringly cold.

"Always wait till she sits," Jane breathes. "Any growls, grumbles, get your hands out of there. She hates being touched when you're holding the rope."

I fumble with the catch. But then I'm slipping it through her collar and it's closed, locked. Wayra spins with the beginnings of a savage growl. I can hear the snap of her throat and the trapped snarl behind her teeth, but my hands are already out and I'm standing, breathing hard, pulling off the latch and swinging open the door.

There's no acknowledgment, just a flick of her tail and then she's ambling away as if this happens every day. For her I suppose it does, but not for me. Rather than going straight to the sentinel tree, Wayra plonks herself down in what seems to be her favourite spot in the middle of the runner. As if she knows she's not walking today and she wouldn't want to, even if she could. Her spot is a little dip of grass between a tall, nimble tree with bark that smells of baked pepper and a patch of knee-high young patuju. It is so well cared for, raked meticulously every day by Jane, that it looks like a garden. Wayra's garden. She rolls onto her side, belly blindingly bright, and looks straight at Jane. Wilderness hangs off her. She might disappear. I'd believe it if I blinked and the rope was gone, she was gone. I make to move forwards but I can't, the force around her pushing me backwards without my feet even moving.

But Jane walks straight up to her. Wayra doesn't hiss or grumble. The wild smell fades, dissipates, flows and then grows even stronger. Jane ducks her head, leans her face down. And the two of them sit cheek-to-cheek, forehead-to-forehead. I have stopped breathing. We've spent five days in the boiling heat and humidity being bitten to shit by mozzies just so we can watch this angry, stubborn cat sleep no more than ten minutes from her cage. I'd assumed that was it. That's what this month would be.

Jane turns, flashing me a smile. "You can come over."

Wayra pulls back, readjusts and sits again, almost in Jane's lap.

"Wayra!" Jane laughs.

Wayra stares up into Jane's face, her eyes wide. For the first time, I see that she is ever so slightly cross-eyed. She tries to lick Jane's freckled button nose. There's nothing but sweetness and affection in the gesture. Jane grins and slides her legs away with a grunt, letting Wayra settle into the curve of her thigh. Jane shows absolutely no fear, despite having an entire puma in her lap. Wayra gives a happy sigh and rests her chin on Jane's knee.

"This," Jane whispers, stroking Wayra's neck, "is where she really learns to trust you."

I nod, not able to speak. I look up at the flat blue of the sky. I feel upside down, in a sea that should be down, not up, the clouds floating little white boats. I'm facing the wrong way entirely. A parrot calls out. It goes against every instinct to sit on the ground so close to Wayra that I can reach out and touch her. Her teeth are the length of half a finger, I know because I've seen her bare them at me. I wouldn't do it, shouldn't do it, if not for Jane. I know that Jane trusts Wayra, and I—in some strange way—am starting to trust Jane.

I sit down very carefully and hold out my hand. I know Wayra is watching me so my action doesn't come as a surprise. Just with a heavy sigh as if to say, *Finally*, she angles herself towards me, and then she's licking. In an attempt to get nearer, she gives a frustrated little grumble, puts one giant forepaw on my leg, immaculately sharpened claws caught in the material of my jeans, and pulls. I don't look at Jane because I know she'll be smiling, but maybe I am too. With my other hand, I reach across and place it on Wayra's shoulder blade. I let it lie there, getting used to the warmth. The hardness of muscle, the softness of fur. Letting her get used to me.

There is a thin patch of fur on her spine that grows in the wrong direction. I never noticed it before. Her breathing is soft, relaxed. I think, by the angle of her ears, that she's listening to me, and I work hard to keep my breathing steady. I run my hand downwards, across her back, over her hip. I think I can feel the steady thump-thump of her heart. I can't hear anything else now, the jungle has gone and it's just this. She twists her head, her eyelashes catching in a burst of sun. I move my hand upwards, stroking until my fingers reach her neck. She's velvet. She leans towards me. She smells of the jungle floor, rain and damp mud. The light mottles, making patterns against the line of her spine, the shades of her fur, whenever I blink. I wonder what I smell like. Sweat and cigarette smoke perhaps. The mustiness of La Paz. Toothpaste. Soap. I let out my breath and then I lean towards her. There's no one left to hide behind. No more Oscar, whose bulk had started to feel like a plate of armour. And Jane too, I sense, has edged away, giving us space.

My breathing is slowing to match hers. She's stopped licking, her strong back paws curled up in the mud, her one front paw still on the edge of my trousers, claws contracted, toes relaxed. Her other paw is tucked under her chin. She's starting to shut her eyes, her breathing deepening. Her chest rises and falls, her eyelashes flutter. She suddenly looks incredibly vulnerable. It floors me. I wonder what she does in that cage every night when we're not here. I wonder if she looks forward to seeing us, or dreads it. I feel dizzy again, as if I'm tilting. Maybe it's the adrenaline. But maybe it's also because I've been spinning for so long. I've felt lost in the lights and sounds and pressures of moving forwards, moving upwards, moving somewhere. The aimlessness of it making my hands shake and limbs desperately tired. I'm tired now but it's different. Now, for the first time in a really long time, with the sound of Wayra's steady breathing and the settling of the jungle heartbeats around me, I feel like I'm weightless. As if I might be coming to a stop. Here in a place I least expected to. With this puma, who I'm starting to realise might not be as brave, or as bold, as she wants me to believe.

Three days later, I'm assigned a macaw to work with in the mornings. His name is Lorenzo. He is blue with yellow belly feathers. There are more than twenty macaws in the aviary, a series of interconnected roofed cages that back into the trees. They're close enough to the comedor that I can clearly hear them calling out as I try to eat my breakfast. *Osito, mi amor! Hola Mila! Fuck Harry!* A few of the macaws are housed in their own cages—Big Red, who laughs constantly and is blind and a little senile, and Romeo and Juliet, a couple interested in nothing but each other, spending their days grooming and gossiping. The rest are deemed sociably acceptable enough to live in one big enclosure, but entering is like going inside a mafia enclave. The massive birds, scarlet and blue, are clumped about in groups, their beaks sharp as flick knives, and when they sense weakness they swoop, cawing and plucking at your head. Paddy and I both scream and run out the door. Sammie—who's training us, me on Lorenzo and Paddy on the rest of the macaws—rolls her eyes.

"¡Cállate!" she yells. The macaws squawk, circling, but retreat to their perches, giving her the evil eye. She turns her sharp expression on us cowering. Two macaws wobble along the ground. They're identical, with delicate masked faces limned with blacks and whites. One of them, the one approaching fastest, has eyes that roll dramatically back in his head. The other waggles his turquoise wings, trying to catch up. Sammie's expression softens.

"Frodo," Sammie says as she bends down, letting them both climb onto her arms. "This"—she holds up the slower one, the one able to hold eye contact—"is Lolo." Lorenzo leans over so far—as if trying to get as close to her as possible—that he falls and is left hanging upside down, his claws desperately gripping her shirt. The other takes the opportunity to climb rapidly up Sammie's back and onto her head, where he gazes around as if he's reached the peak of Mount Everest. Paddy and I look at each other. We've already discussed the fact that neither of us wants anything on our heads.

"Alright, Crazy Eyes," Sammie murmurs, leaning against one of the platforms for him to disembark. "Lorenzo's the only one who goes outside."

Paddy watches the rest of the birds, who are still eyeballing us as they sharpen their beaks on the fence. "Why?"

"Agustino gave him wing extensions after he came with his feathers cut, and now we're trying to see if we can teach him to fly again. It's a trial. But the others get jealous." As if he's heard, the one called Crazy Eyes launches at Lorenzo, who, not yet stable, drops in panic. Sammie catches him, and when she presses him protectively to her chest, a faint pink blush colours his cheeks. I've heard that macaws can blush, but never believed it.

"Eyes tries to fool volunteers. Make sure when you take Lolo out that you've got the right bird."

All kinds of horrific scenarios run through my mind—bird escapes, death by Crazy Eyes—as Sammie and I take the one she tells me is Lorenzo out to the road. She patiently holds him on a stick, slowly waving him up and down in the air to give him a bit of a lift. The road is the perfect training ground, straight and empty as a forgotten airplane runway. Pale puffy clouds lazily drift past the trees sleeping on either side of us. When it becomes clear that Lorenzo isn't going anywhere though, she lifts up his wings to show me the plastic spines Agustino has added to the bottoms. Lorenzo squawks indignantly but continues to grip the stick, his claws wrapped tightly around it as if he can't let go. Why him and not others, I wonder? I guess time, money . . . people. Luck. Lorenzo is going to have me, for the whole hour before breakfast. But the rest of the macaws, they just get Paddy, and that's for just half an hour because of all the other tasks that have to be done. There aren't enough volunteers to go around.

The sky is so big, so blue. The three of us watch flocks of wild macaws fly past in formation, their feathers bright scarlet, cobalt blue, tropical-beach turquoise. How is that fair? I look down at Lorenzo as he gazes after the wild birds that look so much like him, and feel a painful lump in my throat.

When Sammie leaves, disappearing back into camp, the canopy curling around her as if she was never there in the first place, he ruffles his head feathers in panic. We both gaze after her longingly, then back at each other with trepidation. I give the stick a little shake and he turns his head almost three hundred and sixty degrees, shrieking so loudly in my face that I drop him.

Ten minutes later he's on top of the fumador. He hasn't flown, he's crawled, using his stubborn beak to pull himself up on the thatch. The useless stick hangs at my side. He is a bright flash of blue, almost the same colour as the sky as he stretches his wings out. *Screw you and your stupid stick*. He casts one proud sideways look down at me before seeming to forget that I exist, getting down to the business of preening his feathers.

Mila is in one of the hammocks, drinking a cup of coffee. She's been there the whole time and is trying not to smile, but I can see the edges of her eyes crinkling. Every now and then she gives me gentle encouragement, which only makes me more frustrated as Lorenzo moves further away from me. In the end she trots off, returning minutes later with a pocket full of peanuts. I'm so grateful, I hug her.

"Todo es como una cebolla," Mila says, pensively rubbing a mosquito off her nose as Lorenzo happily picks peanuts out of her calloused
palm. "It's like . . ." She snaps her fingers, looking for the English word.
"Onion."

Before she came here, Mila was a waitress. Then she found three
puma kittens in a cardboard box. The pumas are now three years old.
They are called Inti, Wara and Yassi, and Mila can walk them without
a lead. Sometimes she sleeps with them in their enclosure at night. So
I listen avidly to her words.

"Para mí, los animales rescatados son como las cebollas." She
watches me to see if I have understood, but when I bite my lip nervously, she sighs and switches to a slowed-down mixture of English and
Spanish. She is used to having to make herself be understood, I think,
and when I concentrate, I find that I am able to follow more of the
Spanish than I expect. She tells me her theory that, for her, rescued animals are like onions. You work so hard to peel off one layer of anxiety,
only to expose another, and then another that you had absolutely no
idea was hiding underneath. And because all of us really are no different
from any of the animals here, because we're all messed up and broken
in our own individual ways, we're like onions too.

"Y eso es lo que hace el parque," she says with a smile. "And that is
what the parque does, no? Peels off our layers"—she taps me sharply on
the chest—"you and me. One after another after another, and we learn
new things about ourselves, and about the animals that we're with, cada
día. Every day. Juntos. Together. We do it together. Por eso me enamoré
de este lugar. That is why I fell in love, no? With this place. You never
know what is going to happen."

Lorenzo has crawled up onto her shoulder, wiping the peanut shells
off his beak with her ear. She goes back to her coffee, leaving me with
the uneasy—and oddly thrilling—sense that my skin is being peeled off
when I'm not looking. Lorenzo, having finally assented to come back
onto my stick, flaps his wings churlishly. He goes too far and it takes a

while for him to stabilise himself, but when he does, we both look up. A single harpy-eagle is flying from left to right across the sky. It's hard to tell the scale, but I know she's huge, her leaden wings spread wide. She soon disappears, back into the shelter of the canopy, but it feels as if Lorenzo and I watch her for a very long time. I think we feel as if just by watching her, we'll get closer to that feeling of being free.

As the days pass, Mila's words stay with me. When I notice that suddenly it isn't a struggle to pull my jeans on, this small thing makes me indescribably happy. The next day I notice that my feet have moulded to the shape of my boots, and then I discover a dip in my mattress that fits my spine. I fall over and instead of cringing, I laugh. I wake up and the first thought I have is of Wayra. Is she going to be in a good mood today? Is she going to lick me again? Will she be pissed? Lazy? Excited? Everything at once? After another week, I can tell the difference between Lorenzo and Crazy Eyes. I can't remember ever not being able to. Lorenzo rolls onto his back when he sees me, his legs waving in the air. I give him belly rubs. He spreads his wings to show them off and his feathers feel both fragile and strong. He sidles backwards, pushing his neck into my hand so that I rub the feathers around his ears. The first time he flies, wobbling a few metres along the road before falling to the ground with a painful crash, we do a little dance together, lifting one leg and then the other, rolling our necks to the ocean blue of the sky, the green banks of leaves fluttering around our heads. I let myself imagine that the harpy-eagle is watching us as we do this.

At the beginning of my fourth week, I find myself on the road, where my sore feet usually take me. It's the only place where I can see the stars because everywhere else, it still feels like I'm in a drawstring bag made out of leaves and smothering darkness. I think my eyes dimmed when I was living in London. I felt exhausted all the time. I needed thirteen hours of sleep and still it wasn't enough. Now though—I almost don't ever want to shut my eyes again. I walk along the road staring upwards, not caring when I fall into potholes. I'm in a cavern made of crystals, I'm looking into an ocean exploding with phosphorescence.

How did I spend so many years missing this? In a city or a bar. On the Tube. Watching TV. On the computer. Pulling the duvet over my head.

I take off my gumboots and wriggle my toes. The heat of the road is almost too much but even so, I press my hardened heels downwards. I thought I would miss TV. I can't even fathom how I thought that. Every night the constellations look different. But I love being under my mosquito net too, with nothing to do but watch the candles dance, moonlight shining across the patio bricks. I've even come to love the comedor. We play cards by candlelight. Me and Katarina, Jane, Paddy and Bryan, Bobby, Osito, Germáncito and López, Mariela and Juana, sometimes Tom too, sometimes Agustino and Mila. Bobby strums his guitar and sings. And we play silly games. Who can eat the most peanut butter? Who can balance the biggest melon on their head? Who can find the carrot that looks most like a penis? The comedor explodes with laughter. And I join in. But when I'm tired, I can just come out here to be by myself too. And that's OK. Or I can go to bed. There's no shame in going to bed. I love that. We're all exhausted. But it is bone deep and physical and welcome. So different to the mental exhaustion of anything else I've experienced.

My roommates snore and fart, and I listen to the monkeys play-fighting next door. Being in a small room with so many people should horrify me, the sound of rowdy laughter make me flinch, god forbid rats in the rafters and the low tick of spiders crawling the walls. But I just feel safe. It's taken three weeks but I've learnt that Coco and Faustino aren't going to bite me. If they try to touch my breasts, there'll be no hard feelings if I push them away. I can cradle them in my arms with their tails wrapped around my neck. I groom their fur and they pick imaginary bugs out of my short hair.

Today Osito taught me how to swear in Spanish, and I taught him how to say, "My name is Osito. Will you be my girlfriend?" in English. Mariela and Juana showed me how to eat the ends of patuju stalks. "Muy rico, no?" Mariela giggled. The stalks are stringy and taste like cucumber, sliding out of their shoots with a whoosh. She was right. They are delicious. Panchita rubbed her snout along my inner thighs, smearing my jeans with the stench of her stink glands, and I didn't have to concentrate on not being afraid. I held the rope with Wayra, perhaps my sixth time walking behind her, and I never had time to think, I'm walking a puma. Because I wasn't. She was walking me. And it was OK. Walking was what she wanted to do. It was her right. She had a fundamental right to walk in this jungle, way more than I did.

I see the light of a candle flickering now and I hesitate. There's the silhouette of a wave. It's Mila, her silky dark hair spread wide.

"Laurita," Mila calls out, her voice soft.

Sammie and Harry are with her. They lie on their backs, boots discarded. There's the faintest hint of a breeze, and not a single piece of traffic for miles. Mila sleeps out here sometimes, she's told me, when she cannot bear the heat in the dorms. She props herself up now on her elbows and watches me approach, moving over to make room.

"Gracias," I say, dropping down.

Harry lights two cigarettes and passes one to Sammie. Since that one night, weeks ago now, we've had little to do with each other. He avoids me and I avoid him. I sense that he thinks I'm inconsequential, and I try not to watch when his blue eyes assess some other pretty new volunteer as she walks across the patio.

I light a cigarette of my own and take a long drag. I'd intended to quit, when I came travelling. I started at school as a way to make friends. Flicking ash with gothic black fingernails off my fishnet tights behind the gym. Eight years later, I still think I can fool people into believing I'm braver than I am by smoking a cigarette. Here, though, it's different. Here, when there's always some kind of work to be done, when you're busy all the time, smoking is just a moment of exquisite peace.

I think Mila has fallen asleep but suddenly she turns her head.

"Cómo está mi amor Wayra?" Her voice is quiet as a star shoots across the Milky Way. There is no moon. It makes the stars burst. "La cebolla."

I turn on my side and we face each other.

"Increíble," I say, whispering too, unable to stop myself from smiling like a loon. "Caminamos y es . . ." I shake my head. I have no words for what it's like out there. We walk together and the wild smell that inhabits her touches me too. I've been wearing a numb rubber suit for so long I'd forgotten that I was wearing it, and now it's come off, I can move. Actually move my limbs. I can feel things I couldn't before. I can breathe. It's like being on a tightrope that could at any moment snap. It's a gift. Mila has given me this gift, and Wayra. Wayra most of all.

"Ah, sí." She laughs, turns onto her back and stretches, the same way that Wayra does after a long nap. Last night, Mila threw a mango at Agustino's head because he let one of the pigs loose. And I saw her cry uncontrollably for two hours when a volunteer packed up and left. Sometimes I think Mila is as brave and wise as any person I have ever met. Then I think she's also just a little bit broken. Jane told me Mila had a family once, kids, and left them for this place, for her pumas.

Mila turns to Sammie. "¿Y Vanesso?"

"Oh, Mila," Sammie keens. "¡Él es perfecto!" Vanesso is the cat Sammie works with. I know this because she carries a picture of him around in her pocket and spends hours staring at it. She calls him V. He's an ocelot, his fur golden yellow, marked with black rippling shapes. A flawless pink nose and gorgeous striped tail. He was rescued from a

Chinese restaurant. Katarina told me that Sammie arrived here last year with a boyfriend. She was assigned to Vanesso, who was just a baby then. Sick from all the Chinese food, vulnerable, needing a mum. She stayed for a few months, left because her boyfriend wanted to, dumped her boyfriend immediately and came back to look after V. She'll stay now until her money runs out. She walks Vanesso alone. Along the edge of a long lagoon. Through his forest trails. I do not doubt that all that time, one-on-one with the jungle, with him, has done something to her brain. Whenever anyone mentions Vanesso, it is as if just the sound of his name makes her heart crack. I am starting to wonder what the recovery period for an experience like this is.

"Todos los animales son perfectos, no?" Mila laughs. "Jaguaru también."

Harry nods serenely. "Él es el más perfecto."

Jaguaru and Jaguarupi are the only male jaguars in the world that volunteers can walk with, into the jungle. Ru's younger than Rupi. He's more playful, boisterous. He's the reason that Harry has stayed so long. He's the reason Harry has come back, two years in a row. He is the reason, I'm told, that Harry left a well-paid job in engineering. Every night, I see him return, often after dark. His clothes are ripped, he is exhausted, drained, and I have never seen a look like that on someone's face before. It's a look of absolute and utter certainty.

"Laura," Mila turns back to me. She says my name with the Spanish inflection that I love. It rhymes with *flower*. "¿Cuándo te vas?"

I close my eyes. When am I leaving? "Tengo un vuelo en una semana." I have a flight back to England in a week.

"¡Qué macana!" Mila exclaims. "¿Solo una semana más?"

"Wow," Sammie says. "Your month went quick."

I open my mouth to say yes, I can't believe it, but Harry cuts me off with a groan.

"It'll almost be wet season again before we know it."

Sammie yelps and pushes him. "No! Don't even say it. The mozzies will hear you."

They all laugh and I close my mouth, realising it's not about me. My short time here is just a scale to mark the turnings of the year for them.

Mila sighs. "Entonces tenemos que buscar un nuevo voluntario para Wayra."

I sit up with a start and say louder than I expect to, "¿Para Wayra?"

She tiredly runs her hands through her hair. "Sí. Tal vez mañana lleguen nuevos . . . con suerte."

"I . . ." I can't believe it. A new volunteer for Wayra? To take over from me? "No!"

Mila laughs and pats me on the hand. "Así es la vida." She sighs again and starts to get up. "Entonces, me voy a mi cama."

I watch her unfold herself. I'm desperate to protest but I don't know what words to use. No! I don't want you to find a new volunteer for Wayra. Harry and Sammie follow suit, and soon it's just me left on the road. Sammie pauses before they turn in, the path to camp obscured by clumps of overhanging trees silhouetted against the scatterings of stars.

"You could always stay, you know," she says, over her shoulder.

I gaze at her, the candle guttering next to me. And then she's gone, under the canopy. I have a flight, I say to myself. I have a flight.

As Mila predicts, a new volunteer does arrive the following evening. He trots onto the patio, eyes wide and bright, trekking shoes clean. I see him with a sinking heart as I stand on the stoop of La Paz, balancing on Bryan's shoulder, trying to remove my boot. I spent the day convincing myself that leaving was the right thing, the responsible thing. I'd gone over it so many times that in the end, Jane had had to yell at me to go and sit by myself until I sorted my head out.

All of us on the patio look up. He's got long hair, a dark beard. Tall, handsome, nice eyes. Coco and Faustino are sitting, as is their want, on a hanging platform underneath the eaves of Santa Cruz. There's a rare chill tonight, so Agustino has wrapped them in purple blankets and given them hot porridge to eat. Coco is furthest from the door, so I don't hear his grunt or see when he launches himself into the air, but I jump back when his bowl clatters to the ground. Tom and Harry, both of whom are filling water jugs at the standing tap, freeze. Osito, Teanji, and the girls, Mariela and Juana, sitting on the patio, all jump. Teanji falls out of Osito's lap with a beep of alarm. I hear from the direction of the aviary a violent squawk: "Don't do that!"

Osito yells, "Agustino!"

It's Mila who appears, but for once she's too slow. Coco's already lunging. It happens so quickly my brain can't keep up. His fur is so puffed he's double the size, and he has pulled back his lips like a dog or, scarier still, a human entering a fight. His thick muscular arms propel him fast along the ground. Monkeys shouldn't be on the floor. There's something wrong if they're on the floor.

"Coco, no!" Mila shouts, but Coco just snarls. Agustino races out from behind the animal kitchen then, his face flushed. When Coco sees him, the monkey hesitates, giving just enough time for Agustino to grab his tail. Coco howls and tries to leap away but Agustino holds on.

"No. No, chico." Agustino's face twists. "La puerta, por favor."

I right myself, uncurling my fingers from where I didn't even realise they'd been digging into Bryan's shoulder, and push open the door to Santa Cruz. Coco shits violently down Agustino's back. Once the door is closed on him, we all listen as he howls in earnest. Faustino, still up on the shelf, has lain down with his chin in his hands and watches the scene with a look of sad inevitability on his face.

"My name is Uri." The guy's voice is shaking. "What . . ."

Agustino wipes lumps of poo off his shoulder. Mila grips his arm.

"Bienvenido. Me llamo Agustino. Coco . . . the monkey who live here. He's scared of men who look like you."

Uri steps away, taken aback. "That look like *me*?"

Embarrassed, Agustino quickly tugs his own dark hair. "And me, when I first met him. Long hair. Dark. Tiene fantasmas."

"What does that mean?"

Agustino anxiously shuffles his feet, his bright-yellow gumboots incongruously shiny. "Coco has ghosts."

Uri looks around, baffled. "But he lives in a cage, right?"

Osito has come up behind us now, half the height of Uri, and crossed his arms. His young face is set, and Agustino rests a reassuring hand on his shoulder.

I like Uri. Within hours he's teaching Doña Lucia how to make shakshouka. He sings folk songs to Lorenzo, Crazy and Big Red and schools López in the basics of Hebrew so he can flirt with a pretty Israeli volunteer. But Coco doesn't let it go. He stalks Uri everywhere. He eyeballs him from outside the comedor. He slinks up and down outside the animal kitchen. Someone has to lock Coco in Santa Cruz just so Uri can visit the long drop.

It's three days after Uri arrives that I hear an awful scream. I run outside just in time to see Uri sprint out of the showers, blood dripping down his leg. The door bangs and Coco follows, eyes desperate. Uri runs into one of the rooms and out again, wearing the pair of leather gloves that Agustino has given him. Coco comes closer, baring his teeth. Uri steps back.

"No, Coco!" Uri claps the gloves.

Coco lunges and as he takes the leather in his teeth, Uri flings his hand, pushing the monkey back.

"¡No más, Coco!"

Coco circles him. What did they do to him in that hotel to make him do this? How hard did they beat him and how long did they keep him from seeing the sky? Coco drops his eyes, skulks backwards and

Uri lets the gloves fall. He is crying. But then Coco turns, rounding for another attack. I race forwards without even thinking and grab his tail, easing him up onto my shoulders. Coco presses his head hard against mine, wraps his tail around my neck and slaps me. It hurts, my skull vibrating with the force of it. But as I steady his weight, he puts his tongue in my ear, like a wet finger, as if to steady himself, and I hear his familiar grunt. Agustino takes Uri to the clinic and gives him four stitches. Uri leaves on the bus two hours later.

Coco goes missing that afternoon. I find him a little way down the road just as the sun is disappearing, the clouds a deep pink, the tops of the trees red. There is the far-away sound of wild howlers, making their raucous elegy to the dying day. I wonder if Coco can hear them. He is rocking, he pushes his lips out when he sees me and beats his palm on the ground. I try to pick him up but he's too quick. He bares his teeth and crawls a little further down the road. His back is bent, and then he starts beating his shoulders hard with one hand, the sound of the slap harsh and loud. I sit down quietly next to him but he just crawls away and starts again. He refuses to look at me.

The howls of the wild monkeys trail off. The patriarch often brings his troop close to camp to taunt Coco and Faustino. This patriarch is a big male monkey. Coco is bigger. Coco's fur is a darker red, his beard longer and thicker. I know in my broken, breaking heart that if things had been different, if forests weren't being cut down, if tourists like me weren't fuelling the demand for exotic pets, if it wasn't normalised to beat and push down those that are different, then Coco, with all his strength, passion and gentleness, could have been the leader of his own troop.

Coco doesn't move until Mila emerges, a dark silhouette. The sun falls below the horizon and the sky turns from pink to golden red, painting the tree tops bronze. A flock of macaws flies above the road, their wingtips matching the sky. Mila walks towards us slowly, her long plait swinging, her cowboy hat shadowing her face. When she reaches us, she pulls a piece of cheese out of her pocket. Coco crawls into her arms, shoves the cheese into his mouth and presses his face into her chest as if he cannot bear to look at anyone. He is ashamed and he is in pain.

I remember my life before, when animals were just animals, and I hate myself for it. How could I have ever thought this? And how could I have ever thought I was any different from them?

"Mila!" I call as she starts to walk back into camp.

She turns.

"Can I go into town tonight?"

"¿Por qué?"

"I think I will try to change my flight. I want to stay, if that's OK?"

She looks at me for a long moment and then nods. "Sí. It's OK."

Town is like Santa María, only bigger. I go by myself, getting a ride on the bus. There's a little internet café on the corner of the plaza where couples walk hand in hand in the evening, punctuated by popcorn sellers and coffee carts pushed by men in smart white uniforms. Motorbikes race around, decked with youths in their finest, blowing dust about the streets. The internet café burns with the heat of the computers. They work so slowly it's possible to load about one email every half hour. I bypass them, busy anyway with rowdy boys, and go straight to the phone booths to call my mum. Condensation steams the glass and the plastic receiver feels slippery in my hand.

"Hello?" Her voice sounds far away. The line buzzes, like there are bees in the receiver.

"Hi, Mum."

"Hello?"

"Mum, it's me."

"HELLO?"

"MUM, IT'S LAURA!" I shout and then hold the phone away as my words bounce back. I rest my forehead against the mirror in front of me. This is the first time I've seen myself in weeks. My face is pale, pitted with bites. There are hollows under my eyes. My short hair is a clotted mess. My cheekbones stand out more than they used to.

"Laura! Are you OK? We've been so worried!"

I laugh a little, imagining what she would say if she could see my face.

"I'm good. How are you?"

"Fine. Everything's fine. Where are you? How are you feeling about coming home?"

I close my eyes. The bees fade. I don't know when it happened but I've started to think of this place as home. The double-edge of this almost floors me. The last email I sent was a few weeks ago. A one-liner. I'd meant to send others, but I'd not come into town. I'd been going to Wayra. It had seemed, somehow, more important.

"I'm still at this parque."

She waits. When I say nothing else, she asks hesitantly: "And you're OK? It doesn't sound good in Bolivia. There's been riots . . . We've been worried."

"Riots?"

"Yes!"

I shake my head. I guess half the world could have exploded. "We don't get the news here."

"It looks scary."

I look around at the kids on their video games, at the lights of the motorbikes on the softly lit street.

"It doesn't feel scary."

"I hope your flight's going to be OK."

"That's the thing. Mum, I think I'm going to change it."

There is a long, slow silence.

"What do you mean?" I hear Fletcher bark. "You aren't coming home?"

I watch the seconds tick by on the display, every moment adding another dollar to the total. In England the cost of this phone call would be the same as a night out. Here, it is another week with Wayra.

"I don't want to leave."

"Bolivia?"

"This place. It's . . ." I laugh, holding my head in my hands. "It's ridiculous. It's . . ." My mum works in a hospital for personality-disordered women. Wayra, Coco, Panchita . . . they're as personality disordered as they come. I know my mum will understand. I just have to explain it right, but the words . . . I had so many of them when I was planning this on the bus.

"It's amazing."

"Well." She laughs gently. "It's nice to hear you so positive about something."

I reach for the stool and sit down. "It's wonderful and hard. It hurts every day and I can't stop smiling." There's a long pause. I think with a shock she might be trying not to cry. "There's this cat," I continue in a rush. "There's a monkey who bites people." I lean my face against the mirror again, suddenly feeling that I too might cry. How can I put these friends I've made—because they are, I realise, they're my friends—into sentences? If I can't explain every little thing, then I don't want to explain anything. "I'll tell you everything when I get back. I promise."

"When will that be Lau?"

I gaze at the ticking clock. "Three more months maybe?" I imagine her staring out of the window into the garden. She can probably just see the edge of the little wood. I hesitate. "I've met someone."

"Really?" She tries to keep the excitement out of her voice.

I laugh.

"Well, come on. What's their name?"

"Wayra." I pause, just for a second. "She's four years old. She's a puma."

"A *puma*?"

I swallow a lump in my throat.

"I'm happy." I say it so quietly I don't think she hears.

"You know how I feel Lau," she finally whispers. "I just want you to be safe. And I miss you, that's all."

There's an expansive pause. I'm meant to say I miss you back. Before I missed them so much it hurt, but now . . .

"I miss you too," I say, swallowing hard. The truth is I'm not sure if I do. It's not that I don't care, of course I do, but it's just that this place is like the tree roots that suck up all the water and don't leave any room for anything else. Any other thoughts I had, the anxieties, ambitions, the endless circling worries, they've gone. They've stopped breathing and all that's left is this.

On the way home, I hang my legs over the top of a logging truck and watch the orange lights of the town fading, the fields melting, the land rising, evidence of human existence softening, then disappearing altogether. The black sky opens, empty of everything but stars. As we set off, the driver offered me a handful of coca leaves, which I took, chewing them excitedly and trying not to gag as I climbed onto the top of his truck. It's my first taste of coca. The leaves are a cultural staple, sacred. They're meant to give you energy, suppress your appetite, help with altitude sickness in the mountains. But now, the taste is so bitter, the hard leaves so strange against my tongue, that I feel nauseous. Quickly, I tuck the chewed-up wad into the inside of my cheek, as I've watched others do, and swill the taste down with the warm beer the driver has given me. We swerve over potholes, over the broken cracks in the road, and I hang on tight as the magic of the coca beats in my veins. Trees swell, their bulk familiar, the branches of so many roadside witches curving into the starlight like broken, stuttering clouds. I can't stop smiling.

I open my mouth and let out a whoop, startling the hawks perched on the shoulders of the trees. I want to be loud! The jungle makes me want to open my lungs and sing. I don't feel any kind of premonition, no uneasy tingling as I rest against a decapitated tree, its veins coated in centuries-old sawdust. I just watch the forest fly past and I think to myself in my selfish, naïve way that it's endless. I can't imagine the trees not being here and I can't imagine not being here either.

The next day we're at Wayra's lagoon, and Jane has left to go back to camp to bring out a picnic lunch. The lagoon is at the end of one of Wayra's shortest trails, less than a few minutes' walk from her cage. It's milky brown, kidney-shaped, with shrubs and tall, thin trees huddling around the edges. The beach is sandy dirt, the colour of caramel. It angles sharply downwards, and another runner rope—not long, perhaps four metres—stretches parallel to the bank. Wayra stays here for hours. Soft green curtains of creepers trail into the water, which glistens as if made of glass. It smells of vegetation, rich, almost spicy. The ground is peppered with red and black seeds, the kind that are made into necklaces and waved at every tourist. I have a bracelet myself, buried in my backpack, which makes me feel strange when I think about it, like the person who bought that bracelet was another person entirely.

A heron with a black cap frequents the opposite side of the lagoon, her stick-thin legs reflected in the mirror-still water. Macaws, hawks, kites and vultures circle above us. A family of small turtles sun themselves on a half-submerged tree root, and tamarins leap through a favourite clump of bamboo. Electric-blue butterflies land next to us and every so often we see the head of a black caiman gliding lazily by. When the sun starts to set, the whole lagoon turns gold, then scarlet. We can hear Coco and Faustino, sitting as they always do on the roof above Santa Cruz, howling.

Today, though, it is not yet two and the sun is baking, a bright cir-
clet in a blue sky. Wayra has slept here most of the morning but she is
awake now, perched on the edge, looking into the water. The end of her
tail is twitching. Something surfaced a few minutes ago and the ripples
are still going. It must have been something large, I think. Wayra turns
her head as if she's heard me. Yes. It was a very big fish, she agrees, her
eyes narrowing.

"You should chase it, then!"

She turns away as if I'm an idiot, returning her gaze to the water.
According to Jane, Wayra has never been swimming and, although she
can spend hours staring at the reflections, she shows no inclination to go
further. Other cats swim. Yuma, Inti, Wara and Yassi, Rupi and Ru . . .
They each have access to their own lagoons, or their own private spots
on the river that I've been told runs around the south of the parque.
They swim most days with their volunteers, and they would swim in
the wild. I think sometimes that when Wayra's staring into the water,
she's trying to find her courage. But she's afraid. I understand this. The
bravado, the hissing and growling, they're her coping mechanisms, just
as smiling and *being fine* is mine. When I step on a stick, she jumps a
metre in the air. A puma who's afraid of her own shadow. Who's afraid
of the wild.

She gives a sigh and stands, turning her face away and dropping
into a yoga stretch—a cat pose, then a slow, deliberate cow. I'm at the
top of the rise, where over many days I've carved out a spot just for me.
I can see the patted-down outline of my body. Wayra looks off into the
shadows and I think she'll settle down again in the shade, but once she's
stretched, she circles and pads up to the top, where she places herself
down with another sigh next to me.

My heart is beating so loudly she must be able to hear it. The scarlet-
and-green hummingbird, collecting nectar from the flowers, must be
able to hear it. Wayra has never sat with me before, not without Jane
here to tell me what to do. Her face is turned slightly away from the

light and her eyes are in shadow. She leans down with a very deliberate movement and starts to clean her paws, giving me time to take some slow, deep breaths. I think she knows what I'm thinking before I think it. Her back is to me, lying flat on one side like a half-flipped pancake, and I can see each of her individual hairs. I know now that her fur isn't grey or white or tawny or silver. She is all of them, graded through the different colours, giving the impression that she changes colour as the light itself changes.

Pumas hunt from above and behind, leaping onto your back to rip out your throat. You should never drop your guard. But Wayra . . . she's sometimes so calm I think I could press my face against hers. And yet I've also seen how fast she can turn, how angry she can suddenly become. She could be on my back in less time than it would take for me to blink, although this whole month she's never tried. I wonder how many months I'll need, how many onion layers, before I don't feel my heart in my throat every time she's near. I feel easier every day, but I don't know if there are enough days in the world for this to feel normal. I don't know if I want there to be.

"Está bien, Wayra," I say, trying to be calm. "It's all good."

She turns and leans towards me, as if to say: *I know.*

Quickly I roll up my sleeve. She gives a grunt of satisfaction before starting to lick, pulling closer with one giant forepaw. I wince, because the pain of her tongue is so sharp, but I don't move. She's making a soft grumble and I hope this is OK. If the grumble gets louder, then I should move away, give her space, but I find it almost impossible to tell the difference between a good grumble and a bad one. I've got it wrong so many times, and when I do, she snaps or snarls at me, often missing my hands by millimetres. Jane laughs when this happens, telling me that if Wayra wanted to hurt me, she would have done it already. And I have to prove that I trust her. But I don't trust her, and I just can't hear what Jane seems able to sense intuitively.

I clear my throat.

Wayra continues to lick.

"Wayra?"

Her ears move ever so slightly. The hum of the jungle—like a single organism—sounds like an oddly soothing car alarm. Her eyes come up and meet mine, the line on a heart monitor, a single thread of amber that circles her pupil.

"I changed my flight last night. I'm staying."

She pushes my arm away and rolls over onto her stomach, her paws crossed in front of her. She's facing the lagoon, the end of her tail touching my boot. We're sharing the shade of an overhanging banana tree. The water sparkles down below and she watches it. I'm relieved that she's turned her attention away from me, and disappointed too. But as she puts her chin on her paws and closes her eyes, I think, by the angle of her ears, that she's still listening to me.

"Are you . . . listening?"

She pretends to be asleep. I laugh, shaking my head.

"Is it OK with you, if I stay?"

She lazily turns to the side and rests her cheek on the ground. Her nose is scaled with an intricate pattern of dots that I've never noticed before. And there is a tiny piece of dried snot in one of her nostrils. Inexplicably, this makes my eyes sting. It is OK. Of all the spots at this lagoon, Wayra has chosen to settle next to mine. It took a whole month and she doesn't use words as I do, but she knows how to make a point. I'm OK. She's telling me she thinks I'm OK.

"Thank you, princesa." I sniff, trying not to make a big deal out of it.

Wayra gives me a long, scathing look before getting up and walking away.

That evening Paddy and I take it upon ourselves to hitch into the village. He's staying too, Bryan as well, both of them as besotted with their cats, and this place, as I am. We climb the sheer black rocky cliffs behind the rows of huts, the surface so rough it grazes our hands and knees like sandpaper. We laugh absurdly when we almost topple down massive crevasses and reach the top just as the sun starts to disappear. From here, Osito has promised us, we'll be able to see everything. And as the edges of the sky turn orange, like it's on fire, we stand on the lip of an outcrop that has probably been climbed by the people in this community for more years than I can fathom, and stare, utterly speechless. Santa María is a pinprick of speckled lights among trees that go on and on and on like a carpet of moss across an entire world. The jungle sweeps for as far as I can see until it disappears under a layer of pinkish haze. Far away, I can just make out the faint curve of a mountain ridge. I'm on another planet, where no humans have ever stepped. I'm a giant, overlooking a smoky emerald sea, and at the same time I'm an ant whose head is about to explode. The rocks that we're standing on are knobbles that sprouted out of the roots of the earth before time itself was even a concept. There are silvery flashes of water. The long, winding river, and lagoons. Wayra's isn't the only one, of course. I can see ten or fifteen other lagoons from up here, spread out across the horizon, glowing in the early evening sunlight. Maybe there are pumas at each one, watching the daylight fade.

The next morning a cool breeze blows through the window and a shock of water hammers against the tin roof. It's so loud I can barely hear Katarina snoring underneath me, Paddy in the bunk opposite at a slightly higher pitch. Mila, who shares our room too, has just gone, out to walk cats before anyone else wakes. I hear her low knock next door, Tom's quiet answering grunt, the thud of his feet as he gets out of his bunk, the rustle as he gets dressed. Then, a few minutes later, their two sets of footsteps as they set off into the jungle. Tom—awkward, gentle Tom, more at ease with Faustino and Teanji than with anyone else—is the one that Mila takes with her when she's working with the most troubled cats. I wonder where they're going this morning. Then I sigh, staring into the cobwebs. What they do out in the jungle, with cats that I will never get to meet, is something magic, secret and private.

Silently, I roll out of bed and pull on my clothes. No one else is awake. Early morning—this is the only time when camp is still, as if no humans live here at all. This is magic too. My boots are full of water but I push my feet in anyway, letting the cool liquid ooze out through the holes. The sky is leaden and the forest smells clean and hot. This is rain with a steamy heartbeat of its own, picking up the mud and ants and mulch and carrying them away in rivulets, then rivers. A cacophony of drops hits the leaves, thousands upon thousands deep, like I'm in an amphitheatre and all around me, stretching for miles, is the sound of drummers. Already the ground is flooded. Streams make moats around each of the buildings.

Panchita sprints towards me, covered in dripping compost, and rubs her snout ecstatically against my thighs. I give her a scratch and then head for the aviary. Teanji scurries after me, beeping. I pull back the curtains that shelter the birds, unleashing hoots of greeting. I say a quick hello to Lorenzo, who rolls onto his back, oblivious to the scathing looks from the other macaws. I say hello to Big Red, who cackles, I say hello to Dontdothat, who shrieks, "Don't do that!" and then I go round to let out the pìos. Petunia and Patrick sprint out of their house but the others stay inside, wrapped up warm. I collect armfuls of young patuju shoots, food for the monkeys, birds, pìos and tortoises. Teanji beeps from his favourite spot up on top of the aviary door, ready to terrorise volunteers when they start trying to enter with bowls of food.

I leave my finds in the animal kitchen and make a bee-line for the long drop. I meet Sammie on the way, heading in the same direction.

"Poo race, Frodo?" Sammie asks as we fall into step.

I grin. "What's a—"

"First one to finish is the winner!" Sammie starts to run, elbowing me out of the way. It takes me a few seconds to calibrate, but then I'm running too, laughing. The path's slippery and we both end up falling, giggling as we grab on to each other's sleeves. Sammie finally gets free and then she's launching for the new long drop, which Bobby and Harry built just a few days ago to stop the old one filling up too fast. But like many things constructed here, quickly and with little money, it's ill advised—it's too close, separated from the original by not much more than a few feet and a flimsy wall that's already starting to be eaten by lines of hungry termites.

Breathless, I pull open the door to the old toilet, nod a hello to Hagrid, who is spinning rapidly, and undo my jeans. Through the holes in the wall, I can see the edges of Sammie's face. I feel a surge of shame but then she just turns and waves.

"I heard you're staying then?"

"I'm staying!" The toilet armadillo scratches around beneath my feet.

"Good. Means you'll get to be part of team construction."

I pause, mid-wipe. "Team construction?"

"Yeah, we're starting this morning."

"We are?"

I hear her door slam and a whoop of joy. "The champion keeps her throne!"

"Shit." I quickly finish and scurry outside.

"Well played." Sammie winks as she sets off back towards the comedor, whistling a tune between her teeth, saying over her shoulder, "We might make a long-termer out of you yet!"

I'm left standing stupidly on the path, not knowing what to say.

Bryan and I hover next to each other, neither of us liking the look of the scene in front of us. The rain has stopped and now I'm just wet.

Bobby is jovially handing out hessian sacks, standing upon a very large pile of rocks. We're just off the road, a few minutes past Wayra's witch trees. Thick damp grass covers the ground, drying quickly in the hot sun, and there's the start of a winding path heading off behind the rocks. Otherwise it's patuju, palms and banana trees. I think I can just see the start of a lagoon, not Wayra's, a different one, hidden by a brush of ferns.

"I'm not happy about this," Bryan hisses as Bobby claps his hands and does a little dance. There are about twenty of us clumped about the clearing, each of us holding these ominous sacks. "I didn't sign up for this."

"This season's first day of construction!" Bobby exclaims. "Cheer up Bry, it's going to be a long, gruelling slog. You'll hate it with the fire of a thousand suns."

I gaze longingly back along the road towards where I know Wayra is waiting, probably wondering why we're so late.

Our first task is to carry the pile of rocks to the site that we're going to be building a new cage on. Even Paddy looks daunted. I fall into the middle of the crowd, eyeing the pile, and when I gingerly pick up my first rock, the size of a baby's head, I whimper as I place it into my sack. Bobby helps me hoist it onto my back when it's full and I sway, thinking for a terrifying moment that I might just topple over. I enjoy an unexpected flash of the mysterious lagoon, get a whiff of mandarins, then the reality of what we're doing slams back in and the bush crowds over us. I lose sight of the road and pretty soon I can focus on nothing but my feet, the painful rubbing of my thighs and the crippling sack gouging into my spine. The ground is pitted, the undergrowth punishingly sharp, the air dusky and bug ridden. We walk, and walk, and walk. In reality it's not far at all, not much more than a quarter mile, but to me it seems we just keep going deeper with no sign of slowing. I'm used to Wayra's trails. They are short and wide and well managed (we rake them three times a week to keep the jungle from reclaiming them), and even though sometimes they still catch me out, I feel I'm starting to understand them. This is different. This is like the clock has been turned back and I'm a new volunteer again. Like I'm eight years old and I'm in a forest at night. Sometimes I lose the path altogether and it's only the muffled voices, in front of me and behind, that keep me from losing my shit.

Suddenly I hear a new sound, a sound that doesn't seem right. It's a crash and a rumble, not the normal jungle conversation that burrows in the back of my ears. This jars, but I can't stop. My bag is too heavy. I'll lose my grip and it'll collapse. But the noise gets louder and harsher and then, just as I think I need to stop, to look up, to find out what this is, I barrel into Paddy, who's in front of me. Bryan promptly slams into me. My sack spills to the ground and I jump back, rocks cascading around my ankles. I open my mouth to curse but when I look up, I see what has been causing the noise. Paddy is backing away, into me.

In front of us is a cage. It's small, less than half of Wayra's, made of reinforced red bars, a hard shock against the softness of the palms behind, the jungle that my eyes have become so used to. It's set in a clearing not much bigger than the cage itself. Inside is what seems to be the largest animal I've ever seen. A jaguar, dark orange, lathered with black rosettes that make his definitions hard to see. His eyes are amber, his body low, compact. He's ramming his head, which is bigger than mine and rounded as a pit bull's, against the bars. This is what's been making the high-pitched crashing. All three of us take quick steps backwards. The jaguar snarls.

"Go!" Katarina, who I now see sitting on a log on the other side of the cage, hisses. "Keep moving." She's got Bobby's guitar in her lap. I know sometimes the cats enjoy listening to music, but I can't imagine this cat enjoying anything. I struggle to pick up my sack, fear making me useless. His muscles bunch and his eyes go black. Katarina murmurs, just as we do with Wayra. "Está bien, Sama. Shh, chico. Shh."

Once we're past the cage, the jungle rises back up, a mesh of speck-led trunks, lofty patuju and lianas hanging from the upper branches and shielding the cage, and the cat. Under my feet are leaves of every different purple. There is still a trail but it's thinner, cut quickly with a machete.

"Jesus," Bryan exclaims.

I'm speechless. But as we follow the path, I manage to stammer out what Katarina has told me, lying in our bunks at night. This is Sama. He's the cat Katarina works with every day, and she cries when she tells me about him, her dark head shaking in the shadow of the candlelight. He came to the parque when he was young. Not here, but to the organ-isation's other sanctuary on the other side of the country. They hoped to release him, because in those days release seemed a viable option. They found him a territory in Brazil and he went through a form of rehabilitation. He was given live prey, isolated from humans, taught to fear them. Then the government changed their minds. His release was called off, just like that, because without governmental support a release cannot go ahead. Sama's life had shrunk, decided on paper by people who didn't know him, somewhere at a desk far away. Now here he is breaking his teeth on the bars, trying to fight his way out of a life sentence. He's older now, eleven, but jaguars in captivity can live up to twenty-five.

He isn't like Wayra. He can't come out of his cage. He'll never be able to. It's taken two years to raise enough money to even start to build him something vaguely adequate. It'll take us more than six months to complete, using two hundred metres of fencing three times over to make it high enough to be secure, barbed wire, stone, cement, months of digging, carrying, pulling, securing . . . and Sama will be stressed throughout, not understanding. When he's finally released into it, he may have at best half his life to experience it, at worst, less than a quarter.

In one of the hostels when I was travelling, I saw a jaguar skin, pinned up high on one wall. I didn't think much about it then. I do now. It had the same black markings, the same yellow ears with spots to mimic eyes, the same white belly, the same long tail with the black patch of fur on the end. It's luck that Sama is here and not there. That Sama has twenty or so humans building him a new home, when he could be on a wall somewhere, stuck in some museum, on the floor in someone's dining room, eyes cut out, stomach slashed, claws taken. And it's luck too, luck of an opposite kind, that Sama's not free as he should be.

Bryan brings me back to reality.

"Mila thinks we can build something to hold an animal as aggressive as that?" he hisses. "Has she not seen Bobby's attempt at a new toilet?"

When I think I literally won't be able to walk anymore, we find Tom, Harry and Sammie, filthy, dripping with sweat, standing over a tarp of half-mixed cement, looking like they're having the time of their lives. Harry, shirtless, is leaning cheerfully on a shovel. His skin is shockingly pale, the result of months under the canopy, rarely seeing direct sunlight. He nods to his left where there's an emerging pile of rocks.

"On there?" I say, my arms shaking dangerously.

"On there."

Paddy, who hasn't been here quite long enough to have lost his orange glow, optimistically empties his sack. "Now what?"

Sammie pats him kindly on the back. "Now you do it again."

I cannot help but let out a long groan. I cringe as my mediocre offering lands on the pile with a sorry thunk.

"How many rocks was that?" Harry laughs. "Two?"

"Six!" I blush, glaring at him.

Tom shakes the sweat out of his eyes and goes back to stirring the cement. "Six is six more than we had before," he says philosophically.

Tom is strong and short, the muscles in his back and freckled arms brawny. His beard is wildly curly. A golden, almost reddish blond. He's got an ungainly large head, and his neck is so broad, I'm not sure how he moves it at all. But he's got a sweet face. And I've noticed how he struggles to make eye contact with anyone apart from Faustino. His grey-blue eyes meet mine for just a moment and then flick away shyly, back to the cement. It's easy to see the toll the jungle has written on him. Like Harry, there are gaunt hollows in his cheeks, a concave dip beneath his ribs and shadows under his eyes. Despite that though, he's one of the only long-termers who always waves, always says hello, no matter how tired. And I've never seen him say no to any job—however ridiculous—Mila asks of him. Even if it's going out at midnight with her deep into the jungle, just to give one of the ocelots some probiotics.

Sammie too. She's just as bad, going out at all hours whenever required. But with the lack of sunlight, the deficit of vitamins, her hair has started to fall out. I've watched Coco gently pull clumps of it away as they go through their daily grooming. She shrugs it off as a positive—at least she won't have to worry about lice. But as the light catches her face now, there is tiredness engrained in every stretch of her skin. Her flannel shirt is sodden with sweat. Mud and cement cake her body. Her stomach is swollen from eating little but carbohydrates. These people aren't built to survive here and yet here they are. They're somehow connected to this jungle just as much as Sama has been ripped out of it. It's all upside down and the wrong way round.

"I think you should cut the judgement, Harry," Sammie says, laughing. "She's changed her flight, she's staying, for *Wayra*. Has he told you, Frodo?" She picks up one of my rocks and inspects it casually. "He walks a jaguar but he's still scared of a little old puma?"

I stare at him. "You're scared of her? Of Wayra?" I ask quietly.

I'm terrified of her. I never understand what she's telling me. I don't know whether she wants me to come closer or go as far away as possible. I don't know whether she wants to lick me or bite me, whether she's growling because she's happy or pissed off. I continue to feel like I'm risking my life every time I'm within a few metres of her. But . . . this guy? A drop of sweat, brown from the earth, trails down the middle of his torso. He glances at me out of the corner of his eye.

"Yeah." He shrugs. "She's fucking scary."

Sammie nods. "True story."

I narrow my eyes. I think she might be joking, but Tom's nodding too.

"But she just . . . sleeps," I stammer. She doesn't jump on you, like I know some of the others do, or try to play with you the moment you lose concentration. She lets you sit down, she loves to be stroked. She needs a bodyguard, for god's sake, to walk through the jungle! She hasn't even touched me, apart from to put her head on my lap or lick my fingers. She . . .

"She hisses. And grumbles," Harry mutters. "And hisses some more. She sleeps for hours until you lose your mind, and then forces you to gallop back to the cage hissing at you again. She's never happy. She never wants to play. You do one thing and she immediately wants you to do another. She's terrified of everything but acts like a fucking bitch about it . . ."

"She's not a bitch!" I yell, my face suddenly scarlet. "Don't call her that!"

Harry just shrugs again and turns his back on me, picking up his shovel. "Wayra volunteers," he mutters.

I stand there speechless, wanting to throttle him. How dare he? He doesn't know the first thing about her, or me. Finally, when no one says anything else, Paddy and Bryan pull me away.

"She's not a bitch," I exclaim again, gripping Paddy's arm.

He gently pats me on the shoulder.

Later, when we've barely made a dent in the rocks and I'm wallowing in the afterglow of a lunch of four different types of potato, I'm sitting on the patio watching some leaf-cutter ants. About a hundred of them have split off into three circles, one small, one medium and one large, and they are just going around and around as if they will do it until they die. I cannot understand what has happened to them.

"Frodo."

I look up with a start. Harry is standing above me, looking uncharacteristically awkward. The sky behind him is the darkest brown I've ever seen. I gaze back and forth for help, but there's no one else around apart from Teanji, nuzzling in the pockets of Osito's school uniform. The boy is fast asleep under one of the benches. Harry rubs his beard.

"So you're going to come with me this afternoon."

I stare at him, trying to find the joke. But he just sits down quickly and puts what he's carrying, Ru's meat bucket and two machetes, on the bench. "A tree's gone down on Ru's trail and I need help clearing it."

"My help?" I squeak.

He gazes at the ants, grinning lopsidedly as if he can't quite bring himself to use his whole mouth. "I know. Shocker." He rubs his beard again. It's grown longer in the time that I've been here. The blunt edges of his fingers are dark with the stain of cement. I wonder if he'll ever get it out. Finally he turns and looks at me full on, letting out a sigh. "You coming?"

I hesitate. I want him to apologise, for today, for ignoring me for the last month. I could tell him no, I could tell him to find some other sucker to clean his trail. But also, this is the chance of a lifetime. To see another part of the jungle. To see Ru's trail! I think this is the best apology I'm going to get, so I stand up quickly before I lose my nerve.

"Fine," I snap. "Do you know why they're doing that?"

He raises his eyebrows, then crouches on his heels to inspect the ants more closely. They're dark red, their backs and pincers shiny. Some of them are carrying leaves that they've scavenged, as big as my thumb, but show no sign of tiredness despite having been trapped in a seemingly never-ending loop. Harry straightens and the tension in his shoulders is gone.

"They've just gone fucking nuts." He hands me one of the machetes with a laugh and starts to head off down one of the trails, beckoning me to follow. "No different from us really." He looks back over his shoulder and winks at me. "Right?"

It isn't long before the thunder starts in earnest. The slim sheaf of sky has turned from brown to deep purple. Harry has led me away from camp, not over the road but out back, towards where the river is, and where most of the animals have their enclosures. It's only Wayra, Sama and another jaguar—Katie—who live on the other side of the road. I look around, wide-eyed, as we walk. Broad swathes of patuju, young ones that are as light as cut grass, and adults, dark emerald, twice my height, stretch for as far as I can see. Cacao trees twist up out of the plants like black waves on an ocean. Most of the ancient forest was cut down decades ago, Harry tells me with disgust. They were replanted with these cacaos, although the plantation inevitably failed. This is what enabled the parque to buy the land. The chocolate forest remains, intermingled with the rest of the jungle, a ghost of failed economic development. There are still a few of the old trees left, though, trees that survived the cut, that would have been around before the road was conceived of, before even my great-grandparents were conceived of.

The jungle becomes broader, darker, wider, taller, deeper . . . Perhaps it's the impending storm but despite the stifling heat, I shiver.

"How far is it?" I ask tentatively. I'm out of breath, exhausted from the morning's construction, and Harry's a quick walker. He's been here long enough to know the trails like his own skin. We're following the line of a muddy ditch, and it's like walking through a slip and slide. The only way to keep upright is to grab on to whatever is nearest, which often (I learn the hard way) tends to be a tree covered in spikes, a tree covered in fire ants or, even worse, a tree covered in purple poisonous caterpillars. I only avoid them because Harry swings back and grasps my wrist just in time, telling me with an exasperated shake of his head that they'll put me in bed for over a week.

I find myself sticking close to him after that, his thick, musty, sweaty scent overpowering the other smells. My calves and thighs scream with the strain of keeping up.

"You OK?" he calls over his shoulder. I'm trying to extract my boot from where it has got caught under a root. I can tell by the muffled laughter that I'm meeting his expectations perfectly. Why the hell did he bring me then, I think crossly as I finally get free, only to trip again almost immediately, narrowly missing falling face-first into a tree that's more samurai than tree, its spikes so sharp they're like the spikes you'd find on a medieval mace.

"I'm fine." I grit my teeth.

He waits, leaning casually against a sandy termite mound, massive and sculptural as if it's been created by an artist on LSD. In the jungle, I am realising, everything is the same, and yet as I see more of it, it changes with each turn, each valley, each dip, each spin of my head. We've been weaving in between these mounds for the last few minutes and the one Harry has chosen is bigger than he is. It's a city of mud, a million windows and doors, although it seems as if it's been abandoned. Maybe all the termites are asleep, safe inside from the storm that's coming fast.

"Ru's a bit further away than Wayra, right?"

There's a crack of thunder and I jump.

I nod, smiling politely. "A little bit." A fucking lot.

"A few months ago this trail was swamp up to your chest. It was an hour's walk then, every day." He assesses me from his position against the mound, his blue eyes twinkling. "Maybe two for you."

I scowl. "Well, I can't think of anything worse than walking through swamp for an hour every day." I know, though, it's not just an hour. That's just the walk out there. The cats' trails flood too, so there's no respite for the volunteers working with animals in the flooded sections of the parque. They're in swamp all day. I don't think I would have lasted. I definitely wouldn't have extended. That's why I was so surprised at Harry's vehemence earlier. Wayra might be emotionally hard. But she lets you nap all day! Your feet are dry! She's a ten-minute walk from camp, tops! I shudder, looking around and trying to imagine what would have happened if I'd been assigned a different cat. And then, for the very first time, I wonder if Mila did it on purpose. Whether it wasn't just that Wayra needed someone but that Mila clocked me on arrival. Did she think: Maybe this strange, shy girl might be a good match for a cat like Wayra? I smile at the thought.

"You don't really know yourself until you've spent months in the swamp," Harry says quietly, pushing himself off the mound. I watch as a cascade of tiny mud balls fall to the ground. I roll my eyes, trying to remind myself that this is the worst kind of macho bullshit and I shouldn't be impressed. The wind has started to pick up and the jungle has gone quiet. We walk on, the only noises the creaking of the branches, the rasp of my laboured breathing and the crack of my knees. I stare at Harry's back. At where his jeans are tucked into his dark-blue boots, the rip along the arm of his shirt, which I think may once have been red but is now a mouldy brown, at the line of taut muscle along his neck. There's a spikiness that seems to make the air around his broad shoulders warp, like it would hurt if I tried to touch him. Warning bells should be going off but they're not. I'm too caught up in how it feels when his eyes twinkle at me. Over the electric hum in my belly, it's hard to hear anything else.

After we've been walking in silence for another twenty minutes, más o menos, Harry stops abruptly. We've come out in a small clearing. We are surrounded by a thick brace of bamboo, the colour of dark wine bottles. I open my mouth to ask where we are but Harry stops me, putting his finger to his lips.

"Ru's just through there," he whispers, his whole countenance changing, the spikiness melting away. His eyes gleam as he points through the bamboo, and I squint, hoping to catch a glimpse of the enclosure. But the bamboo is just too thick. I won't get to meet Ru, but on the other side of that jungle lives an animal that Harry has spent every day with for the last six months, that made him leave his job, his life, his home, that made him fly across the world more than once. It's been driving me crazy, wondering what that creature must be like to have elicited such commitment from someone like Harry. As we keep going, there are signs of his presence everywhere. Paw prints in the mud, larger than my hand. Trees with deep, oozing claw marks, patuju barrelled over, scrape marks in the dirt.

When the air starts to feel different, Harry pauses. There is a spark in his eyes that makes me catch my breath.

"Have you ever seen the river?"

"No," I whisper. I've been dying to walk out here to see it, since the first moment last night when I saw the twist of its spine from up on the rocks in the village. Río San Pablo—it twines north through forest after forest, meeting human settlements here and there, meeting with other rivers, the Beni and the Madre de Dios, to become the Madeira and then, eventually, the Amazon itself. But here it's still minor, a slow-moving offshoot that marks the border of the parque on the southern edge. Bobby told me he canoed it once. There were so many twists to it, it took him an entire day to get from Santa María back to camp.

The river that I see though, as Harry steps back with a full two-sided grin, feels anything but small. It's fifteen metres across at least, and the wind is roiling to make sharp, pointed waves. The water is coffee-dark, and there's a track that takes us down to a long beach, paw and footprints layered among one another. At the edge there's an old, battered canoe, tied fast to the bank.

"That's where we sit together sometimes," Harry says, pointing, grinning.

"In the canoe?" I exclaim. "With Ru?"

He nods, full of that certainty which I find so startling. I gulp, looking back at the broad expanse of water. Some part of me suddenly feels that I'm not meant to be here. I'm trespassing. This is Ru's. Maybe he knows we've come here, from all the way back behind that brace of bamboo, and he's pacing the fence even now, smelling my uncertainty on the breeze.

"We should keep going," I say quickly, turning away. But Harry catches my arm and I stop, staring into his face.

"Wait."

I glance back at the river, the canoe trailing desperately in the hard current.

In England, I used to feel like that canoe. As if I were swimming against something I couldn't fight. I was going round and round and everyone else I knew seemed to be OK with it. None of my friends were talking about the fucking loop we were all in, like those insane ants.

I couldn't see how to get out. I couldn't see how to make it stop.

But now Harry's hand on my arm feels like the cutting of a tether.

"Why did you bring me here?"

"To cut down a tree," he says softly. "What else is there?"

I know full well what else there is. I'm about to answer when there's another crack of thunder, a flash of lightning, striking the darkness as if someone has set off an emergency flare. The skies open. Harry grabs my hand, pulls me up the bank until we're under a cacao tree. Its branches rattle wildly.

"These trees," Harry yells over the storm, "during cacao season when the pods come out, they turn the jungle orange, like it's on fire."

I stare upwards as the rain cascades down. The gods have upturned their bathwater, and it smells like that too, hot and heady. It's been stewing for days. I hold out my hands, feeling the hard patter of it against my skin. Within heartbeats I'm drenched. I pull my arms in, under my shirt, and we huddle down, our backs to the trunk, which has been warming all day and now gives out delicious heat. Harry nudges me and points upwards. In the branches, only a few metres above us, two little black creatures are huddled. Their eyes are big and round as polished brown stones.

"Oh!" I mouth. Night monkeys! I've never seen night monkeys before. They're notoriously shy but they've come here, just like we have, for shelter. Lightning sets off the sky again, so close that I can feel the reverberations in my spine, and the monkeys' eyes widen with fear. Mine do too. Fear and awe and disbelief that I've somehow found myself at the heart of a forest I can imagine once spread its roots across the entire expanse of South America.

"You cold?" Harry asks.

I'm shivering, my shirt plastered to me like an extra layer of skin. I nod and he puts his arm around my shoulders. His beard is dripping and it tickles my cheek. When I laugh, he looks down with a grin, and then leans his head back against the trunk. I nestle against his arm. We watch the rain. I can't even see the river now. It's all shrunk to a pinprick. The world is just me and this guy and this tree.

"Are you really scared of Wayra?"

He growls under his breath. "Sammie loves to bring that up."

"So you are?"

He sighs. "I'd be an idiot if I wasn't."

"But . . . you walk a jaguar."

"Yeah, so? I'm scared of him too. If you're not, there's something wrong with you." I sense that this isn't it though, so I wait. And after a while: "But Wayra . . ." He pauses, thinking. "I'm sorry I called her a bitch. I haven't worked with her enough to be making claims like that. But . . . And don't let this go to your head, you're still a clumsy idiot, but I do respect anyone who finds a way to work with that cat."

I twist my neck to look at him, but he just looks away, out at the rain.

"Never tell Jane I said that."

I continue to watch him.

"It's not so much that I'm scared she'll hurt me. It's more . . ." He takes a deep breath. "She's just in so much pain. I can feel it on me, you know? I come back from a day with her and I can't get it off my skin. She's so different from all the rest. Jaguaru . . . Ru is always having fun. Yeah, he had a shit life but now . . . he's happy. He *loves* walking. He loves the jungle. He loves his trails. He loves his volunteers. It's tough, it's long days, sometimes he'll want to run for miles around his trails, sometimes he'll jump on you so many times you forget what's up and what's down, but all he asks is that you trust him. Your instincts do the rest. But Wayra . . . I feel like she needs more. More than what I can give her. She's unpredictable! She's *in her head*. It's all thinking. It's all about her. You'd never even consider sitting on the ground with another cat! Or giving any of them a bodyguard. Fuck. Someone walking in front, it would be a nightmare. They'd just treat that person as a toy. But not Wayra. It's all about her confusion, inability to feel safe. You have to be pretty strong to be able to handle that."

He coughs awkwardly and looks down at his boots.

I swallow hard. I'm not strong. I worry, every day, that she'll look into my soul and find me lacking. That I'm not what she needs. That someone better, braver, bolder could make her happier. I come back from a bad day, when she's been so scared she hasn't wanted to leave the runner, when she's hissed at shadows and spent a whole afternoon desperately cleaning, when we've given her food and she hasn't eaten any of it like she's got stress-induced anorexia . . . and I haven't been able to wash it off me. I've lain on the road chain-smoking, just because I can't bear to go to bed and listen to her hisses echoing through my skull. In those moments, I'd do anything not to go back out there. But every morning, I find a way to do it. And when she licks my arm, it makes all the rest of it seem somehow more important and—at the same time—more bearable.

I grin, elbowing Harry in the side. "So what you're saying is that I'm stronger than you?"

He snorts. "Don't get ahead of yourself, Frodo. At least I can walk without falling over."

I roll my eyes. "At least I'm not so dead inside I feel the need to fill my empty soul with every pretty new volunteer who gets off the bus."

He is silent for a moment. "Touché."

I laugh and then, suddenly, we're kissing. I don't know who initiates it. It might have been me, or not, I'm not sure. It doesn't matter. The rain falls and the thunder drifts. The night monkeys settle. The earth is warm underneath me and soon, I don't care about anything but the taste of his mouth, the hot smell of his sweat, and the heavy, delicious feeling of his body on top of mine.

A few weeks later I move next door, into the dark, dank room where the monkeys sleep. Jane helps me to move the hay mattress that has come to fit the contours of my body into Oscar's old bunk. On my first night, huddled into my new bed, I'm delirious with happiness. Coco is snuggled against my chest and Faustino is hogging my pillow, pressing his soft, fuzzy bulk into my face. A photo of Wayra that Mila has printed out for me is pinned to the wooden window frame. I can't sleep because I'm so hot. The monkeys are perfect hot water bottles. My sheets and skin are orange from their sweat, but somehow these things only make it better. The next morning, we go to Wayra and spend the whole day at the lagoon. The storms keep coming, making the smells different, the world wetter, hotter, closer. She comes up to the top of the bank and turns her angled cheekbones in our direction. A low, panicky grumble turns into a high, contented moan, and then a snore as she lays her head to rest on the ground between our boots and the new, young shoots of patuju that have sprouted up overnight.

I sit at the cracked, back table in the comedor and laugh as loudly as anyone when Bobby finds a papaya shaped like Coco's face, makes a crown for it out of leaves, and enthrones it up in the rafters. Jane and I go out at dawn to rake Wayra's trails and the sky is golden around the edges. I learn how to hold a machete without it slipping out of my hands and hitting Jane in the forehead. I don't push my worries into my stomach. Everyone's hair is messy, everyone stinks—the animals don't care, so why should I? The constant hum of social anxiety has gone. I smile only when it's honest. My brain is silent, filled with just the hip-hop beat of the jungle and the soundless conversations I have with Wayra. For the first time in my life, my bowel movements are normal! I don't do laundry. I wear the same clothes and press my nose up against them, committing to memory their mouldy, crusty smell. They have Wayra's grey fur caked around the sleeves, orange patches around the shoulders, where Coco and Faustino sit, blue feathers in the pockets from Lorenzo. I cannot imagine the tight tailored suits I used to wear, the smart leather bags I carried. When I come home from work to find Mila squeezing a lump the size of an apple out of a girl's back, thousands of jellied spider's eggs exploding across the patio, I elbow my way in to get a better look and offer to hold the tweezers.

I spend a lot of time on the road with Mila and Agustino, and the kids as well before they're sent to bed. Osito and Juana play stupid games, running up and down the tarmac, finding frogs to hide in people's boots. Germáncito—he wants to play too, but thinks he's too old for it. López flirts insatiably with Mariela, who does her homework in the fumador and ignores him. I spend time with the other long-termers too: Katarina and Jane, Paddy and Bry, Tom, Bobby, Sammie, Harry. We laugh together, sharing cigarettes and stale packets of chocolate, watching the stars shoot across the blackness, talking about the dorms Panchita and Teanji have broken into, the food they've stolen, the volunteers they've harassed, the infinite minutiae of what each of our cats has done that day. Once it gets late and the others go to bed, if we're not too tired, Harry and I walk together. When we get far enough away, we kiss. His beard scratches my face and the sweaty, dark smell of him clogs my nostrils. I remember what he said about Wayra and I convince myself that I'll never ask him to be anything more than this.

Soon though, and I don't remember when or how it happens, I start to sleep in his bed. More than I do in mine. It feels as inevitable as a wave that's taken me down a tributary. I can't find it in me to find my way back. Even with the cloying heat, the single bunks, the four other people in the room and the two monkeys who cuddle between us and make it impossible to do anything other than just hold hands, it's been so long since I've slept with someone else that I grow reckless with it. Jane warns me. We sit in the comedor by candlelight, eating peanut butter out of a jar, and she tells me not to get attached. I brush her words away. I don't feel scared. I'm terrified every day, of course—of Wayra, snakes and spiders, getting lost, hurting myself—but for once, I'm not scared of myself, of the bad decisions I might be making. There are no decisions to make. Weeks pass and I cuddle into the hot crook of Harry's arm, one or other of the monkeys snuggled on our pillow. I listen to the rise and fall of their chests, and I imagine that this can go on forever. I have forgotten that nothing lasts forever.

The jungle withers and the forest becomes more brown, yellow and beige than green. The moss and fungus that I thought would never stop growing ceases, curls up, is sucked back into the dirt, leaving only cracked leaves and sticks to cover a hard, hot and parched earth. I'm approaching the end of my three-month extension. It's September. I think I might miss my flight back to England. I've already told my parents I'm thinking about staying longer. They're trying not to be too worried, I think, when I tell them I have no plans to book another flight, when I tell them I've overstayed my visa, when I say it's fine. They can hear how happy I am.

We're doing construction three mornings a week. Sama's fences have sprung up like the vivid mushrooms that emerge out of nothing. It still feels endless, Bobby practically crying as another day goes by and it's not finished. Sama grows more upset too, pawing the ground, biting the bars, as if someone has told him that we're going slowly on purpose. How can I leave? We're tying the end of the top roll of fencing now, having to make our own ladders out of the forest as we go. If only we had a few machines, a few more skilled people. I hear Mila, whispering through the fence. "A few more weeks. Only a few more weeks, mi amor."

Despite the time off for construction, every day Wayra seems calmer, more at ease with me. It's hard to say why I think this, it's subtle, but I'm beginning to read her subtleties now. I see it in the length of time she looks me in the eye, in the firmness with which she licks. The less she hisses. The more she walks. The more confident she is away from the runner, the more affectionate. The frequency of times she sits next to me rather than by herself in the shadows, the less time she spends licking invisible dirt obsessively off her paws, the more she eats, the more she spends in silence rather than making the low grumble that has become so familiar I hear it when I'm asleep. I don't think to worry about whether she's getting too attached to me, to us. Because if I do, I'll have to think about the fact that at some point, flights and visas and money will combine, and both Jane and I are going to leave.

At some point. But it's not going to happen yet. And so I don't think about it. I don't think about anything at all, other than this moment.

Leaves crunch beneath my boots. Jane and I are heading back to camp. It's late and hazy patches of yellow sky are quickly turning to bronze. Wayra caught a jungle rat, but she couldn't kill it. Had no idea how. In the end, Jane cut its poor, fractured throat with her penknife. Wayra then carried it around proudly for the rest of the day, burying it and digging it up, bringing it over to show us as if each time she dug it up, she couldn't believe her luck.

We put her back in the cage just as dusk began to fall, that time when the edges of the world begin to crinkle. The sky is eerie. I mop my brow, catching the sweat before it falls into my eyes. Jane, fanning herself with her hat, suddenly looks up.

"What's that?"

"What?"

"Coooeeee, coooeeee, coooeeee!"

My head snaps up.

"*That!*"

I stare dumbly into the trees. "Was that—"

"Three cooees."

"What does that mean?" I hold my breath, listening. Without phones, without radios, cooees are our only method of communication. One means "Be quiet." Two, "I'm lost." Three . . .

"Emergency."

We both start running.

The moment we emerge onto the road, we see a crowd of people, shadows against a queer sky. They are by the fumador looking north. There is an odd smell that I can't quite place. Mila and López are just swinging off the motorbike, hair ruffled, dark ashy spots across their foreheads.

"Hay fuego," Mila snaps. "Hay fuego en la montaña."

Smoke, I realise as my heart drops. I can smell smoke.

It takes half an hour, walking away from camp, not towards the village but in the other direction, before we see the line of the mountain ridge on the horizon. It's dark now, and roadside hawks sit on the tops of trees, screeching. The sky is a sooty orange and there is a hush over everything apart from a low crackling that I may or may not imagine. The top of one of the mountains is red, flickering ever so softly. Harry silently takes a cigarette from me, and we pass it back and forth. We stand in clumps, twenty-three of us in all, and watch as the line of fire across the sky grows. There are no stars and I know there'll be no moon. There's a scarlet glow over Harry's face, making him look like someone I don't know.

"I don't understand," Jane finally says, her arms around Mariela. Mariela is crying.

Agustino runs his hands roughly through his hair. "Four years ago, these months were very dry, like now. Las montañas quemadas. Farmers over the mountain, they set fire to their fields, because then they'll grow more, ¿sí? And they have to grow more. But it spreads. It didn't happen again, because there's been more rain every year. But this year . . . not much rain . . ." He stops, looking back towards camp.

"And there weren't any cats on that side of the road back then," Harry finishes, his face white beneath the red. He rocks forwards on the toes of his old boots, needing to move. His hands pull into fists. A shiver runs down my spine.

"So what . . . ," I start. "You think it might—"

"Spread?" Agustino's jaw tightens.

López looks up at the sky. Tom follows his gaze, his light-blue eyes crinkled with worry.

"Sí, el viento . . . ," López murmurs, his dark-brown eyes clouded. I stare at him. He's gotten taller since I've been here. Every time I look at him, he seems bigger. It was his birthday a few weeks ago. He turned seventeen, and we cracked raw eggs on his head and pelted him with flour. A Bolivian birthday tradition. He's almost an adult.

"The wind." Tom grimaces. "Soon, it will pick up . . ."

"But then what happens to . . ." I trail off.

Mila gazes back down the road as if she can see through the trees, right to their cages. Everyone is very still. I watch the hollow in Agustino's throat working as he tries to swallow.

"Are there people who can help?" The question comes from Nicole, a nurse, a new arrival just this morning. "Like, the government?"

Mila says quietly, "They won't help."

"There are volunteer firefighters in town," Agustino says, his head bowed. "If it burns here . . . maybe it burns in other places. I will ask, but I don't think they'll come."

I gaze at Agustino and Mila. "It's just us?"

Agustino's head falls further. The gold in Mila's eyes has disappeared.

"Siempre somos solo nosotros," she says. It's always just us.

The sky has started to bleed, leaves of ash raining, turning white as they fall. Robert, a scout leader who's been here a few weeks, is the first to speak.

"It's just the eastern side of the road, right?"

I look around and see people nodding.

"Camp side is OK," Robert continues, "because there's the river to protect it. Then we've got the road, which is a natural firebreak. So we've just got to cut our own firebreak behind the cats at risk. That's—"

"Sama, Katie and . . ." Harry looks first at Jane, then at me before he says her name. "Wayra." I take a deep, shaking breath, and Jane and I reach out, our hands gripping each other so tightly I feel our bones move.

"A firebreak?" Mila frowns. Juana and Mariela have both migrated to her and she has her arms around them both, their faces squished painfully against her chest.

Sammie translates quietly. "Un sendero de fuego."

Bobby grimaces, rubbing back his hair so violently it's as if he's trying to rub back the jungle itself. "It would need to be huge. Fifteen feet wide and a foot deep, at least. We'd need to cut everything. Trees, plants, roots. God."

Robert nods, almost apologetic.

"There's six hundred hectares of jungle on that side. So we're talking a trail . . ." Bobby hesitates, calculating. He's wearing, I suddenly realise, the same T-shirt he was wearing that very first day we met. The one that used to make me so mad. Now I could kiss it. He's calm, working the problem out in his head, when I'm just hearing the white noise of panic. "Seven kilometres, más o menos."

"That'll take weeks!" Sammie scoffs. "And would it even work?"

Osito and Germáncito are gazing between us all, trying to follow what's going on. Even though the English is too rapid, their shoulders are set, determined to take on whatever. Agustino places his hands on their shoulders. Osito lets him, but Germáncito ducks away.

Robert grimaces. "I've seen firebreaks work. The wind's blowing away from us, but if it changes and the fire crosses that dry desert of grass—it's called the *curichal*, right?"

Agustino nods.

"Well." Robert bites his lip. "That curichal, the dry desert, is like a tinderbox. And it's between those mountains and your land. You won't have a chance without a firebreak."

Agustino is walking back and forth now. "If the fire spreads, we can move Wayra and Katie, but . . ."

Our faces curdle, all at the same time.

"What would happen to Sama?" Katarina glares accusingly at Agustino, as if she thinks he's suggested something unconscionable. No one answers her. We watch the flames, and eventually Tom puts his hand softly on Katarina's shoulder.

The next morning we start as soon as it gets light. López goes ahead with the chainsaw, bashing through raw forest. Osito, Germáncito, Bobby and Agustino follow with machetes. Then come Mila, Harry, Robert, Sammie, Tom and a handful of others stronger than the rest. Behind come the dregs, tiny black flies sticking in our eyeballs. We carry rakes, spades and pickaxes, chopping back what the others are forging. I am blistered, bruised, spiked and crawling with ticks. Fire ants catch in my hair. I brush an acid-green caterpillar with my left shoulder, which swells up and burns for days after. By the time Mila calls lunch, I'm encrusted with sweat, dirt and blood and we've cleared less than a hundred metres. The sky burns ochre.

We only see our cats in the evenings, but we hear them crying. Rupi and Ru are loud enough to hear from camp, chuffing in distress. We eat our dinners in silence. We can hear Sama and Katie calling as we work on the trail. It makes us work harder. When I go to feed Wayra, smoke clings to her clearing. She looks up at me with wide, fearful eyes. It's the first time in months that I haven't spent every day with her. I feel bereft, as if I'm floating, and it makes it worse that I have no idea whether she understands this at all. Jane and I bring down wheelbarrows of wet blankets to hang around her cage. I don't know if they stop the smoke from choking her. I offer to help Katarina do the same with Sama, but she tells me he'll just pull them down and shred them. His enclosure is not finished. He's stuck behind his bars, with nowhere to hide but a wooden house. If the fire hits, we'll have a choice: open the door—letting him out, but breaking the law and risking him killing someone—or leave him in there to die. We rake, cut and wait. Rake, cut, wait. Our trail grows like a highway. We scour it to the dirt, exposing fresh lines of mycelium, secret dark homes that bugs have built under the illusion that they'll never be disturbed, and root systems that blow my mind. But even after all that, palm trees still meet across the divide, desperate as lovers. Branches fall where they're not supposed to. And every day, new patuju grows.

Animals watch us with wide-eyed panic.

The wind holds.

The mountain smoulders.

About three days in, Harry, Sammie, Katarina, Tom and I stand on the road.

"Have you noticed how quiet it is?" Tom asks, swinging his machete. He jumps up and down, his boots making a heavy, resounding clunk on the tarmac. I feel it too. The adrenaline. There are strange animals on the move, mostly small ones—tejones, capybaras, rats, birds, monkeys, snakes—but some large too. I found giant anteater tracks by Wayra's lagoon. Katarina saw puma prints circling the aviary. Bryan swears he saw the end of a black jag crossing the road.

Sammie frowns. "When did the bus last come?"

"I can't remember," I say miserably. "Never."

"Did the meat come today?"

Harry picks up a rock and throws it angrily against the side of a tree. It makes a hard thunk, pings back and narrowly misses Sammie.

"Hey!"

"Fuck!" Harry yells. "Sorry." An angry blue vein on his forehead pops out and starts to throb. I watch it, fascinated, as he picks up another rock and tosses it from hand to hand. "The meat didn't come. Agustino's taken the bike to see what's happening."

It's a few hours later that Agustino returns, carrying a bag of dead chickens and a radio. He sits down wearily in the comedor, putting his head in his hands.

"Hay bloqueos."

I've been in Bolivia long enough to know what *bloqueos* means, long enough to feel sick at the word. Harry kicks the door-frame, the sound bouncing off the walls, and Mila glares at him sharply.

"¿Bloqueos?" one of the newer volunteers asks. She sounds particularly nervous. I think she only left London a week ago.

"Road blockades," Sammie mutters. "It's how people protest here. They set it up, have a party, burn tyres, get drunk, but it's effective. It can go on for weeks. Entonces, ¿qué pasó, Agustino?"

"Es por el precio del gas."

The people out there who can't afford gas, who don't have proper homes or heating. I can't even see them in my mind right now. I run my hands through my hair. All I see is that fire, and I don't know what the people in this country are thinking or feeling. If there are fires here, are there fires in other places, ripping other people's homes apart too?

I'm suddenly wildly angry. At this place, at the farmers who slash and burn, at the blockades, at Bolivia's government that turns a blind eye, at corrupt governments around the world turning their own blind eyes, my own government—my own useless, capitalist, war-causing, resource-consuming government. I've had the luxury of a sheltered life, to have been complacent about politics, apart from through the remote-seeming conversations around the dinner table that I was never interested in following. But suddenly, my brain is swimming. How could I have not listened to those conversations? I should have been listening!

"What about food?" Katarina's voice cuts through and my head snaps up. We're already down to the bare bones, fruit and veg beginning to rot.

"And gas," Paddy says slowly.

I look at him. If we have no gas, we can't pump our water. We'll have no water. Never mind the people out there. We'll have no *water*.

Agustino holds up his hands. "We'll buy food from the village, OK? Meat for the cats. Gas too. It's more expensive but . . ." He grimaces. "We can pick fruit and leaves. And water . . . we'll ration. No showers."

There's a long silence.

"Uh, are you serious?" One of the younger girls, Hannah, fresh out of university, pales. I've watched with fascination as she diligently layers makeup on her face every morning, but she works hard, and even those of us who can comfortably go for a week without a shower are only just getting through the long days with the dream of cold water at the end of it. This news hits everyone hard. Doña Lucia, who has to walk for two hours now each day rather than get a lift, by the second day is feeding us just dry rice with bottom-shelf dusty cans of tuna. It makes us all ill. On top of this we're drinking as little water as possible. Some days it tops forty degrees and we're doing construction from sunup to sundown. Nobody complains, because in the end Agustino hasn't been able to buy gasoline. We have two tanks left, enough to run the water generator for perhaps a week. We fill all spare containers with Wayra's lagoon water and leave them covered by the fumador. I am terrified now, more than angry and tired. Bone-scared, as the smoke grows thicker and the cries of the animals louder.

"Está viniendo," Mila says ominously one day as we stand together in the early morning—the madrugada—clutching our coffee cups and a bag of coca, watching the sun trying to cut through the thickness. *It's coming.*

Night watches begin. We're assigned shifts, four hours each. I'm paired with Jane and we go out in silence at midnight . . . wet bandanas over our faces, panic in the tight grip of our sweaty hands. Ash lies across the ground and we cannot see the moon.

Five days after the blockades start, Agustino is finally able to get gas from a friend and we're able to shower again. Thirty seconds each. I let the freezing-cold water run over my face. My arms are shaking so hard, I can barely hold the soap. Faustino sits in the rafters above the shower, curled up in the darkness, and howls.

The trees are creaking. I am barely awake, cuddled in my bed next to Coco. He's staring up at me questioningly, his little fingers wrapped around my wrist. Harry and I haven't shared a bed since the fires started. I'm too afraid and he's too angry, his face closed and tight, as spiky as he was when I first met him. He snaps at everything I say and I do the same in return. We toss and turn by ourselves. Tonight I've been watching him lie awake in his bed an arm's length away from mine. The branches bump against one another, sharp fingernails scratching the roof. We've almost finished the trail, but it's impossible to know where the fire will hit. That it will hit, none of us doubt. Every night, patrols walk the highway. Four hours, there and back. We see wildlife fleeing the mountains, hundreds of little eyes reflecting in our torch beams.

I'm listening to the wind when Harry turns over in his bed.

"It's changed," he whispers. We gaze at each other, his eyes dark in the light of the one candle that is still flickering. Then we both sit up. Coco grunts as he falls off my chest, but someone is banging on doors and then I'm tumbling out of bed. When I open the door, the smoke is so thick I almost choke.

"It's moving off the mountain!" I hear. "We have to go!"

It's five in the morning. We stumble dazed onto the patio, collecting tools, wrapping bandanas around our mouths, soaking blankets, throwing them over our shoulders because we only own one broken wheelbarrow and we have to take it in turns to push it. Agustino and López, Tom and Mila speed off on the bikes. I look at my spade, my single jug of water, my blanket that is so heavy I don't even think I can carry it. My feet are so swollen they barely fit in my boots. I have blisters on blisters on blisters. We're living on coca leaves and cigarettes. I'm not even sure if I *can* walk. But suddenly we are out of the trees and moving across open grassland. The mountain is in front of us, a crackling mess of red, the wind blowing in our faces. We push blindly through the undergrowth. On the side of the mountain it's hot, hotter than I could ever have imagined. We lose our minds a little then. At first we spread out one by one, trying to cut a break along the bottom. It should be getting light, but the sun just meets a burnt-brown sky.

Nobody knows what to do and the fire is everywhere. So we forget everything Robert has told us. We scramble up the sides of the mountain and lose ourselves. I am on my own, snuffing out coals. Dousing. Shouting. I stamp on burning logs and calm steaming dirt. But I need more water, more tools, more blankets, more *help*. I know Agustino has asked people to come. But there are fires everywhere. We're not the only ones who need help.

The danger line—where the fire advances, where it starts to meet the dry grass of the *curichal*—gets closer. My blanket is burnt to scraps and everywhere there's the crackle, pop and fizz of flames. Animals howl. I'm in hell, I think, as a huge, bleeding and blackened tapir hurdles out of the inferno. She is so panicked that when she sees me, she just turns around and runs right back in. I'm not sure anymore what I'm fighting for, to put the fire out? I don't think it's possible. It's going to keep burning forever. When it starts to get dark, I think it's just the smoke and confusion. Where are the people who started these fires? I don't know how I realise hours must have passed. I can barely see my hand in front of my face. It's only then that I leave the blaze and race blindly through the ashes. Tears are running down my face. The first person I find is Jane. Flames from the thousands of tree fires are leaping above her head.

"This is crazy!" I grip her arm.

We hop as the soles of our boots melt.

"Where is everybody?"

"I don't know. Do you have a torch?"

She shakes her head, perhaps for the first time noticing that it's night-time again. I let out a loud cooee. Holding on to Jane, I drag her through the falling cinders until we find Sammie and Harry.

"We need to get out of here!" I shout.

They both look at me as if they don't know me.

"Come on!"

"We can't leave this!"

"Look around! We have to go!"

I push Sammie downwards. Praying that everyone else has the sense to do the same, I stumble over burnt brush and thorns, stepping over carcasses of dead animals. The earth is blistering and the mountain is creaking. Stupid, I curse again and again, stupid, stupid. When we come out onto the edge of the grass, there is a group of people waiting. They count our heads. We're the last. When we turn, we see that the whole mountain is alight and we watch as where we've just been goes back up in flames.

That night, fire ripples across the curichal, killing everything in its path, and by the next morning it's in the parque. I'm checking Wayra when I hear three cooees. I meet a group of ash-covered figures, bandanas around their faces and machetes over their shoulders. I don't even recognise most of them. The sun has been blotted out, wind whips my hair and I can already see some red flickers down the road. With shaking hands I find a wet scrap of T-shirt to put over my mouth and a blunt machete that lies forgotten on the ground. When I reach the point where the firebreak intersects with the road, I just stare. It's burning. All of it. Agustino and Harry are hacking at the trees.

"It's hit the break on this side!" Harry yells. "It hasn't crossed but it wants to. This wind!" His eyes are wild, the vein on his forehead stark. "Go and help the others. If it stays low, we're OK, but look at this!"

I just gaze up into the crackling palms.

"I don't know what's happening in there. Go!"

He pushes me, and I go.

Trees, flowers, palms, vines, fungus, insects, animals, everything that was alive on the wrong side of the trail is dying. I stumble blindly through the smoke. Occasionally I see shadows, volunteers—some no older than eighteen—battling as the blaze tries to cross. I join them, spraying water, muffling embers with my clothes. But then another call comes from further along and I run on. All hope of putting out the fire is gone. The jungle on the far side of the trail is gone. But our side is salvageable. It has to be. We will save it because if we don't, our friends will die. Sama will die. Like that tapir, he will die.

I can't hear, the noise is so loud. I'm almost crawling in search of a cooee I think I've heard. And then, with an almost careless flick of my head, I see it. A flame. I nearly pass it by. I stare for a moment, dumb. Then I yell. I shout as I bash off the trail into the jungle. Our side of the jungle. I retch. I'm not made for this, this isn't me. A patch of patuju about seven feet in diameter is burning and I honestly don't know what to do. It's crossed. I have no water, no blanket. All I have is a spade someone else dropped and my bandana. If this is burning, who knows what other fires there are, deep in the trees. I have nothing left. I'm so close to Wayra's trails here, I know it. I recognise landmarks. That huge fallen strangler tree, that bush of blossoms that smell—even now—like mint, that patch of electric-blue seeds that pepper the ground. I drop my spade and crash backwards onto the firebreak. Mila and Sammie are by a fallen tree not too far away.

"¡Fuego!" I grab their arms. "Fire!"

Sammie stares at me as if I've lost my senses. Silently she puts a machete into my hand and pushes me towards a burning log. I shake my head in frustration.

"No! No. ¡Fuego! It's crossed the firebreak!"

Eventually I make them understand and then we're running. We reach my twinkling flame, but by this time it's grown exponentially. Mila and Sammie don't even think, they just start to cut. When my brain computes that they're making a new firebreak, just for this one fire, I'm finally able to help. I beat away with my spade. I pull the heat inwards, again and again, trying to contain it. There are vines that seem to go all the way under the earth and together, Sammie and I use my spade to slice them off at the steaming roots. I can't bear it. I grab Mila's arm.

"Wayra . . . ¡estamos muy cerca!"

Her eyes are rimmed red and she's wheezing.

"Sí, Laura. Estamos seguro ahora."

"Pero, ¿qué hacemos si hay otros fuegos? Más cerca de su jaula . . ." My Spanish collapses. "That we haven't seen?"

I have to check Wayra's cage. That is all I can think. I have to. I have to be with her. We hear another group of shouts and our heads snap up. It's over, I think. We're losing. We've lost. Mila looks back at me, body sagging.

"OK. Cuida a tu gato."

I'm already gone. My home crumbles around me. Burnt and black and red and alive and dead. I'm running, wiping ash and dirt out of my eyes, when I collide into Hannah moving in the opposite direction. I grab her wrist and point behind me.

"The fire crossed the break! Back there. There's just Mila and Sammie. You have to help them."

She laughs desperately, already shaking off my hand.

"Join the club! It's crossed everywhere. They need help over there too!"

She waves her hand towards the road. I start running again, but it isn't long before the heat springs up and I stumble backwards, pulling my shirt over my face. Flames soar and I can't even distinguish where the firebreak is anymore. It seems to lead off to the left. I know this part of the trail, and that's not right . . . I turn down the new path and soon I can make out shapes of people, bent over, coughing, hacking and frantic, Agustino and Harry, Osito and López, Nicole and Tom, nothing but shadows against ten-foot walls of red. They're cutting a new trail because the old one has gone.

"Welcome to Death Alley!" Tom coughs. He's ashen from head to toe, streaked with charcoal. He's wearing shorts. I almost laugh. It's a panic response, but I can't stop. I have to keep going, I have to get to Wayra. I run past, almost at the road, when someone grabs my wrist.

I fall, stumbling into Harry.

"Where are you going?" His face is raw, parts of his beard gone.

"I have to check she's OK!"

"What?"

"I have to—"

"You have to stay here!" he yells over the noise, holding my wrist so hard it hurts.

"I can't—" I stumble, gulping dry tears.

He pushes me away. "You have to. We need you!"

"It's too . . ." I choke, not able to say it.

"What? Hard? Guess what *Frodo*, life is hard!"

It feels like he's punched me in the face. He looks away with disgust.

"You're not going to check on her. You're running away! What do you think you'll be able to do anyway, just you, even if she is burning?" He picks up a forgotten spade and shoves it into my shaking hands.

I stare at him, raising my arms to the jungle. "We've lost!" I splutter. "We're done. Our paradise is gone!"

"We're not fucking *done*." He glares at me so savagely I have to step back. "I thought from the beginning that you wouldn't last, that you were too fucking soft and spoilt, and it looks like I was right. Do whatever you want. Quit like you told me you always do. I don't care." And then he turns away, his body silhouetted against a palm tree burning high above his head. I watch as the hard muscles bunch around his shoulders, cutting, breaking, digging. I look around at the people who are my friends. They might die. I might die. Harry's right. He's right about everything. I'm so terrified I just want out. Suddenly I hear a horrible noise. Turning slowly, I see Osito retching on the ground. I watch helplessly as Tom drops his spade and picks the boy up. The moment Osito is off the ground he starts hitting Tom.

"¡Bájame!"

"¡Osito, no! I have to get you out of here."

Osito breaks into another coughing fit. Tom throws the boy over his shoulder, tears turning to sobs, and then I lose sight of them in the smoke. As if waking from some kind of fit, I grip the hot metal handle of Tom's spade and start to dig.

It goes on all that day and the next. We lose track of time, lose track of eating, sleeping. I don't know how but at some point, the flames finally drop. No longer sailing through the canopy like a ship that's lost its course. The wind dies a little. The threat changes. It doesn't stop, but it's different. It's no longer lurid, vivid like some disaster movie, but slow, creeping, crackling. It's no less traumatic. It's a nightmare with no end. We sleep in shifts, sometimes collapsing on our watches as the flames sputter and spit at our feet.

There is an end of course, perhaps three weeks after that first scent of smoke and the fire that lit the top of the mountains red. The wind turns away. The smoke drifts and the flames move, perhaps towards someone else's land. It is only then that we're able to breathe properly, and it's only then that we can truly see. Our trail, the highway, divides two different worlds. Closest to the mountain, it's a sprawling grey-black desert. The only things left are occasional trees, limbs scorched like survivors of a dark apocalypse. Vultures circle in ever-decreasing clumps, shadow creatures hunched over for the feast. But on the other side . . . I can't believe it. It's the jungle as I know it, thick, endless and baffling, shining from the inside out with a glow like sunlight through glass. The only clue that things aren't right is the silence. Other than the caw of the vultures, there is very little noise at all. There aren't any frogs or crickets. No monkeys, owls and butterflies. Everyone has gone.

Wayra is pacing when we go and see her. The runner hangs unspeaking and still between the cage and the sentinel tree, as if the clearing still feels it has to hold its breath to keep from choking. I know the feeling. Wayra's body looks shrunken. She slides through the still-heavy air on tiptoes. She's surreal, otherworldly. Her eyes are red and the floor of her cage is white, as if it's been snowing.

"Alright Wayra," Jane says. "Let's get you out of here."

Wayra shoots under her house, making herself as small as she can. Her paw prints stand out starkly among the crumpled pieces of ash. I look at Jane.

"I'll be bodyguard?" she asks.

I nod. It's better when Jane is in front. Wayra knows Jane better, trusts her more. I take the rope down from the runner. My heart beats fast. I've done this so many times and yet, even after so long, even though it's amazing every time, I truly haven't come to terms with "walking a puma." But when I look back, she's at the door and she looks so terrified that I forget my own fear. I've become so used to fear, so much more these last weeks. She's hissing, pacing fast and slamming her paw down as if she demands an answer. As if she's been sitting here knowing the world was collapsing and there wasn't a single thing she could do about it. She couldn't even run.

"I'm sorry," I whisper.

Then she's clipped on and sprinting, swinging her head back and forth with violent snarls. Jane runs in front, checking that we're OK, and the rope tethers me. I hang on, grounding myself with the familiar rough feeling of it. Wayra passes the sentinel tree, turns an immediate sharp left, sprints over the rise, across the fallen log, under the yellow blossom bush, up the bank and straight to the lagoon. The water has a haze over it as if it too has been in stasis. Wayra powers down to the edge. I have the rope in one hand, uncertain, not sure what she wants, and then she's dragging me forwards.

"Wayra, what . . ." I stumble. Wayra turns once, gives me such a violent snarl that I jump backwards, and then she's lunging for the water. She's pulling against the rope, her paws submerged, her belly, her back, batting and snarling at the sticks in her way, and then I'm down the bank too, leaving Jane helplessly behind, and the water is over my boots. I hiss, stumbling, up to my knees in it, a nasty surge of bubbles cascading from the invisible bottom, and then she's swimming. She's swimming!

I squeal. The water swallows me up. Boots, jeans, shirt . . . I'm chest high, neck high, billowing like a useless sail. She's paddling desperately. She tries to keep her head above the water, her legs working, neck craned, air snorting and bubbling through her nose.

"It's OK, Wayra," I say more calmly than I feel. "We're OK."

At the same time, I turn my head, spinning. I've never been *in* the lagoon. It feels colder than it ought to be. I know there are caimans out here, piranhas perhaps, prehistoric fish. Ours is the only beach, all the way around. The rest is a net of greenery, creepers, brutally knotted trees, sharp dark edges darned with root systems, their legs and arms submerged in the reflective brown like golden spiders. The haze floats above the ripples, so thick that I can almost move my hand through it. I can feel the heavy push of the sun. It's like we're in a bowl, Wayra and I. The water warms. Wisps of white, like feathers, streak the sky. I remember how to breathe. The ripples spread in ever-greater circles and Wayra pulls me on. I let her. My limbs are so sore and scorched, I almost moan.

"Don't let her get to the other bank!" Jane shouts, panicking. "And they swim with their claws out! Don't let her attack you!"

Oh, I think. *Right.* Then Wayra turns her face towards me.

"I think it's OK," I whisper.

All I see is her head and the line of her back. She belongs here, just as much as the caimans do. Wayra is not soundless like they are, she has to snort as she breathes, but she folds through the water, grey and sinuous. She comes so close that her fur brushes mud across my arm. I stay very still. If we're in a bowl, then we're all made of glass and this whole dream could shatter. She swims forever, her pupils so swollen I can barely see the green behind. On land, she spends a lot of time not looking at me. I don't know if it's because she wants to forget that I am there or that I simply don't factor into her thoughts. But now she is looking at me as if she cannot believe what has happened, as if she can't look away. What we have done. I cannot believe it either.

The water holds pockets of heat and the mud is clammy, catching in my clothes and holding me. I can still smell the cloying scent of smoke far away on the breeze, but mostly I just smell water and earth and the faint tang of lavender. A troop of squirrel monkeys, yellow, small as pointy-eared rats, watches us from the top of a mapajo tree, one of the tallest trees in the Amazon. Its hoary branches spread like wings.

Perhaps it was the weeks in the cage alone. Perhaps it was the lack of control. Perhaps it was the heat and the fire and the fear. Her instincts would have told her to go to water perhaps. I don't know. All I know is that she's done this thing that she's been too scared to do for all the years she's been here, sitting for endless hours at her beach. I am so proud of her, it swells in my throat and I find it difficult to swallow. All I can see is the back of her head, brown in the sun, splattered with water droplets and lagoon sludge, the slick pale tips of her ears and the dark tuft of her tail swishing through the water. Everything that I feel for her swells up too, unexpected and completely flooring. I'm absolutely wrecked, my body broken, my mind shattered. Is this love? I don't know. All I know is that I've never felt anything like this before in my life.

The sky is a light-blue blanket of soft cotton. The clouds float around our chests in distorted patterns of an upside-down sky. Wayra gives a tired puff, shoots a last glance at the far bank, swims one more contented, proud and happy loop, then circles in, coming so close that I reach out and touch her. It's what she wants. She presses against me, so tightly I feel the weight of her skinny, fragile body. We exchange a long look, her eyes just above the level of the water, before she turns and paddles wearily back towards her beach.

Back at the cage, I clip her onto the runner. She turns away with a humph, with a wet flick of her tail, and drops into a patch of sunlight to dry herself.

"She swam!" Jane exclaims, her cheeks flushed.

I laugh, shaking all over and struggling to get my boots off. When I pull one, the seal breaks and a flood of mud, sticks and sludge cascades onto the dirt. Wayra shoots me an irritated look. I can't stop laughing now, nodding too. I wouldn't have expected any less from her. After the expanse of the lagoon, the peace, floating under a sky that we haven't been able to see for days because of the smoke, it's hard to come back under the heavy heat of the trees. Disorientating almost. I am wet, grey cloying clay clumped into every line of my skin. Wayra is too, curled up small under the tree that smells of pepper, shivering, a sour look on her face, fur stuck ungracefully to her bones. But when I look around, I feel reassured. I remember the other lagoons that I saw, so long ago now, from up on the rocks with Paddy. I think they must still be there, silver in the sun, maybe with cats just like Wayra swimming in them too. We are part of that green plateau. Stretching into forever. Trees don't end. Trees that burn grow back, bodies press. Here there is always someone listening, breathing. There is always someone becoming part of us, making us part of them. This is a belly that holds on, that keeps us alive.

I turn to Jane to tell her all this, to tell her how we've done it, we've survived! When I see that she's crying.

"Jane!" I throw my arms around her shoulders, brown water squelching down her back. She laughs but also pulls away, sits and presses her face against her knees. All I see are her shoulders shaking. Out of the corner of my eye, I see Wayra watching Jane carefully, tail half in, half out of her mouth, a look of concern on her face.

Finally, Jane raises her head. "I think I want to leave."

I stare at her, as if I haven't heard correctly.

She starts again. "I think—"

"You're not serious." I cut her off, going back to my boots. I don't believe her. But when she doesn't say anything else, just stays like that, her head back on her knees, turned towards me with tears running down her cheeks, I start to feel sick. "You're serious."

She nods.

"*Why?*"

"Lau . . ." She shakes her head wearily. "I'm so tired. I thought I might have it in me to stay till Christmas but you know what, I don't. The fires . . ." She looks over at Wayra and wipes her eyes again angrily.

I stare at her, shocked. I don't know when but the jungle seems to have got its voice back, or perhaps my ears are just able to hear again. The high purr of the crickets and the hum of the bugs settle back into my stomach. Behind Jane, the sentinel tree stands tall and watchful. Wayra gets to her feet with a low growl, sensing something is going on. She turns. When she sits back down, the dark line down her back is all we can see.

"But what about—"

"She'll be fine. There'll always be volunteers."

I blink. She's serious.

"What about Sama and his cage? Don't you want—"

She takes my hand. "I've got three months left on my ticket. I thought I might go up to Colombia, then Ecuador. Paddy and I were talking. Maybe we could meet him and Bry on the beach for Christmas."

"We?"

"We think you should come with us."

I stare at her. "Me? I can't . . ." I drop her hand. The elation I felt minutes ago plummets, leaving me cold. Months ago this was all I wanted. A friend to travel with, laugh with when I puked my guts out, hitch with so I didn't have to sit on the side of the road by myself. Now I don't know what I want. I want this to be my life. I don't want this to be temporary, something I can leave behind like just another memory. I want to be *here*. But maybe that's stupid. Maybe I should grow up.

How could I be here without Jane? Just me and Wayra? Or would Mila give us a new volunteer? Would I have to train them? How would I even begin?

Jane looks away, back at Wayra. "Just think about it, OK?"

We stay until after dark. Once Wayra has cleaned herself off to her liking, she settles on the patch of ground between us, her scrappy, still-matted rabbit-like back legs on me, her head in Jane's lap. Just before she closes her eyes and drifts into whatever dreams she has, she looks at us both and purrs. Neither of us have ever heard her purr before.

Jane can't stop crying. Neither can I. The fires, the fight with Harry that we still haven't spoken about, Jane leaving and now this. When I get back to camp, tired and wrung out, I do look for Harry. I've been spiralling, but I think if we can talk about it, it'll be OK. We'll be OK. But when I look, I can't find him. I go to bed that night alone, not even with monkeys for company. I should sleep like the dead but I don't. I toss and turn and in the morning, when I look across at Harry's bed and see that it's still empty, I feel something horrible drop in my stomach. When Sammie takes me aside and tells me that he spent the night with Hannah, I have a moment when I think I'll be sick. I can't breathe it hurts so much and when Sammie awkwardly asks if I'm OK, I just nod, swallowing until it's pressed down deep. I swallow again. The shock, the shameful recollection that it's not safe to trust anyone, the embarrassment of my naivety.

This isn't paradise. We're all broken, just as Mila said. My stupidity and shame settle inside me. Then I go and find Jane and tell her yes, I'll go with you. Of course I will. We'll train someone else to take over with Wayra. A new girl has just arrived. Funny, calm, patient. And there are people who know Wayra. Mila and Agustino love her. Sammie could do it, she's staying. Tom . . . Jane's right, Wayra'll be fine. She'll understand.

And I'm just fooling myself, thinking that something like this could last forever. This isn't my life. I could never belong in a place like this and nothing that I do matters to anyone here, least of all to Wayra.

Our goodbye is short, and painful. Wayra stares at us through the cage on our final day. We've stayed two weeks to train our replacements. Wayra is happy. She is swimming every day. She is affectionate, calm, and she seems to look at me with absolution as she gazes down from her throne, her eyes a wide, fathomless green. Why, then, do I feel sick inside? There is no reason for me to stay. I repeat this to myself as I stumble back up the trail, my legs shaking, Jane's choked tears meeting the purr of the jungle sounds. I raise my face to the cool green shadows. And I feel numb. Empty. That night, we get on the bus and by five o'clock the next morning, we are in the city. And the jungle is gone.

PART TWO

I press my forehead into the hard plastic of the partition, it is cold and it makes me shiver. I pull my fleece around me, huddling down on the wobbly plastic seat.

"Mum?" I murmur. I am in booth six, halfway along the line of stalls, each containing a phone, each loud with Argentinean voices.

"Laura," she says.

I open my mouth, but I don't know what to say. It is cold here, in Buenos Aires. Chilly. But every time I wake, sweat seems to stick to me like a membrane, soaking me, leaving me clammy. It's been over a year since I left England for what was meant to be a three-month trip. I told my parents I'd be home in time for Christmas. Then it was my birthday, the end of January. It is April now, 2008. It's been almost seven months since I left the parque. I've been staring all morning at flights, prices flickering on the whirring computer screens. What have I been doing since I left the parque? Moving restlessly around a continent, through Brazil, Colombia, Ecuador, Peru, Chile, Argentina. I travelled with Jane, then Paddy and Bryan, then on my own. Worked in hostels, had one-night stands, was seduced by Argentinean guitar players, coasted on a force field of cigarette smoke, fried cheese and smiles. I've had a good time. I'm different than I was. I've made friends, I've studied Spanish. I've proven that I'm tough enough to travel on my own. I'm not going to collapse into a heap.

It's time for me to go back to England.

But . . . but . . .

I've been circling Bolivia, like a crazy ant on the patio. And every night the parque comes back to me. Every night, I lie in bed, grooming Coco when he's lonely. I chat with Hagrid in the baño and help Panchita hide her stolen underwear, I walk through the sunlit shadows with Wayra and think those times the most precious. And then I bury her, again and again. Ashamed. Ashamed to feel this much, to miss these animals, quite so much. It's not what is supposed to happen. The parque was just something I did when I was travelling, a cool thing, an adventure, and now it's over.

Christmas Day after leaving. Ecuador, in a sunny beach town. I woke early. I wanted some time before Paddy, dressed as Santa, started the militaristic prep for our turkey barbecue dinner, complete with all the trimmings and tequila slammers. I wandered down to the hostel computer, thinking I'd send some Christmas messages, and logged on to Facebook. Paddy, Bryan and Jane found me there later, minutes, hours, I couldn't say. I was still staring at the screen, at the pixelated picture of his face. From far away, I heard Jane's sob. Paddy's long, horrified silence. Bryan's gasp.

> Coco, our friend. It's with regret that we have
> to let you know that Coco has been hit by a
> car and killed outside of our home. Always a
> part of our family. Coco, we hope now that
> you are finally free.

The grief tore through us. By day I seemed to watch the world through a film, trying to laugh, drinking mojitos with Paddy and Bry, reading the final Harry Potter on the beach with Jane. But at night, Jane and I pulled out Coco's picture. It's one of the ones where he's lying backwards on the motorbike, his tail curled possessively over the red gas tank. His hands hang over the end of the seat and his toes cling onto the sides. His long dark face is resting on Agustino's favourite leather cushion. He's got porridge in his whiskers and his eyes are downturned, focused on the ground beneath him, as if he can't bear to see his own reflection in someone else's face.

After Jane left, on a plane to Australia in January, it was just me staring at his picture.

My lower spine feels tight with grief. A few months ago, it jarred under the pressure and it hurts all the time. I lie in hostel bunks, gritting my teeth in pain. I've been in Buenos Aires for over a month now, working at a hostel, high on painkillers, trying to figure out what to do. I don't have any friends here, and no reason to stay. There is a flight home tomorrow, $450 to London Gatwick. I've just enough left in my bank account, eked out from my savings and the pittance I've made working. Tears squeeze out through my eyelids and I brush them angrily away with my sleeve.

"Lau?" Mum's voice is low, far away, lost in a bad connection. Last month, she came to visit. We travelled around Argentina. I miss her. The bluebells will be out in England now, flooding her garden. If I book this flight, I could be back by the weekend. I'll see my dad, my sister, my brothers. Maybe we'll all have Sunday lunch together, out in Mum's garden if it's warm enough. Then I'll see a chiropractor and when I get better, I'll find a job. I'll put Coco's photo up on the wall and with time, maybe it won't hurt so much.

His face hovers in front of me, porridge stuck in his clammy whiskers. Wayra, her face. Slightly cross-eyed, looking up into the blinding blue patches of sky. I can stare at photos of her face for the rest of my life. But I'll never hear the warning call of the birds that she's turning her ears towards. I won't smell the musty damp of her fur. Or feel the touch of papery leaves over my skin. My thighs stick to the horrid plastic of this chair. I don't want to spend any more time staring at photos. I don't want to waste any more time, feeling sad that I've missed out on something. Afraid to write a line in a diary for fear of making a mistake. Reading other people's stories rather than being brave enough to make my own.

"Mum . . . ," I say again, and in the way she breathes, I know she knows what I am going to say. I press my forehead again into the wall. When I speak, it comes in a rush.

"I want to go back."

I catch my breath, expecting I don't know what. I think she will be angry, sad, or disappointed. But when she speaks, all I hear is relief.

"Then go back," she says firmly, and through the phone, I hear her nodding.

My hands are shaking when I replace the receiver. It takes me all of a day to be ready to leave. The next morning, I'm on my way to the bus station. And for some reason, I cannot stop smiling.

It takes more than sixty hours and eight different buses, and it feels like it takes a year. But then, in no time at all, I am dropping stiffly onto the tarmac. Shimmering heat waves make strange, blurry shapes along the road. Jungle meets above my head, thicker than I remember, knotting to block out the sky. I just stare for a moment. The muddy twisting track by the fumador has been widened, pressed down by footsteps. Coco's sign is gone. A bright, beautifully painted banner now sits in its place, scrawled with the words BIENVENIDOS EL PARQUE. I think for a second that among the distorted shimmers, I see Coco feeling the breeze on his face. I shake my head, pulling myself in check. The jungle twists across the road and I can't remember it being so green. Was it this green before? The sun shines white through the fanned, fluted leaves, reflecting emerald, olive, sage, lime, moss, jade, turquoise, viridian . . . colours I cannot name, across my face, across the silvery-gold branches of the trees. For a moment it is so beautiful, I cannot move. Too terrified to blink because if I do, maybe I'll wake up and I won't be here at all. I'll have made a different choice. I'll be in England behind a desk, nervous that my hair is out of place.

"Laurita!"

I spin. A smile spreads across my face. Suddenly, ridiculously, there's Mila. I drink her in. Her luscious dark hair caught in a plait. Her old, battered cowboy hat. Her shoulders, are they more stooped than before? I can't tell. I'm just so relieved to see her. I drop my backpack and take a step, thinking she is going to hug me.

"Laura." She doesn't hug me. She barrels into me, gripping my arms around the tops so hard it hurts. I stare into her brown eyes, gold settling in a pond.

"Wayra's gone." Her fingers tighten, but I don't feel it.

My heart has stopped beating.

"*What?*" I whisper.

Her eyes start to well and one tear slides down one cheek, which I see now is bloated with tiredness. The light catches her, splayed as if through a prism. The jungle, shimmering in waves, seems to whisper and then it puckers in the heat. The lines all over her face, which I swear weren't there last year, crease and, as I stand there watching, crack beneath my fingers.

Mila is speaking but I don't know what she's saying.

I shake my head. "Qué . . . ," I murmur.

"She ran away, Laurita."

I sway. A slight mist is easing off the tarmac. There is air, I think, in my throat, but I can't seem to swallow. An animal whines. Above us, a macaw screams. Mila does hug me then and I stand immobile in her arms. She smells of musty sweat and the road smells of burnt rubber. I can taste the salt from her skin on my lips. She's gone. Wayra's gone. This is all I can think. The forest repeats the alarm. Wayra is gone. Gone. Gone. Somewhere far away, someone whines again.

I visited the zoo yesterday. In my breaks between buses, in the closest major city, eight hours from the parque. I needed to stretch my legs but also, I just needed to see it. Some of our animals, I knew, came from this zoo. It was a sprawling place in the middle of the city with concrete paths, hot, glaring sunshine, popcorn carts and cages packed in tight. It was flooded with families, school groups, tourists, couples holding hands. The laughter of kids and the vivid snap of camera lenses. Everyone seemed to be having a great time.

When I reached the felines, I found a line of semi-subterranean enclosures, little more than boxes really, side by side like glass-fronted packing crates, each about four metres across, that you look down on, hanging over metal railings. People crowded in, reminding me of gulls at a feast. A lynx. She was pressed up against the wall, shaking. Next to her a male puma on concrete, his muscles clenching horribly each time someone took a photo. You could tell that he should have been huge. But his body was shrunken, his tail obviously broken a long time ago, his fur matted in tufts. There was an ocelot, curled up on a single leafless branch, nothing in her eyes at all. Jaguars, most of them immobile, hunched in corners as if they hadn't moved in years. The people, however, a mixture of travellers and locals, were moving. Pointing, laughing, crowding, pushing, ooh-ing, aah-ing.

At the end of the line, a slight female puma was pacing, deathly quiet. I stayed for a long time, the railings pressed hard against my freezing-cold belly. There was something about the way her fur faded from silver to grey, the angular shape of her cheekbones. The way she was sliding, a ghost on tiptoes. It took her about three steps before she had to turn and start again. Turn and start again. Turn and start again. I don't know how long she'd been doing that for. Turn and start again. Years perhaps.

I didn't know what to do. Chain myself to the fence, campaign against the zoo, call the local and national news? That's what Juan Carlos would have done, I'd heard, the Bolivian volunteer who helped get the parque off the ground. He goes around the country now, chaining himself to fences, shutting himself in cages in town squares, carrying broken-legged pumas out of circuses in his arms. Before I walked away, because the zoo was closing, I didn't do any of the things I thought about. But I did make a prayer, my knuckles so tight they turned white. I prayed that someday, if that puma could never have the life she should have, if she could never be free, then I prayed that one day that puma would end up at the parque.

I don't want to talk to anyone. I avoid the crowds of laughing volunteers. Faustino is on top of the comedor glaring at them all. I'm desperate to say hi to him but I don't want to do it in front of these people I don't know. I look around for Panchi but I can't see her. I see Mariela and Juana though, doing each other's hair like no time has passed at all, and we wave to each other shyly. They are trying to push a larger, significantly fatter Teanji out of the way, and when he beeps indignantly, I manage a weak smile. But the knot in my chest grows. A black-furred, small-headed, gangly monkey that I don't recognise, a spider monkey, lanky and long-limbed, streaks by. People squeal, pointing. There are so many people. Were there always this many? There must be close to fifty or sixty. Tents are haphazardly erected along the paths. The colours are strange, reds, blues, oranges. There can't be enough beds for everyone. What if there isn't a bed for me? I start to panic. The bowed edge of the pìos' enclosure comes into focus. Petunia and the rest are nowhere to be seen. It won't be long before night comes. The aviary is silent too. I'm about to turn away when suddenly I hear a squawk. I swing my head, craning my neck.

"Lolo!" I exclaim.

The bright macaw, from wherever he's been hiding—how he's even outside the aviary, I don't know, but right now I don't care—swoops, dive-bombing my head. He lands so gracelessly that I laugh out loud, soothing the pain inside, just beside my heart. I collapse onto the dirt.

He spreads his wing feathers, ornately pleated and perfect, and waddles into my lap. Then he flops, as he's done so many hundreds of times before. I reach for him, my hands shaking, to scratch the tickly feathers under his belly. He remembers me! He really does. He waggles his spindly legs. The way he flew—he doesn't need someone with a stick anymore! I laugh again as he flips back over, spreads his wings, takes off and cruises upwards, showing me what he can do. The sky is starting to turn red, the jagged peaks of the canopy black. He's a blue streak, the forest a wilderness that he navigates seamlessly, a sailor in a storm.

"Frodo."

I spin as Lorenzo lets out an exuberant shriek.

Sammie stands at the edge of the path, just in the shadow of the animal kitchen, grinning. "You let your hair grow."

My hand self-consciously flies to my straggly ponytail. A leaf falls out and I hold it carefully in the palm of my hand. She smiles, rocking back on her heels. She's gained some weight, dyed her hair a darker shade of blond. But she's still wearing the same dirty red flannel shirt that she had on when we said goodbye to each other last year. I feel a little strange, shy.

"When did you get back?" I ask. I heard she'd left, not too long after Christmas.

"About a month ago." She eyes me carefully. "Have you seen anyone else yet?"

"Mila." I try not to let my voice crack. "She told me about Wayra."

She nods, biting her lip. Then she reaches out a sweaty hand and I take it, letting her pull me up off the ground. We don't hug. We just stand there awkwardly together, waiting for each other to say something.

"Who else is here?" I finally ask.

"Harry got back yesterday," she says.

I nod. I knew that, had been informed by Facebook, and am trying to be cool about it. The reality is, Harry feels like a lifetime ago.

"Tom's been here a few weeks," she continues quickly. "The rest of the volunteers are new. And there's hordes of them! Fifty or something ridiculous like that." She laughs. Lorenzo hears it. He lands on her head and sticks his beak tenderly in her ear. She reaches up a finger to stroke him. The light is dying rapidly, turning us all into little more than dusky shapes. She takes a step towards the aviary and struggles to open the door. The latch to the macaws' cage was broken when I left. I reach out to help her. It's still broken of course. I shake my head with a despairing laugh, waving a number of mosquitoes out of my face.

"He's semi-free now," she says quietly. "Did you know that?"

"Free?" I stare at Lorenzo, his claws wrapped possessively in her nest of wild hair. "How can he—"

"Just during the day." She smiles proudly. "He can fly by himself and find his own food."

He puffs up his wings. He knows she's talking about him. *Free.* Not entirely wild. But not lost either. As we enter the cage, the last of the dusk seems to refract off the fencing squares, sending a criss-cross pattern of shadows across the dirt. The rest of the macaws are quiet, asleep in their night houses already, built in a higgledy-piggledy array around the walls. All I can hear is the occasional soft rustle of a feather, the stroke of a beak against a wing, night dropping outside, like a blanket falling over the world. Sammie turns to me then, her face white. A frosty cold shoots into my chest.

"What?" I whisper, bracing myself.

She gulps, her eyes flicking away before she clenches her jaw, Lorenzo pressed up against her pale cheek. Someone else has died, is all I can think, the panic coming back in a rush. *Wayra.* They've found her . . .

The trees are just darkness now.

"Panchi." Sammie's voice breaks. "Last week . . ."

I just stare at her. Her eyes fill up with tears and she angrily wipes them away, nudging Lorenzo gently into his own little house in his quiet corner of the aviary and pulling the curtains shut.

"She died. She got hit—"

"A truck?" I exclaim. "Another fucking truck?"

She nods grimly. "Logging truck. There are so many of them now. So many more than last year." She pauses, swallowing. "She died instantly." She reaches over and takes my hand, a gesture so unusual that it makes me jump. I think Sammie and I were friends, last time. But we were never close. Not like I was with Jane, or Paddy. "We buried her next to Coco."

The feeling of her hand in mine is too strange and I pull away, my palm clammy with sweat. And I think if I speak, something inside me will explode. My insides will hang from the branches of these spiky huicungo palms, like the giant seed pods that fall slowly to earth for the birds to pick off one by one. So I don't speak. I just hobble with Sammie out of the aviary, my body seized up and miserable after the endless buses. I close the door behind me. I think I can see what might be the first star, pale in a flat sky. I stare up at it, blinking back tears, listening to the high-pitched whine of mosquitoes and the drone of amphibians in the murky wet grasses. The canopy is black, ragged lines of shadow. Only the last hints of red still cling on. The savage coal-dark needles that coat the trees and the ground bleed together. The air is suddenly as heavy as I feel.

I remember how I felt when I first came here. I couldn't sleep. The jungle was so loud, full of raging sharp heartbeats. Now the heartbeats I most want to hear, the ones I've dreamt about for months, they're not here. I'll never hear them again.

I stare through the drapes of the mosquito netting. Sammie has let me share her bed. A bottom bunk in Santa Cruz. The person in my old bed now—I don't know them. The room is full and stuffy. Sammie has been kind, otherwise I'd be in a borrowed tent. There are ten bodies in here, including my own, squashed into the six tiny beds, Tom and Harry amongst them.

Sammie has pushed herself up against the wall as far as she can go and I am huddled on an inch of mattress, almost falling out of the gauzy net. Faustino is between us in paroxysms of miserable delight, occasionally and surreptitiously licking sweat off the side of my neck. His small hand is pressed against my heart. I touch his frizzy, damp fur. He's asleep now, his lips pursed, his breath making his whiskers tremble. It's strange, knowing that of these ten bodies, none of them is Coco. I cannot imagine how Faustino feels. Lonely, I would think. Sad. Confused. Gently, I press his hand a little closer and feel his fingers curling into mine.

Wayra's collar broke. Yesterday. Sammie, Harry and Tom told me in snatches as we lay on the road together, ignoring the strange looks from the other volunteers. She scaled a tree and came down through a vine, catching herself and snapping her collar. After she fell, she just ran. But she never learnt how to navigate, not like Lorenzo. She couldn't watch other pumas and learn how to do it. When she needed her mum, her mum was taken. All she had was us, and we could never show her. Never teach her how to hunt. To protect herself. To not need humans for food, or love. Animals like her are not released for a reason. She has no good options, out there. She could starve. She could be killed by another cat fighting for territory. She could be hit by a car. She could be recaptured and sent to that awful zoo in the city or chained up as a pet. She could be shot.

I place my hand over the silky thin skin across Faustino's ribs and watch as he breathes, very softly, in and out. I just want them all to be safe. Rats scurry along the walls. Mosquitoes whine outside. An owl hoots shrilly, telling other owls where he is. I look back at Foz and a wall of tears convenes in the back of my throat. I rub my nose hard and an unsanctioned choking noise escapes. My breath catches and suddenly I can't breathe at all. I grit my teeth, holding my hand over my mouth. I feel Sammie shift quietly, the hay mattress undulating underneath. I dig my fingernails into my palms but it does no good. Everyone can hear. The people trying to sleep, the rats, the wasps in their old nest outside the door. The spiders running over the walls. The palm trees, the owl up on his perch, Teanji in his little house above the roof. The wild monkeys sleeping in the canopy, the night-time creatures going hunting. Tears are running down my cheeks now, unstoppable.

I hear Sammie roll over onto her back. Faustino does the same. They do not say anything or make any move to touch me. Sammie is one of the last people I'd choose to hear me cry. I'm self-conscious around her. She's too funny, too loud. But she stays quiet now, the only sound the rush of my tears. It takes a long time for my choking to ease but finally, when I am just starting to breathe normally again, Faustino crawls into the pit between my shoulder and neck and touches his hand to my wet cheek. He puts his arm around my neck and squeezes. Then I am crying again. Not like before. This time it's just tears, slow and hot, squeezing out of the sides of my eyes and onto his fur.

Sammie turns her head. I see the silhouette of her nose and the dark nest of her long hair by the faint blue light of the moon shining through the netted window.

"It's just so strange," she whispers. "Without them."

A tree, right behind the wall, touches the roof. It makes a soft scratching. I imagine the moon gleaming off it like melted silver. The beams bright in the darkness. I nod rapidly, trying to laugh, but it comes as a mangled sort of croak. Finally I manage to choke out, "Who's going to steal our underwear now?"

She laughs. "You might want to check up in the rafters. I reckon Fozzy's still got a good collection of bras. I'm missing at least four."

I laugh, wiping my nose with the back of my hand. We both stare into the darkness. I think she goes to sleep, but then I hear very quietly:

"I was in the States working four jobs just to get back here. I was on antidepressants. I was more miserable than miserable."

I turn slowly, swallowing my surprise. Very gently, she touches the side of my arm.

"The very worst day here is still better than any day back home."

I gulp. Faustino resettles, melting into the gap between us, his tail wrapped around her neck, one of his arms slung across my legs. I stare at the pretty shape of her cheek, the billows of her hair, and I feel a swell of gratitude. I relax sleepily against the pillow.

"Do you think he misses Coco?"

Sammie sighs and shifts again, the bed creaking. "Yes."

After a while, I ease his hand again into mine. At first there's nothing, then I feel the slight pressure as his thin, hairy fingers tighten around me.

The next morning, I sit on the bench with Mila. Faustino is by himself on the roof, howling to the sunrise. The sky behind the dorms is a pale pinkish rose, the trees stained bronze. Without Coco, it just sounds desperately lonely. Mila's face looks almost soft, the dawn light tinting the slightly crooked curve of her nose, her long hair unbound, hanging gleaming around her jeans. But there is a tight frown around her mouth and the lines across her forehead are etched deep. She looks exhausted. Her eyes settle on Morocha, the spider monkey, who is spread-eagled across the patio, picking up ants off the floor and flicking them at unsuspecting volunteers. Mila sinks back against the wall, her cowboy hat gripped tightly in her lap, her face falling into shadow. She lets out a resigned sigh.

"Ella era una mascota. Como la mayoría."

She used to be a pet. Mila tells me Morocha only came here because she wrecked her family's home. They didn't want her anymore, it wasn't any fun, so they left her here. Motherless, friendless. Her fur is black and fluffy. She's got long, disproportionate limbs, an insane tail as functional as a hand, and a face that's pink, eyes like spectacles. She's young, but not young enough to forget that a bed is more comfortable than a tree. At five o'clock this morning, she broke into Santa Cruz, pulled down everyone's mosquito nets, pissed on my pillow, and it was only after she'd thoroughly destroyed everything that we managed to get her out, using Tom as bait, sitting outside on the floor and waiting for her to crawl into his lap. Her eyes had been jubilant as she'd hugged him, or wicked, I'm not sure, dark brown in a sea of pink. Mila says we'll keep her until we get permission from the government to transport her to our other sanctuary, where she can be with other spider monkeys. Here, our monkey population numbers just two: Faustino and Darwin, a new howler, a baby who was thrown out of the window of a passing car and who cries constantly. Faustino hates him.

I turn away to stare blankly into the trees. For a moment, I let myself imagine that she's out there. Not gone, real, her fur the colour of slate-grey shadows, of a brown sky. The smell of a wind kicking up dust. Eyes the colour of patuju, lined with black. Looking back at me. Her tail high. Her paws crossed under her chin.

Mila stands, shouldering her backpack, and puts on her hat. The trees blur, two-dimensional again, nothing but fog and shapes.

"Vamos," she says.

I don't know where she wants me to go. The fog gets thicker, shapes of people walking past but I don't see them. They're a blur of beards and flannel shirts. Faustino's booming howls rise, then fall. Vaguely, from the direction of the aviary, I hear Big Red laughing, Teanji's high, aggressive beep and then, at an even higher pitch: "Don't do that!" I hold my shirt cuff between my fingers, gripping it so tightly the button makes a white indent in my skin. When I let go, the blood floods back in, turning it scarlet. And then I nod, standing up too. And I follow her dumbly out of camp.

I hear all the noises of the jungle but somehow, I can't hear anything. There is a hollowness that I'm stuck in and it's soundless. The sky is bowed and veined like a blue shell, pressing down hard in the brief segments of canopy that it's managed to push apart. The jungle seems confused, the smells familiar but not, thicker than it was, wetter, sweeter. The pervasive rot, the slickness of new growth, the waning of another rainy season that I've again missed. I don't care that rainy season sounds awful. I just wish I'd been here. The path trails in front of us. At first all I can feel is the weight of it pressing on my shoulders. I stagger along with a bowed head, gazing at the backs of Mila's yellow gumboots. We walked down the road in silence, past Wayra's witch trees, and in at the turning by the big lagoon. I can't think where she's taking me. Not to Wayra's, anyway. And other than that, I don't think I care. I will never see her again. The sounds pass me by, the smells. I think my feet are on the ground but otherwise, I'm not there. I could be back in Buenos Aires, lying on that sticky plastic bed, or on a flight to London, drinking wine and watching mind-numbing, awful reruns of *Friends*.

My fingers trail over leaves. The ones that hang over the path seem to be intentionally in my way. I instinctively reach out for them, lightly, touching velvet, slick, papery skeletons. Some are wet, giving me tiny electric shocks. Some are beaded with dew, sticky. When I meet a young, furled patuju, I unconsciously pull it out of its stalk and the noise, a familiar soft swoosh, makes me jump. I bring the tightly coiled white end to my mouth and bite. The crunch, the wet cucumber liquid oozes over my tongue. I shiver, give a small smile, and look up.

The jungle is dark. The sun must have gone behind a cloud. Slowly I adjust to the hazy, grainy gloom and the furious whine of mosquitoes, the painful stabbing of their attack. There's a pool just to my right. It's a syrupy coffee black, matted with bamboo and lianas. The braided hair of sleeping giantesses. The bamboo shoots are such deep greens. They stand so straight, they could be spears, topped with fluttering ribbons. The water looks like a place where anacondas and caimans live. It's got a swampy, sweet smell. Then the sun suddenly comes out and the pool twinkles glassily. A cascade of purple orchids scatters the mulch-covered wet ground and the smell of vanilla wafts up my nose. There's a long, low log that hangs over the water, and I imagine Wayra lying on it, resting her cheek against the warm bark, watching the light as it catches the surface of the pool.

I turn to see Mila watching me, a half smile on her lips.

"Creo que a Wayra le gustaría este lugar."

I smile bitterly. Wayra would like this place.

"Do you think she's OK?" I whisper, barely daring to ask.

Mila's about to answer when a low, throaty roar explodes, coming right out of the trees. I jump, grabbing her arm.

"Mila!" I exclaim. "¿Qué es?"

Her face falls, all the pleasure in this place slipping out of her eyes. The roar drops to a bark and then an echoing, miserable choke. I let go of her arm when I realise that the danger is perhaps not imminent.

"It is Iskra," Mila finally tells me. "El león."

"Lion?" I exclaim, as she starts to walk again. I follow quickly on her heels, trotting to keep up. There aren't lions in Bolivia!

"Laurita," Mila sighs. "When you leave, how many cats we have?"

I think about this. "Sixteen?"

She nods, her hair casting a shadow across her face. All I see is the hooded expression in her dark eyes, the harsh frown on her lips. "Now, we have twenty-one." My mouth drops. Five more cats? They've had to find and make enclosures for five more cats over this wet season, while I was sunning my way around the continent? She turns to me with a look that fixes me to the spot. "Iskra came from the circus. The government will ban all animals from circuses, I think. Soon. We will be the first country in the world to do it. But those animals." Her eyes are heartbroken. "Where will they go? Here?" She snorts. "Iskra is a lion from Africa. She is in a cage smaller than your dorm. How are we meant to build an enclosure fit for her? But how can we turn her away? Where would she have gone, then?"

I think she wants me to answer. Her eyes rake my face, as if searching for any clue as to what she should do. But what can I tell her? A useless art student. A foreigner. In the end, we just start walking again, her shoulders slumped. The light filters through pitted canopies of leaves like stars. But all I see is a lion, crying in a cage on the wrong continent. A baby jaguar, being driven away on a speeding motorbike, because two days after Iskra arrived, Mila tells me, she and Agustino did the unthinkable. They turned that tiny jaguar away, because they literally had no people, and nowhere for him to go. They listened to him mewling as the bike disappeared into the distance.

Wayra, wherever she is. I hope for the breeze and the sun on her face.

The next time I look up, I realise I know where we are. There's that brace of spiky thorns, the clump of walking palms, the huge strangler fig that reminds me of an elephant's face. I don't know how many times I've walked down this path. By the end of last year, it had been widened through months of construction. But it's had a full wet season to recover. The jungle is dark green, red with the petals of patuju flowers. I turn to Mila, my mouth open.

"Sama?" I whisper.

She smiles.

I just feel a rush of panic. She's assigning me to another cat. To Sama! The angry, ripping crash of his head, the snarl as he clamped his teeth on the bars! Katarina's frantic tears every night in the fumador. I turn my head desperately, brushing the massive scaly root of the old elephant. The bark is cold. I can't do this. This isn't why I came back. I can't do this again. I can't—

"Laurita." Mila touches my chest hard with the side of her machete. I take a number of deep breaths. She waits. I hear the faint echo of Iskra's roar and then an answering bark from somewhere else. The lines of exhaustion around her eyes are awful to see. Her face is stiff with pain. I thought it was bad for me, not being here, not seeing Coco's face when he died. But I left. Mila is the one who stayed. That was her choice, if you can call it that. Sama didn't even have a choice.

Mila watches my face change. I take a very deep, steadying breath, and then we're walking again.

After a few more seconds, Mila calls out, "Hola Sama!"

"Hola Sama!" I repeat, my voice cracking only slightly.

The path hits the enclosure head-on, so quickly it is a shock when I see it. The fence is more than double my height. Its thick diamond links shine in the sunlight, pulled taut, angling in at the top where the fence posts curve. I'd forgotten how impressive it is. A thin, well-trod pathway winds away in both directions, around the exterior of the fence. I can't see the corners and I can't see the other side. Something catches in my chest. Awe. I remember the dimensions. The perimeter is more than two hundred metres. Inside it is more than half an acre. It's not square. It's a weird meandering shape, his old red cage boxed on the side like an afterthought. When I left, it was still a building site. Now it looks like . . .

"Jurassic Park," I whisper. A massive, sprawling dinosaur-proof fence, shiny, not yet bowed or rusted, and the jungle! It's a weighty thing, to fence in such a large piece of forest. The tree tops explode out of it, cascading over the sides. There'd been arguments during construction. Some of these trees are over a hundred years old. They are massive. They feed countless species of birds and monkeys and insects. There's a troop of squirrel monkeys, even now, spiralling around the branches of one of the mapajo trees. They're so excited it's like they've taken a huge hit of speed.

Some people, Harry, Paddy, Bryan—foreigners mostly—wanted to cut these trees down. If they fell—and trees do fall, a lot—they'd smash the fence. The fence we'd worked on for months, the fence that cost thousands of dollars. But with Mila, Agustino, Osito and the rest of the kids in charge, there wasn't a chance these trees were going to be cut down. For them, the risk was worth it.

I feel a shiver of fear, even though the late summer heat is making my jeans and shirt into a wet suit. I look around for the extremely dangerous jaguar. I'm expecting growling, hurtling, snarling. All, however, seems quiet and Mila has crouched down calmly by the fence. I peer into the undergrowth, my eyes scouring the darkness, patuju bursting out of it in disorientating flashes of green. When I look back at Mila, opening my mouth to ask nervously—Er, where is this guy, then?—I jerk back in surprise, my heart flying into my throat.

Sama is lying on the other side of the fence, inches away from Mila's face. The way the light is falling, it would be easy to miss the fence and think he's a normal cat, just a very large one, enjoying a patch of sunshine with a friend. He has patted down the patuju and made a nest for himself. His markings, amber gold melting into hay yellow and then white under his belly and chin, mottled with liquid-black rosettes, camouflage him with the dappled, mulchy ground. He is silent. The expression on his face is the furthest thing from rage I have ever seen. His eyes are squinting into the sun and his ears are tipped, turned towards something in the bushes. His head is cocked, ever so slightly, to one side.

Mila places her hand on the fence. He turns to look at her. His eyes are almost the same colour as hers, only a couple of shades paler, bright amber. I brace myself. The last time I saw him, he was trying to dig his way out, wanting to kill me. But he just gives a long, slow yawn, his tongue curling languidly. Then he sits up on his haunches, stretches the muscles in his front legs and shoulders, places his enormous paws side by side, leans forwards and starts to lick Mila's palm.

I let out a noise of shock. Mila flicks her gaze to me, and Sama pins me with those eyes. It's like being raked through. I can't move. He knows I'm afraid, he knows I didn't want to come here! I see him turning me over in his massive mind. *Who is this, then?* Before, when he was screaming, trapped and in pain, I think he couldn't hear anything. Now he can hear everything. I flinch when he opens his mouth, shows me his gigantic broken canines, then flicks his tail with disdain and just walks away. The black patterns of his rosettes move with his muscles. Two yellow spots, stark in the downy black of his ears, watch me like eyes. My breath rushes out, my head spins. I don't even notice the mosquitoes whining around my ears. He crosses the open patch of ground in front of me. The bushy patuju plants seem to part and then close behind his swaying tail. Then he's gone, into his jungle. I hold my breath, scanning the leaves.

"Will he come back?" I whisper.

Mila turns, and her expression is long-suffering, and patient. Waiting for me to figure it out on my own. My heart sinks. I realise that he probably won't. Why would he? Not unless I can prove to him that I want to be here. That I'm worthy of being here. I'm not sure what I want to say, but I cast around for the words.

"He's finally happy?" I say *happy* under my breath, as if I don't even dare to say it out loud. She doesn't hide the tear that's sliding down her cheek, coupled with a broad, beautiful smile.

"Creo que sí." Then she hesitates, pulling herself up on the fence. "I think so. He has a choice now, no? He can walk away if he wants. He has dignity. This is all any of us can ask for."

A thicket of head-high patuju is swaying, far off to the right. I think maybe this is where he's gone. And the squirrel monkeys are squeaking with alarm, scurrying away, leaping through the branches and out, chasing new, safer horizons. Lines of ants seethe around my boots, making their way in the opposite direction, into the enclosure. The leaves they've carried here gleam, as if they are shards of painted porcelain. I shake my head, unable to keep the smile off my face. Then I laugh. I can't wait to tell Katarina. She's in London now, working in her job as a dentist. A dentist! I never even asked her what she did, until we started emailing. I feel a swell of emotion. This place. This is why I've pushed my bank balance into the red and disappointed all my friends and family. This is why I've come back.

"Gracias Mila," I say quietly.

She nods, her brown-gold eyes sparkling. We worked so hard to get this enclosure built. And it was worth it. All worth it. We start to walk around the perimeter, Mila in front, me following on her boot heels.

"Así es como le damos a Sama su caminata por la selva," Mila tells me over her shoulder as we make laps. This is his version of a jungle walk. "He can follow if he want, no?"

Somewhere, I hear him call. It is a beautiful, huffing bark. The sort of noise that belongs here. He is busy right now, I think he's telling us. If he's even thinking about us at all. Around us, the jungle doesn't pause, doesn't cease, but it listens, always. The ants continue to carry their loot, monkeys scream and play and search for food, giant rodents scuttle about their burrows, spiders make their webs, snakes sleep quietly in tree knots, fungi grows—living, composting, making rainbows—roots expand.

Wayra . . . I don't know where she is. Is she out there, somewhere, amongst all those roots and rainbows? Or is she dead and gone? Is she filling up with worms, fungus growing out of her eyes? I may never know. I look out at the jungle. It knows, somewhere. Somehow. It is listening, and it knows what has happened to her.

The patio is a glaring yellow, flooded with midday light. Groups of volunteers are sitting around on the benches laughing hysterically as a very tall, gangly Danish volunteer in his forties, called Dolf, tries to race a very short, very sweaty, foul-mouthed Kiwi, called Ally, around the dorms and back. Both are pretty out of shape, although right now Ally has the edge. Various obstacles have been set up. A dip through a swamp containing last night's compost, for example. A climb over an old fence while doing your best impression of a pìo, and a hare-brained rummage through the washing lines to retrieve the most brightly coloured piece of clothing you can find belonging to your competitor. The finish line has been marked out between the comedor and Faustino's favourite tree. Faustino is on my lap, however, watching morosely as Teanji, who seems to have taken ownership of Faustino's tree, watches the contestants avidly with his stripy tail in the air, like some kind of strange referee. The laughter increases as Ally, going for the win, lunges for Dolf's legs. She topples him, leaving him squealing in the dust, brandishing a pair of bright-gold, compost-covered hot pants. Just as she races for the finish line, however, Morocha swoops out of the trees and rips the slippery hot pants out of her hands. The sound of cheering resounds as Morocha streaks across the finish line.

"And Morocha takes the win!" Harry and Sammie yell as one, the foul architects of this nightmare. Mila and López, from up on the roof of the comedor, both wolf whistle. I hear Dolf groan as Ally collapses on the ground next to him, swearing copiously.

"Not feeling tempted?"

I look up as Tom plonks down next to me. He is still slightly flushed and out of breath. He ran the race before this one. Osito beat him piteously, but he was a gracious loser. Much better than Harry, who, when beaten by Mila, threw a papaya at a tree. Faustino and I have stationed ourselves strategically out of the way, underneath a mango tree, where we hoped we could avoid detection.

I laugh. "Not likely!" And Faustino grunts in agreement, pursing his lips.

Tom wipes his face, his soft-blue eyes not quite meeting mine. His freckles are dark in the bright sunlight, and his beard looks particularly ginger today. I think it's grown redder, somehow. Maybe from the sun. Or lack of it. I'm not sure. He gazes down at Faustino, who has rested his chin in the crook of my shoulder, then looks away, swallowing. I watch his throat bob.

"Sensible," he says with a wry, shy smile. "Someone's definitely going to get hurt soon, and my money's on Harry."

I laugh. "Oh yeah, he'll get bitten. I'm just not sure if it will be by Teanji, or Ally."

He grins. "It was a good idea though, right? We needed a laugh."

I nod, although we both know the real reason for this. Last year, Agustino would have been the first to sign up for something this stupid. He would have been tearing out in front, doing his world-famous pìo impression, wearing nothing but sparkly jaguar-print leggings and compost, followed hot on his heels by a joyous Coco and an incensed Faustino, intent on derailing the proceedings. However, like Coco, Agustino is not here. He is nowhere to be seen. Not even this could draw him out of his bedroom. I've been back a week now, and I've only seen him once. I barely recognised him. His grief over Coco, over Panchita, was written all over his face.

"How's it going with Sama?" Tom asks quickly, changing the subject.

I smile. "Awful."

He chuckles. "Ignoring you?"

I nod. I've spent the week walking endless laps around his enclosure. I see him once when I arrive, when he shoots me a scathing look and disappears into the undergrowth, and once when I leave, when I give him his food. The rest of the time, it is just me and the jungle.

Tom shrugs. "He's testing you."

Slowly, I pick a piece of muck out of Faustino's fur. He grunts, grabs it and places it, like any of the best connoisseurs, on his tongue. I know Sama is testing me. I think he watches me as I walk around and wait.

"Do they all do this?" I ask.

Tom looks towards the sky. There's not a cloud in sight. "They're all different. But they all test us, in different ways I think."

I remember how long it took before Wayra began trusting me. Then I wonder, Did she ever really? I did leave her in the end, after all. Jane too. Do they all just know that at some point we're going to leave?

Is that why they make it so hard? Faustino, sensing my mood, glares at me. Then with a disgusted huff, he clambers off my lap and lands with a thud in Tom's. Tom buries his face in Faustino's fur. Faustino wraps his arms around Tom's neck. I sigh. Maybe they don't make it hard enough.

"Who did you come back for?" I say quietly, looking at Tom's fuzzy beard. It is thick, and the same colour as Faustino. I almost cannot tell where he ends and Faustino begins. I realise that I've never asked him. He's always just been in the background. Mila's go-to volunteer. Unlike the rest of us, I've never heard him talk about "his cat."

He shrugs, without lifting his head. "I don't know. All of them, I think."

I stare at him. Then I say, almost desperately, "But how do you have space in your head for that? I can barely fit in my own anxieties, let alone Wayra, and this guy"—I nod at Faustino—"and now Sama! I think I'd explode with anyone else."

With extreme gentleness, he holds Faustino's chest in his hands. Faustino nuzzles against him, his whiskers trembling. "I suppose my head must be pretty empty otherwise." Then he laughs, blushing a furious pink, and looks towards the now emptying patio. "I think the spectacle is over. What do you say we go and find out what Doña Lucia has made for lunch?" He wipes his forehead dramatically. "There's nothing better after a sprint through a sauna than a nice warming bowl of soup."

"¡Laurita!"

I jump up off the bench, tumbling Teanji out of my lap. His orange tail bristles, the rings bright like hoops of fire. The sun is sinking below the trees, the day almost gone. There are candles being lit in the comedor, the smell of dinner wafting over the patio. Mariela is helping Germáncito with his homework, huddled by torchlight on the opposite bench. They look up as Teanji gives a disgusted beep, shakes himself and waddles away, but I'm already running. It's a week since the races, two weeks since I got back, two weeks and one day since Wayra escaped.

"¿Qué pasa?" I yell.

Agustino is sprinting up the path to the road, beckoning wildly for me to follow. His limp black hair flails in the breeze. The extra pounds that he's gained in the months that I've been away have made his face bloated, and some of the blood vessels around his cheeks have burst. His hands are shaking. We stop on the edge of the road, just in front of a gloomy, empty fumador. Agustino raises his hands, and then drops them again. Dolf, the gangly Dane who lost his race so spectacularly, is waiting for us, bouncing up and down on his toes. My eyes flick nervously between him and Agustino. Dolf waves his long arms, his thinning blond hair frail across his egg-shaped forehead. I frown to follow what he's saying, his accent thick as eating marbles.

"Agustino says one of the hunters from the mountain has seen her."

I feel a wild surge of joy before I look again at Agustino's worried face.

"No sé qué pasa," he says.

I just stare at him, taking this in.

"He isn't sure what happened!" Dolf's words tumble out. "He doesn't know—"

"Doesn't know what?" I hiss. But I don't wait for an answer. I spin, taking a step up the road as if right now, I'm going to run all the way to the mountain. The sun is almost gone. The shadows are lengthening. Soon, they'll be gone entirely. Horrible possibilities run through my mind. Guns. Blood. Cages. Chained up in a nameless backyard.

I look around in panic. When Dolf grabs my hand, I pull away unthinkingly. He's Wayra's volunteer. He's the one who was with her when her collar split. He's the one who's been helping Mila look for her, every day out in the jungle, even though he was only assigned to Wayra two days before she ran. Suddenly Mila appears with a backpack and starts sorting confidently through ropes, carabiners, head torches. I give a sigh of relief to see her, but when she snaps her head up, and

I see the tightness around the edges of her eyes, I feel sick. Sick to my stomach. She claps her hands and then is running towards the motorbikes. Wordlessly, Dolf and I follow, leaving Agustino behind on the rapidly darkening road.

The bikes swerve violently over deep, cavernous potholes. I cling helplessly to the back of Mila's shirt. Wind rushes around my ears. My eyes are watering. My face stings. These potholes are massive. Gaping scars. I swear they weren't this big last year. It must be the rains, washing away the tarmac . . .

Evening has fallen and the stars are just emerging in a deep-blue sky. Dolf is on the second bike, just in front of us, his lights stuttering. When I see him veer suddenly, I bury my face in Mila's back. She veers too, almost throwing us both, and we choke on the cloud of rocks and dust that's hurled into our faces as another giant logging truck thunders past, blinding us with its headlights.

Mila mutters angrily, "¡Borracho!" Drunk.

I crane my head around to count the trees on the back. Five. Each as wide as I am tall. They've been attached to the base by heavy chains, like giants that have had their heads and feet chopped off and yet still they need to be restrained. I watch them bounce, trying to jostle free as the truck crashes through another pothole, but the chains hold. Last year, one logging truck would pass once a week at most. Now they seem as common as the flocks of wild macaws that fly overhead. Another reason for the potholes, I guess.

I remember facts teachers parroted at school. Three football pitches disappearing every minute, children! We need to plant some trees! A sponsored cake sale to save the Amazon! I've seen the cattle ranches spreading across this continent now, like oceans, and I've stopped eating meat. Ice cream has lost its joy. But saying no to ice cream feels almost as useless, sometimes, as those cake sales.

Now, back in the thick of it, I can almost smell the smoke of the fires again. It makes me feel like the jungle is being eaten alive. Everything—the ants, monkeys and giant rats, the spiders, snakes, fungi and roots, and people—being eaten with it.

I turn back just as Mila starts to slow, then she's pulling to a stop at the base of the mountain. Its bulk looms darkly above me, cutting out most of the sky. I look around, back the way we've come, disorientated. The last time I was here was when the whole thing was on fire. But it was jungle. Jungle, then grassland, then forested, scrubby mountain. I turn, turn again, almost falling off the bike. Where has it gone? Where have these fields come from? They seem to stretch as far as I can see. The stars should be consigned to the ribbon of the road, yet they spread now, uncontained. Young crops, monocrops, row after row after row. They rustle eerily, reflecting the low light of the moon. It's as if someone has shaved the earth.

"Is it rice?" I say quietly. Farmland. Spattered along the roadside are a few stately trees that have been left, refusing to be moved. They open their limbs like the nests of enormous birds, dressed in mourning black. It's only a little bit before the sanctuary's boundary line that the jungle starts again. There's a small pale sign to mark our parque's land. No barbed wire, no fences. Just trust, that no one will come in and take our trees too. But the sign is old and battered, almost falling down. Written on it are the words of a Native American proverb. CUANDO EL ÚLTIMO ÁRBOL SEA CORTADO, CUANDO EL ÚLTIMO ANIMAL SEA CAZADO, CUANDO EL ÚLTIMO RÍO SEA CON-TAMINADO, SERÁ ENTONCES QUE EL HOMBRE SE DARÁ CUENTA QUE EL DINERO NO SE COME . . . When the last tree is cut, when the last animal is hunted, when the last river is polluted, it will be then that man will realise that money cannot be eaten . . .

When did this happen? How did it happen so fast?

"Arroz." Mila nods bitterly. "Girasoles, choclo." Rice, sunflowers, corn. "Some are local farmers but many . . ." She pauses, her face stark in the torchlight. "Many are big contracts. Shipped overseas."

I can't look at her after she says this. I just stare at the place where the jungle used to be. A dirt road, which wasn't there before, now runs along the bottom of the mountain. We dismount from the bikes and start down the road on foot in silence. Mila is in front, Dolf behind, me behind him. The rising moon makes our shoulders pale. Dolf is hunched. Tension radiates off him. It makes the hairs on the back of my neck stand on end. He's barely been here two weeks. If I'd been dragged out into the jungle at nightfall to chase after a puma only a fortnight into my stay, I would likely be peeing in my pants by this point.

The track looks ghostly and the fields stretch with an uncanny silence, just on the edge of my torch beam. The mountain feels menacing on my left. Soon the road thins, tightens, and climbs, and we're climbing too, our breath coming in sharp bursts. Fields drop away and the jungle crowds back in. First it's a relief, until scraggly trees, whose branches are monstrous hungry spiders, start to block our way. They smell like roots, dug out of the earth, and moss. We have to fight through pillars of bamboo, vicious knots of palms and curtains of rubbery vines. There are streams, I hear them tumbling over rock falls.

The jungle at night is impenetrable, incomprehensible and disorientating. I can see nothing but the blinding beams of our torches. The ground is uneven, ragged with stones that make walking difficult, pulling painfully in the small of my back. Crickets scream for their mates, an incessant whirring made by the rubbing of their wings. Insects hiss. And animals. A lot of animals. Wherever I shine my torch, I see eyes looking back at me. Each one: Wayra? *Is it her? Is she here?* But most are too small, low on the ground or high, peering down creepily from tree branches. More than once I hear Dolf stumble and then whimper. I find myself reaching out to catch him, an act that has been done for me so often that it almost makes me smile. But then I let go of his hand, suddenly awkward and angry, and thrash at the mosquitoes.

Mila is walking ahead of us, violently swinging her machete, and I think I will ask her where in all the heavens we're going. But just as I open my mouth, I hear a dog barking. She holds up her hand quickly. The dog barks again and Mila lets out a low whistle. After a few seconds, there is a returning whistle, the rustle of undergrowth. A man pushes his way out of the bushes, and Dolf and I instinctively stand a little closer together. The man is short, about the same height as Mila, half a head shorter than me, about two heads shorter than Dolf. He's got a serious, heavy-set look, his eyes almost hidden by deep lines, and he is watching us warily. I quickly lower my torch. I can't tell how old he is. Older than I imagined, older than Agustino. He's wearing a Boca Juniors football shirt, jeans and ragged trainers, and he's chewing a ball of coca the size of a fist. There are green stains engrained around his lips and a shotgun slung over his shoulder. A machete wedged in his belt. Two ratty terriers are snuffling around his feet.

He and Mila speak, fast and clipped. I frown, trying to understand, but soon get lost in the unfamiliar syllables, the buzz of the insects a constant ringing at the back of my ears. They're speaking Quechua. The local language is Guaraní, but many people around here don't speak it. In the eighties, during a stark economic crisis, whole communities were relocated from the altiplano, the cold highlands near La Paz. They were poor, their Indigenous cultures mountainous, Incan, pre-Incan, and they came wind-hardened with different languages. The government said they wanted to redistribute the wealth, promising that farming would be better down here. But divides between the collas, these migrants, and the cambas, people from the richer, eastern lowlands, are stark and difficult. Mila, Agustino, the kids, many of the proud, toughened people from the local pueblos . . . they speak Quechua. They don't talk about where they come from.

I gaze between Mila and the man. They've stopped talking and the man is staring hard, almost belligerently, at his trainers. I look at his bowed head, his slicked black hair. Is he one of the men I've seen speeding past the fumador on a motorbike, a dead jaguar slung over the back? The jungle rustles around us ominously.

Mila sighs, finally turning to us. "Alfredo has been hunting here for years." She pushes one of the dogs away as it sniffs her boot. "He knows this land."

I try to read her face. I know how she feels about hunters. But I also know she's been working with some of them for years, trying to teach them about endangered species, with some success. With all the will in the world though, she can't stop people hunting. She can't even stop people coming into parque land. It's forbidden to hunt on private ground, but it's not forbidden to use the waterways. Our lagoons and rivers are public, and of course, isn't that how it should be? She takes a long, deep breath. Come on, Mila! *What did he say?* My eyes flick anxiously between her and Alfredo. "Last night," she continues, "he saw a small puma, just here on the track."

"She's alive?" Dolf cries. He's grabbed my hand. I'm grateful for it. I find my legs are shaking.

Mila nods curtly. "He almost shot her."

"But he didn't?" Dolf exclaims. "He didn't shoot her?"

When Mila nods again, I think I almost faint.

"He said if she had attacked him, he would have. But when she just disappeared into the forest, he let her go."

I turn to Alfredo, nodding my head. "Gracias. ¡Gracias! *Pachi!*"

He looks up, meeting my eyes for just a second. His gaze is soft, reminding me suddenly of Tom, and he breaks into a wide grin at my use of the local Quechua when I say *pachi*—thank you. It makes him look years younger, and I smile back. Maybe he's never shot a jaguar. Maybe he lives out here, just him and his dogs. Or does he have a family in town? Does he have babies? Has he tried to farm, but was pushed out by those low-paying, slave-labour multinational contracts Mila talked about? He starts speaking again, this time in Spanish, gesticulating wildly, but his coca wad and his speed make it incomprehensible to me, and to Dolf, who is trying so hard to understand he looks like he might be about to have an aneurysm. Mila finally laughs.

"He says we can go with him tonight and look for her, if we'd like."

"Yes!" I nod rapidly.

"¡Sí!" Dolf exclaims. "¡Por favor!"

She smiles. "Entonces, ¿vamos, Alfredo? Mis hijos quieren encontrar un puma."

The man grins, cheerful now, and whistles for his dogs. Then he sets off at a speedy pace. We follow after him, and as we wind our way further and further up the side of the mountain, there's the murmur of waterfalls, the dark whisper of the canopy and the thrill of animals on the hunt. And maybe, I think wildly, amongst all that, a small greyish puma with wide, slightly goofy green eyes.

The next morning, I see Dolf eating breakfast by himself and I quietly slide onto the bench next to him. When he looks up at me, his eyes are red. We walked for hours through the tangled darkness, trailing Alfredo and his dogs. By the time we got back to camp, the sky was turning tangerine orange and we'd not seen a puma.

"She's ghosting us." He laughs miserably, rubbing his face, stretching out his exhausted feet. I look down. His boots are too small. He's had to cut the ends off an old pair and cover his toes with duct tape. We sit together in silence, watching Morocha tearing across the patio. The morning is startlingly bright, and the trees seem to shine with a particular brightness, hurting my bloodshot eyes. Morocha's long prehensile tail flails and the hair on top of her pink heart-shaped face stands up as if she's forced one of her doting volunteers to spend the morning back-combing it.

After we finish eating, Dolf and I walk outside together, neither of us keen to endure the chatter in the comedor for a second longer than we need to. Morocha lets out a squeal, at first I think because of us, but then I see Teanji waddling towards us covered in some kind of faeces. He's taken to swan-diving head first into the baños, much to the horror of anyone who wasn't here for Panchita's shit-covered rampages. I smile, knowing the pig would have been proud.

Morocha, who seems to find both faeces and Teanji irresistible, launches for his orange tail. The tejón spins and beeps furiously in her face. He's surprisingly fast for his now above-average weight. He's found a way to break into Agustino's bedroom, a happy discovery for him. This is where our breakfast bread is kept. Morocha lunges away, only to start spinning furiously by her tail from a rope that's been tied up outside the comedor. I can't help but laugh at what is now just a blur of black fur. Teanji is clearly unsure what to do. When she stops, landing dizzily in the middle of the patio and holding out her arms for someone to hug, he springs at her. She manages to jump out of the way, but behind her are a crowd of flip-flop-wearing volunteers. Not half as agile as she is. They've been eagerly watching the drama unfold. Unfortunately, though, they've severely misjudged the situation and as a ball of tejón hurtles directly at them, they all scream.

"Don't run!" I yell, but they don't hear me. Teanji is in a fit of exquisite rage now. One particularly slow boy, squealing in terror, trips over a loose brick and falls, spread-eagled over the mud. I leap for him but Osito, just coming out of the comedor, gets there just before Teanji takes a chunk out of the boy's leg. He manages to scoop the tejón up into his arms and they walk away, Teanji nuzzled safely inside Osito's shirt. I watch with a twinge of sadness as the volunteers all start muttering about "health hazards" and "crazy animals that should be in cages." Morocha watches from the dorm roof, a fascinated expression on her

face. The sheet metal shines in the sunshine. Faustino, from the opposite end of the roof, glares at Morocha with disgust, his tail wrapped
protectively around himself as if he's afraid she might try to hug him
too. Coco would never, ever, have tried to hug him.

"I know," I say as he crawls down and drops morosely into my
arms. "There's no respect anymore." He grunts in agreement, scratching his stubbly beard. I can feel the slow beat of his heart and there's
the faint stench of burnt hair, where he's been burning his beard on
the candles again. I lean my head back and look up at the sky, a dazzling blue. A flock of macaws, their tail feathers fanned scarlet, sail
high overhead. I'm about to sit down on the bench when I hear from
somewhere far away:

"Wayra!"

"She's here!"

Dolf and I grab each other's hands. Time stops. Just for a heartbeat,
and then I'm carefully shutting Faustino in Santa Cruz, trying to be
calm, trying to breathe, and moving in the direction of what is now an
uproar coming from the pìos' enclosure.

"She's eating Matt Damon!"

Dolf and I race around the comedor, past the animal kitchen and
the aviary. My breath comes in ragged gasps. By the time we get to the
pìos, it's chaos. Matt Damon—Matt, or Damon, nobody really knows
anymore—has not been eaten. He has, however, jumped over the fence
and is now, somehow, in the pigs' enclosure. The pigs Panapana and
Panini are racing around his legs, squealing. Matt Damon is lifting
his massive wings and hissing, his scraggly head feathers ruffled and
upset. He's my height, his neck as tall and skinny as a rake, his ample,
shapely feathered bottom swinging from side to side. Panapana and
Panini are no bigger than Alfredo's terriers, but Matt is spinning in
desperate circles. *Get me out of here!* his beady eyes implore. The birds in
the aviary are screaming, their wings flapping in panic. The rest of the
pìos, thankfully still enclosed, are running in frantic circles. Agustino

is trying to herd them into their small wooden safe house, but the situation has obviously got the better of him. A clump of red-faced, uncertain volunteers are just standing by the fence. Agustino pants, his arms spread wide in an attempt to collect the birds into a manageable unit.

"She run, go that way!" He waves in the direction of the comedor.

"Help him," I say to the other volunteers, their eyes wide. "But don't shout! We don't want to scare anyone."

The thousand different greens, sharp as glass, blur before my eyes. She's alive. She's *alive. She's here!*

Dolf grabs my hand. Just as we duck behind the animal kitchen, we hear from three different directions:

"Wayra!"

"¡Aquí!"

"Cooee, cooee, cooee!"

Dolf spins. Before I can stop him, he drops my hand and sprints back towards the birds. I stand there alone as the world reels. Leaves mist into a kaleidoscope of colours and I take a long, slow breath. A feather, silvery white, flutters to the ground. It settles amongst the mulch. Somewhere, clouds move across a blinding sky. Where are you, princess? My heart beats in time with the forest and its oceanic pulse. Wayra is out there somewhere. I turn and then I'm walking. My hands are very still as I take the path out behind the baños. The jungle noises, the common everyday speech, quietens until all that is left is the beating of my heart. And the beating of her heart, somewhere. I step carefully over a little bridge, its rotten planks sagging at the core, and round a corner. I'm at a junction, swathes of bamboo clouding out the sky. I know where I am. If I go left, I'll get to the monkey park, where platforms and ropes in the trees teach the monkeys how to be monkeys. If I go right, I'll get to the enclosure where Bambi and Rudolfo, two baby deer, live. Straight over will take me to quarantine. I take a moment, listening again to my heart, and I go straight.

I've never been to quarantine before. The first rule that Mila drills into us is to never, ever visit areas of the parque that we aren't assigned to work in. It's for safety, ours and the animals', and for their privacy. Quarantine most of all. It's where our most recent arrivals live, animals that are sick, or traumatised, or both. And if Wayra gets there first— she's looking for food. She must be. Quarantine is where our most vulnerable live.

"Princesa?" I call tentatively, as I step out into a wide, open clearing. Quickly I glance around, taking it in. It's about the size of a large tennis court, surrounded by a shaky waist-high fence. Inside I see lines of small temporary cages. Sammie works here in the mornings, and I've listened avidly to her stories about the residents. There's Shakira, the tiny Amazonian parrot who's completely enamoured by Alice, a baby sloth as small as two fists. There are three tortoises who escape every day. Shelly Minnelli, Shelly Raffaelli and Shelly Machiavelli. There's a tapir who has a finger-sucking fetish. Herbert Ezekiel. He narrowly missed being eaten by a family in town. Then, finally, there are two baby pumas. Found in a cage in a market in the city. Sammie has told me Juan and Carlos are each no bigger than my forearm, covered in tawny spotty fuzz, and they play with each other, rocketing about their cage, mewling for hours. She feeds them milk from a bottle and they nuzzle up inside her shirt, thinking she is their mum.

I stay outside the fence, and the rope that I always carry now, just in case Wayra appears, bangs at my side. A few clouds, coming out of nowhere, cover the sun. I shiver, a rush of cold running up my spine. I can hear the rustle of feathers, the soft mewling that might, I imagine, be Juan and Carlos. The dirt around my feet is damp, still wet from the morning dew. Suddenly I can no longer hear the pumas. There's an implacable stillness. I can't hear anything.

Not more than twenty metres away is Wayra. Her fur is almost the same colour as the shadows. She's stick-thin. She looks like she hasn't eaten in months. Her ribs are harsh, her head shrunken. There's blood on her haunch from a deep gash, blood on her ears, her nose. Jesus, could this be her? But then she turns her head and I see her eyes. Green, even from this distance.

"Wayra," I whisper, stepping forwards, not thinking anything other than that this is her, she's here, it's really Wayra, she's the most beautiful thing I've ever seen! I take another instinctive step. Her pupils swell, then contract. She remembers me. She must remember me. She must know I've thought about nothing but her for months! Her ears flatten. Then they disappear entirely. *Does she not remember?* There's a sharp, slinking fear in her eyes. She's so small. She flinches backwards, as I've seen her do so many times, but this time in my panic I step forwards again, holding out my hands in some insane, inarticulate act of supplication. The jungle falls deathly silent, the canopy sagging, its leathery leaves almost touching the back of my neck as if to say: *You fucking idiot.* I don't even realise that the rope is still in my hands. I open my mouth to murmur her name again but it gets caught because the moment she sees the rope, I hear from outside of myself a deep, guttural hiss. She's cornered, squashed like an alley cat in a trap. The fence is at her back and the cages are behind, the canopy on top and me in front of her. Her eyes go bright green, then black.

I don't see her launch, but I know she does. Her mouth clamps down and there's the flash of teeth, the rush of a snarl. Pain, somewhere. Blood. Drops fall, staining my boots red. She shrinks, waifish and feral, her eyes horribly panicked. Wayra. It's *me*. I don't have time. There's a shout from somewhere, over by the gate, the pounding of feet. She rises back, snarling at something over my shoulder. Then she's running, her paws not quite touching the earth. Over the fence, through the mess of cages, over the fence on the other side and back into the forest. The trees close around her, a sheet of bamboo that she slides through, her long tail sweeping, and then she's gone like she never was.

Agustino holds the needle. Darwin, no bigger than a squirrel and the same burnt-red colour, is clinging to his neck. Faustino is here too, curled up in the rafters. The "clinic" is no more than a storeroom. The old clothes, blankets, mosquito nets and fancy-dress costumes—pulled out on special occasions—are separated from the medical supplies by little more than a threadbare curtain. The day has passed in a blur, setting out traps in the nearby jungle for Wayra, and now it's starting to get dark. Agustino is wearing a head torch and there's a candle flickering on the rickety table. Faustino is gazing longingly at the hot flame, stroking his beard in anticipation. Shadows dance across his fur, the dirt floor, my arm. I can't not look at it. The skin is turning purple now. There are six holes, each of them deep, two on my thumb and four on my arm. I can see tiny globules of yellow fat where the skin has torn. The whole side of my hand has gone numb. I wonder if her teeth hit a nerve, or a tendon.

"¿Lista?" Agustino asks me. The very long, sharp syringe glitters. I gulp. I think I might be sick.

"Is this going to hurt?"

Agustino just looks at me. "Sí."

Darwin's liquid eyes are wide.

I grip the side of the table with my good hand. "OK."

He leans forwards, the shadows guttering across his face showing deep worry lines that are so ingrained I'm not sure if they'll ever go away. Then he inserts the syringe into the first hole. I jerk as stinging iodine squirts into my flesh, staining my ragged skin orange. I watch, every muscle in my body shaking, because I cannot close my eyes. I bite down on my tongue so hard I taste blood. I feel dizzy, nauseous, for a moment I can't see. Fire spreads up my arm. I lean my head back. It's a mistake. This makes me feel worse. From a distance, I hear Faustino grunt and I try to speak, to tell him I'm alright, but I can't make my mouth work. It's only when I hear the clatter of the syringe being placed back on the table that I manage to sit back up, holding tightly to my shirt, ripped and stiff now with brown blood, as if this will keep me stable. Then Agustino reaches for his sutures kit.

"Mira," he says gently, touching his right canine. "¿Su diente está roto, no? Her front tooth is broken. That's why it tore like this. Es por eso."

I stare blankly at the gaping holes as Agustino begins to stitch. The colours are a grotesque combination of scarlet, dirty purple, white. As I watch, I feel disassociated, as if it's not my body I'm looking at. I've never broken any bones or had a major operation, but when I was sixteen, I spilt a pan of boiling water over my lap. I ended up in hospital, struggled to walk and missed months off school. I still tense up when I think about it. I have scars on my thighs and belly. And I felt a bit like this then too. Blank. As if my body wasn't my own.

I wonder, as if from a distance, if this will get infected. I'm sure I've heard stories about people getting blood poisoning . . . of people dying from animal bites. Maybe I should be asking Agustino about antibiotics, about possible infections. But I can't bring myself to. I wonder if I'm in shock.

Agustino pats me on the back, giving me a sad smile. Darwin starts to cry. He wants his milk, his mother. He's only a few months old. Agustino thinks, by the look of his teeth, someone fed him potato chips and chocolate. His bones are so weak, he woke up a few days ago with a broken arm. Agustino's wrapped it in a tiny cast.

I look at Agustino, biting back tears.

"Do you think . . ." I stop. I don't know what I want to say. The gash on her back, her weight, the tightness of absolute terror around her eyes. She deserves to be free. Wayra was always meant to be *free*. And she won't survive it. I understand now, properly, for the first time. And I don't care that I got injured. All I care about is that if we don't find a way to bring her back, she'll die. She's going to die. Agustino puts down the sutures and inclines his head.

"You have to trust her to come home."

"But will she?" My voice breaks.

"I don't know." He reaches a hand up to Darwin, who is still crying.

I hear the ticking of his watch as he reaches for the milk powder. Faustino swings down and goes straight for the candle-flame, thinking we're distracted, but I grab him before he can get there and I blow it out, leaving just the light of Agustino's torch. He places it face down on the table and a thin beam trickles out, falling across the wood and staining it yellow. Faustino settles in my lap. Darwin has finally gone quiet. Agustino has sat on the stool next to me and all three of us listen as the baby monkey suckles. He turns off his torch with a low click. It is so dark, I can barely make out their shapes. I feel Faustino reach out to take the milk bottle, but Agustino gives a grunt, which makes him pull his hand away miserably. My arm is really starting to throb now. I can just hear the low murmur of voices outside, the scratch of branches along the roof, the squeak of Darwin's throat as he drinks. I try to imagine where Wayra is, but I can't.

We stay in the clinic for a long time. It seems none of us can find the energy to move. It's only when the moon is high above the patio, casting trembling shadows across the floor, that we uncurl ourselves. When we hear the desperate shout of someone stuck in the showers without water and then the following clunk and whirr of the water generator being kicked into life, when I smell fried garlic and then compost as someone takes out the bucket for the pigs, when Iskra's nightly roar begins, when the jaguars start in response, when the cicadas start to rattle and the frogs chirp on a higher frequency, when the toads and the bats slide in between them and the leaves move in tandem, the whole thing rising and falling like waves on a shore, gradually gaining momentum, when Teanji snuffles past, when one of the birds cries, when Faustino begins to snore, his lips pressed against my shoulder, when Darwin reaches the end of his bottle and drops it with a clatter, and when he snuggles under Agustino's shirt, up against his heart.

The next morning, Sammie spots her near the pigs. A day after that, Mila almost trips over her on her way to the monkey park and López sees her on the road just as the bus pulls up to take them to school. He tells us coolly that she fled across the tarmac, barely visible in the sunshine, before disappearing again, lost in the greens and golds of the forest.

She is circling camp. A shark, desperate and hungry. Like I circled, when I was out there on my own, not sure if I was able to find the courage to come back.

Two days later, I'm walking home from Sama, swinging his empty meat bucket at my side, the road wide and bright and baking after another long, hot day. I keep my eyes peeled, scanning the verges for anything that resembles her. It's been a good day. For the first time, Sama has wanted to do something other than slide in and out of the dark jungle and watch me apprehensively from the shadows. I've stopped walking so many laps and just started sitting. There's a log which I like, and I've been reading *The Lord of the Rings* aloud, just in case Sama is a nerd like me. It turns out, he is. Four chapters into *The Two Towers*, I watched him—careful not to let him see me watching him—slink out of the trees and come to rest, mere metres from the fence, from my log. When I kept reading and he didn't move, I took that as a good sign. His eyes closed after a while, his cheek resting lazily on his paws. Relaxed. And I gazed at him, my heart in my mouth, as his eyelids fluttered gently in his sleep.

I squint, seeing a person now standing by the fumador. With a few more steps I see that it's Harry and he's waving, a grin on his face so broad it makes his beard look like it's levitating.

"Frodo," he calls. His beard is short now, trimmed from his time in Australia working a "real" job.

I walk towards him. "Hey."

"How was Sama?"

I grin. "Great!" I put down my meat bucket and pull out a cigarette. "He let me read to him! And get this!" I exclaim, jiggling on my toes.

"When I stopped reading, he gave me this look of *total* disgust and was going to get up, but when I started reading again, he stopped. He stayed. He sniffed my hand. He *sniffed* my *hand*! He likes reading. He likes me reading to him! He likes . . ." I trail off, staring at Harry. He is looking at me strangely, his mouth pulled into an uncharacteristically gleeful shape. He, also, is jiggling on his toes. "What?"

Harry grins, punching me in the arm. "She's back!"

"What?" I whisper.

"She's back! Back in the cage!"

When I say nothing, he opens his hands as if to say, *Well, come on then. React.*

I just stare at him.

"Wayra!" he finally exclaims. "She's home!"

Suddenly I'm kicking him so hard that he's squealing, racing away from me, laughing. Then I'm laughing too, my hands shaking so much I drop my cigarette. When I try to pick it up, I can't do it. He has to help me, and he hands it to me with a sheepish grin.

"You're such a dick," I say.

He nods, still grinning, and sits on the tarmac. I sit next to him and for a while, I just stare at my cigarette. It's gone out, and I can't quite remember what I'm meant to do with it. The sky is a searing blue. With a sigh, he takes the cigarette back and lights it for me. It's only when I take a long drag that my head finally clears.

I turn to him, shading my eyes. "*How?*"

He pulls his knees to his chest and looks at me sidelong. He looks so much younger now somehow. Maybe it's the beard. Or, I don't know. Maybe I feel older. He taps the ash off his cigarette and puts it to his lips. He's got coca stains around the edges of his mouth and a paunch, perhaps from losing so much weight and then regaining it so quickly when he went back to an office job. His blue eyes flicker, a little nervously, and he rubs one hand over his beard. Since he's come back, Ru's been giving him a hard time. Not as affectionate as before.

Picking on him. Playing with him, but not like before. Playing hard. Jumping hard. Getting out his claws, when last year, Ru would never use his claws. Harry makes light of it, but I see him coming back into Santa Cruz some nights, his hands and legs shaking from exhaustion, frustration, self-recrimination. His mood seems unnaturally tied to Ru's, but of course—who am I to talk? The certainty that I found so attractive last year—it's a shock to realise that it's not there anymore. Or maybe it wasn't even there in the first place. Maybe it was just in my head.

"She went into the trap by the pìos," he tells me. "Around three I think."

That was when Sama and I had been fighting orcs at the battle of Helm's Deep. The traps are just small transport cages really, about two metres square, with raw chicken inside. There's a weighted board on the door that's supposed to release the moment someone steps on it. We've already caught a few things, and a few others have escaped.

"So it worked?" I say incredulously.

"Yup. They're just carrying her back now."

"Mila will make me wait till tomorrow, won't she? To go see her."

He pulls a face. "You can guarantee it." Then he laughs, leaning into me and nudging me gently in the side. "Can you wait?" I look at him for a moment, and then I laugh too, running my hands through my hair. It's the first time we've laughed together since I've been back. It releases something I didn't know had been tight inside me, and when I gaze up into the sky, I'm smiling. I also realise that my back no longer feels so stiff. There are a few clouds, soft tufts blowing along the road. My arm still throbs every time I lower it below the level of my heart. I haven't told my parents what happened. I don't want to hear what they'll say. I hug it to my chest, the bandages that I change every lunchtime soaked with sweat, dirt and the oozing pus of infection. Maybe I should be more worried than I am. But Agustino says it'll be OK.

"I can't believe it," I finally whisper, nudging Harry back.

He grins. "She's home." Then he shakes his head. "Fucking Wayra."
I nod, wiping the tears off my face with shaking fingers.

The faint whirr of bugs' wings, the rattle of cicadas, the high, sonorous
whistle of a screaming piha bird. Insects boil across the jungle floor,
making a sound like a long-range radio transmitter. I am standing on her
path, just in front of her sign. HOLA WAYRA PRINCESA. The hoary
strangler it was nailed to came down, months ago by the looks of it. The
sign fell too, and has been propped against one of the vines that wrapped
the tree like hair. The vine is now stretched taut, fading from ochre to
silver, then a deep burnt brown. The path to her cage has had to move
to avoid the dead tree. I trail my eyes along its trunk, smelling of decay.
Tiny white and yellow fungi burst out of the rifts. A thousand insects,
microscopic spiders, furry neon caterpillars, ants, beetles, strange things
that belong in books, not real life, have found homes there.

I take a deep breath, then I'm walking down the bank. It's sweaty
this morning. Although the mosquitoes are starting to ease, going to
sleep or dying in preparation for the dry season, they still hurt. I come
up in massive, itchy sores. I'm wearing two pairs of ripped second-hand
leggings, knee-high neon-orange football socks under soft, pliable gumboots. An oversized plaid buttoned-up and collared shirt over a T-shirt
with a picture of a house cat wearing a crown and eating cake. The
dirt is sandy and it crumples under my feet. I walk, as I have done a
hundred, a hundred thousand times before, over the little mound, past
the other strangler, bark scarlet like maples. The rotten log has gone,
stamped down in the mud, all that's left of it is the same sweet, cloying
smell and an indentation in the earth, a patch of darkness, where it lay.

"Wayra," I whisper, feeling an oh-so-familiar shiver of fear as I
step towards her and grip the fence. My hand burns as my fingers curl
around the metal. She lifts her head, opening her eyes into slits. She's

on her highest platform, her paws resting on the edge of the wood, her face angled away. The sky is cloudy, dark and speckled like snakeskin, preparing for rain. I think it might be one of the last rains of the season. The air seems to hang around the edges of her cage, weighty and expectant. Bursts of leaves are already wet, oozing with moisture, and dripping onto the floor. She's curled up. She looks so small. Folded, almost nothing more than a lump of fur. But the dappled sunlight catches her eyelashes, betraying her. There's dried blood on her nose, and that cut on her side has stained her fur dark brown. Her skin is stretched so tightly over her bones she looks skeletal, her ribs like sticks. She's Wayra but not. She's a parallel Wayra that has slipped in from another place. I cannot believe this is the same cat I left behind. She was happy. She was safe. Fuck, she wanted to be free. And now she's this. I press my forehead hard against the fence.

I was always scared of her. Even when she lay across my boots, licked my arms, I never got rid of the voice inside that whispered that this was a predator. And I was prey. Now though . . . I lay in bed last night, panicking that I might never be able to be close to her again. Panicking that the fear would be too much. I stare down at my ragged arm. At the bites that look ugly, and *angry*. Was it my fault? If I hadn't been holding a rope, if I hadn't stepped towards her, if I hadn't cornered her . . . if she hadn't stopped, if those people hadn't come, if it had been worse?

"Princess."

She turns her head, just an inch, to look at me.

I shake my head. It was my fault. She didn't want to hurt me. She doesn't want to hurt anyone! She's just . . . *scared*. I grit my teeth. Even so. I feel like I've stepped backwards, back to that place I was in at the very beginning, when she was nothing more than a puma and I was nothing but a massive stinking ball of fear.

Her eyes stare blankly, big and dark as the bottoms of the canopy. Then she turns very slowly again so that she is facing back towards the jungle, her tail hanging listlessly, lifelessly, off the platform. I wait for the fluffy end to flicker, to jerk at the mosquitoes flying around her head, but there is nothing. No movement at all. She puts her head back on her paws, curls herself up even tighter, and closes her eyes. Her chest rises and falls, and I listen to the barely audible sound of her breathing. The clouds drop even more and the clearing is stained a dreary deep grey. The noise of her, slowing down until I think she falls asleep, is easily swallowed. The crickets' wings, the creak of branches, the rustling thunder of overgrown patuju, the hum of insect life—it's so loud. The colliding of palm trees, the cacophonous caws of the birds, the grating hoots of so many monkeys and the thundering, persistent beating of my own heart. She's right there, and I'm so afraid that I've lost her entirely.

"How's Yuma?" I ask, sitting down on the step.

Sammie grins. The light falls across her round face, painting her cheeks with a red flush. It's a perfect crisp Saturday in May. She wraps her shirt gleefully around herself. Dry season is in full swing. The temperature has eased, hinting at the winter that's on its way, and her eyes sparkle. I know what she's thinking. I'm thinking it too. For once, isn't it glorious not to be a sweaty mess?

She sits down next to me. Together we watch as Morocha helps Darwin up onto her back. Morocha waits patiently until his tail is wrapped securely around hers before setting off into the trees. His cast came off a few days ago and Morocha, surprising us with her gentleness, has started teaching him how to climb. They're going up to her house now, a box Osito made for her high above the patio, where they like to sit, Darwin in Morocha's lap. She runs her long fingers through his fuzzy ginger coat, clumsily showing him how to groom.

I was right, the rain a few weeks ago seems to have been the last. Since then, the skies have been cloudless cotton blues and the stuffy heat has given way to a drier cool. The mozzies have pretty much gone.

Ticks, yellow flies and brutal stinging bugs that look like miniature batmobiles have replaced them. I don't mind too much. They're going about their business, same as us.

Most of the volunteers have gone into town. There are still so many, eighty-two at last count! So today, in a rare moment of stillness, camp feels like it's finally able to take a breath. It is glorious. The kids are meandering about, doing their chores. Mila is in quarantine, Agustino is playing with Faustino. I don't want to jinx it, but it feels that maybe . . . *maybe* . . . in the last few days, the old Agustino has started to re-emerge. Still exhausted, still overwhelmed, still grieving, but with Wayra back, and with so many volunteers to help with his workload, as Faustino chases him around the comedor, and as I hear his pealing childish laughter reverberate off the trees, I cannot help but smile.

Doña Lucia is cooking lunch. The mouth-watering smell of fried onions is wafting through camp. I've been painting a portrait of Coco on the wall of the showers. His sad, anxious eyes have been staring at me all morning. Sammie is wearing a T-shirt that says "Retired Hooters Girl." There's a picture of an owl on the front and massive breasts on the back. When she sees me looking, she rolls her eyes and laughs.

"I think it was Bobby's. I found it on the floor. I'm wearing it ironically." She stretches her muscular arms out in front of her, her freckles sun-darkened, her thick tangle of hair nearly gold. She's been helping Paddy with Yuma's new enclosure. He turned up a few days ago, full of gusto, even more tanned than usual, having just horse-trekked solo across the Bolivian plains to fundraise for the dream that he left here with: a new home for his crazy puma Yuma.

"It's going good," Sammie says. "I reckon it'll be a few days before Paddy's boundless and entirely groundless enthusiasm sends Harry into a spiral of self-hatred and the two of them have some kind of bust-up."

I laugh, nodding. Then she smiles, picks up a small round pebble and holds it gently in the palm of her hand.

"How's Wayra?"

I close my eyes.

"Still doesn't want to come out?"

I shake my head. "She sleeps and she eats. She doesn't growl. Doesn't even hiss. Doesn't do anything! She just ignores us, staring off into the middle distance."

Sammie shrugs. "If I got my ass handed to me in the jungle, it would take me a while to readjust. It was a big deal, what happened."

I grimace. "Eighteen days she was out."

"It's a long time. Maybe she's got some thinking to do."

I see Sammie's shuttered expression and I know what she's not wanting to say. Right now, Wayra might be coming to terms with that fact that she had a rare, possibly her only, chance to be who she's always wanted to be. And she couldn't do it. The thought of her even thinking that—it breaks my heart.

"Do you think . . ." I hesitate, rubbing my arm. It's finally started to heal, the holes closing over with satisfying crusty scabs. Sammie waits, throwing the stone carefully between her palms. It makes a soft thunk every time it lands. "Did Mila ever tell you," I start again, "that thing about onions?"

"Oh, of course. The layers theory? Many times." She grins.

"Do you think it's true?"

She thinks for a while, staring at the pebble in her hand. I watch as Faustino and Agustino play their version of hide-and-seek. Faustino races yet again around the comedor and launches up onto his favourite branch, poised for ambush. Agustino appears a moment later, panting desperately to keep up, and leans against the side of the comedor to catch his breath. I watch as Faustino sets himself to launch.

Sammie yells: "¡Corre!" *Run.*

Agustino leaps away from the comedor, his eyes alight.

"¡Ayúdame!" He squeals, but he is giggling at the same time and it is impossible not to laugh as Faustino scrambles off the branch, grunting excitedly. Agustino feigns a run, his arms windmilling dramatically, but he is going slow enough to let Faustino catch him, which is of course what they both want. They set at each other in a flurry of grunting and teeth, and Faustino scampers up a nearby tree and hangs upside down, using his long arms to bat at Agustino's head. Agustino continues to squeal, but his grin is as wide as his face.

Finally Sammie looks away and shrugs, gazing behind her at the wall, where my seven-foot-high painting of Coco glistens in the sunlight.

"It probably is true."

I stare at her for a moment, almost having forgotten what I asked. The layers.

"So," I say slowly, "do you think when the layers come off, we never get them back again?"

"Fuck," she says. "I hope not."

My nose itches and I rub it, smearing myself in paint. "So the Wayra I knew last year, she'll never come back?"

"I don't think so. The jungle gets too deep." Her lips tighten, then she laughs out loud, making me jump. "Come on, Frodo. That useless kid, that girl who was wound up tight as a spinning top, that Laura who was here last year, you reckon she'll ever come back?"

I stare at her, then I laugh a little nervously. "Fuck, I hope not."

"Well then." Sammie looks back at my painting. At the oh-so-impressive reddish-brown beard, the downturned mouth, the scraggly black fingers and toes clinging for dear life to his branch, the tousled whiskers. It looks like him. I turn to Faustino. They have finished with their fight and are now curled up in a ball together, Faustino on Agustino's lap. The man gently runs his fingers through Faustino's fur. The monkey's eyelids flicker with pleasure.

But I sigh, suddenly angry. "This world's so fucked!" I exclaim. "Wayra can't be free. None of them can, not really. How do we ever know what layers come next, in the face of that? Mila says we don't know what's going to happen, like it's a good thing. But how can we ever know what to do?" I crane my neck desperately upwards. My eyes land on Morocha. She and Darwin have fallen asleep together in the patch of sunlight that shines onto the front of her house. Their tiny hands are touching, Darwin a ginger patch across the black of her stomach. The trees all around, I stare at them too. No two are the same. Flat-topped, tall. Broad with squat, shiny leaves. Dumpy, bold, imposing. Needy, small, retiring. I feel Sammie looking at me, sardonically raising her eyebrows.

I raise my own too.

Sammie sighs. "Isn't the good in this world worth fighting for, Mr. Frodo?"

I nod, rolling my eyes. "Yeah, all right, Samwise Gamgee."

She grins. When she laughs, the sound reverberates off the canopy roof. A parrot, somewhere, squawks eagerly in reply. "What do you say we two hobbits go and help Doña Lucia?" Sammie holds out her hand and then pulls me up off the ground with a grunt. She rubs her stomach eagerly. "I think I'm just about ready for my second breakfast."

It takes me another week, but when the idea of going into the cage with Wayra comes into my mind, it bubbles up in a fizz that I can't ignore. Heady and intoxicating. I've felt too helpless for too long. Jane was the one who taught me to go inside the cage. We'd do it only if Wayra went back in there early, or if she'd had a particularly bad day. She was never possessive of her cage, not like most of the other cats. It would just cheer her up, our being in there with her. Another way to prove that we trusted her. We'd stretch out underneath her platforms. Wayra would wait a few minutes, just to show she didn't care, before strutting over, swishing her tail. Then she'd rest her white chin on one of our boots and curl her limbs underneath herself into a tiny, perfect ball. She'd go from being the picture of cool to the most vulnerable thing, in one strange, precious moment. Outside, the jungle would be silent and loud, the greens would dapple. And Wayra would fall asleep with us, trusting us, as we trusted her.

I loved being inside that cage. It felt like a secret, like hiding in a cupboard when you were a child and tapping the back to see if you could reach Narnia. It felt like the whole world had stopped. I think this as Dolf and I walk down, the morning bright and clear. Mila cornered me yesterday. I couldn't believe the time had gone so fast. I'd completed a full month with Sama, a little bit more, and she gave me a choice. Wayra or Sama. I couldn't have both, not with so many volunteers waiting to be assigned cats. I chose Wayra, it wasn't really a choice. But it was hard to say goodbye, harder than I thought. I gave the next girl lucky enough to be assigned to Sama a stern talking-to about reading aloud, despite the strange looks she gave me, and forced my copy of *The Lord of the Rings* onto her. I wouldn't need it. I've tried reading to Wayra. She can't stand it. I'm pretty sure she thinks it's beneath her.

I take a deep, shaking breath. Around us, the clearing watches. It's grown up since last year, the boundaries suddenly jumbled and uncertain. The mahogany and rubber trees are where they always were, the strangler figs, the huasaí and huicungo palms, but behind me there's a lemony bush that used to come up to my knees. Now it reaches over my head, its shiny, fragrant leaves shaped like hands, and it almost cuts off the route to her door. It makes the clearing darker. The patuju, where it used to be semi-contained, has rewilded itself, sprouting up and elongating. Her garden doesn't even exist anymore. I sigh, looking at it all. It's going to take a lot of work to get her world back in order.

Dolf stares at me as I take the key out from around my neck. I slide it into the old, rusty padlock. Wayra is underneath one of her back platforms, the line of her spine dark against the sharp geometric shadow cast across the ground. She flicked her ears back when we arrived, but no more than that.

"Come on," I say, unhooking the padlock. My hands are shaking but I don't want him to see, so I shove them into my pockets.

"You're going *in*?" Dolf breathes.

I nod. A few months ago, when I was swanning around the continent, it was wet season here. And everyone who has experienced a wet season has told me that it's shit. There are bugs and floods, worms that burrow under your skin. All the animals' routines are messed up. There are no full days with a single cat. The animals get a few hours, here and there, because volunteer numbers are so low. But even though I know all this, and even though I've listened to Mila tell me how difficult wet season is for everyone, not just Wayra, I still feel terrible. Angry. Frustrated. I've read the notes that volunteers have made in Wayra's "diary" while I was away. They say Wayra was tetchy, in words that do not hide their own misery. They say she was stressed out, miserable. They say she stopped walking entirely. I can't see any record that anyone was able to clean her trails, go inside her cage with her, or sit in her runner space. No one went swimming with her. Maybe no one knew they could. She had a different volunteer every few weeks. And in their notes, they all sound terrified.

I look down at myself. A bedraggled twenty-five-year-old wearing leggings with a hole in the crotch and a T-shirt that says: "Winner of Pennsylvania's 2003 pie-eating contest." A twenty-five-year-old who last year was a scared little kid.

Dolf's already on his feet, excitedly straightening his thinning, wispy blond hair and wiping a streak of dirt off his forehead. Surreptitiously, I straighten my ponytail and attempt to brush off some of my own dirt. It makes me feel better somehow, ready to greet her properly, and then I'm ducking into the doorway, closing the outer door behind me.

"Hey, Wayra," I say quietly. "I'm just coming in, OK?"

She turns at the sound of my voice, craning her neck around with an incredulous expression. When she sees me, sees what I'm doing, her dark eyebrows pull together. Her eyes widen, goofy in the way that I

love, totally incongruous, even as her furry grey ears slam back against
her head. Her paw cranes to get the reach she needs to see me without
expending the energy to actually uncurl from her self-made ball. I hear
the low murmur of a growl and release a shaky breath. We're doing this,
Wayra. She narrows her eyes, then looks away, back down at her paws,
as if they are suddenly very interesting and she doesn't have the time to
engage with any sort of people right now, thank you very much.

"What if she . . . ," Dolf whispers from outside, then hesitates.
"Will she attack you?"

I have another awful flashback of a whirl of grey, a flash of bared
teeth, a swipe of claws, and for a moment I falter. She could cross this
cage in less time than it would take for me to blink. But then I look at
her again. She's started to clean her backside with avid concentration,
somehow grumbling and licking at the same time with a low *num-num*
noise. I smile and raise my chin. I've swum with this cat. I've felt the
sharp dent of her elbow digging into my stomach as she's fallen asleep.
I've closed my eyes while lying in the slippery mulch and been sure—
surer than I've been with a lot of humans—that she's not going to hurt
me. I stand up straighter.

"She might." I look straight at Dolf. "It's a risk. You don't have to
come in."

He gazes down at me, then gazes at her. She's finished with her
backside and has started with her tail. She's got it half in, half out of
her mouth, the black tip in her teeth. She is managing to look deeply
annoyed, as if she is certain she will never be entirely clean and it is,
without doubt, my fault.

"I'll come in," he says firmly. The straightened wisps of hair have
clumped again across his wide forehead. I nod, looking around. The
cage looks very different once you're inside. The platforms spread, a bit
like a jungle gym, at various heights. Most of them are semi-rotten with
green growing out of them, the effects of building in the jungle rather
than in cool, sterile places, where termites and mould don't thrive. The

central tree, a wide dark-barked friend, spreads out overhead providing shade. Outside, the jungle tangles, curling up and around the tension wires. The fencing around the bottom has been made living with the tiny vines that constantly spread towards the light, despite the maintenance that we do. The whole thing gives it the effect, which of course is true, that the cage could be pulled down by the forest at any moment. It feels temporary and yet, like it's been here forever.

I take a step towards her. She immediately stops licking and flattens her ears. I hesitate. Her eyes are wide in the shrunken, dishevelled contours of her face. Her pupils are early-morning swollen. There's still that patch of dried blood on her back, although she's licked most of it off by now. Her nose has a crusty scab on it, healing, and the backs of her ears are pitted with scars, layered beneath new bloody ridges from the yellow flies. Even now I can see at least ten swarming around her. She flicks her ears irritably and hisses, attempting to snap at one of them. Then she sighs miserably, lies her head back down on her paws, and waits. Her pupils contract, making her eyes soft again. The same as the forest leaves, all their colours mixed into this single one, fluttering gently in the breeze.

I relax and then I'm walking towards her. I don't think about it. I know if I think, maybe I'll stop, and I don't want to stop. The adrenaline pulses hard. The cool shadow from the tree at the centre of the cage falls across my face, its whorled branches rustling. I can hear the beginnings of another growl starting in the back of her throat, but then I'm there and I'm crouching down, putting my arm in front of her nose. If she doesn't remember me, and I'm still not sure if she does, I'm hoping she'll remember this.

My dad, a few years after he and my mum got divorced, took me and my sister out to dinner. We went to our favourite restaurant, the one by the sea that we used to visit every Saturday. It had been our ritual. I had the fried potato skins, which was part of the ritual. And the taste of it—the crispy, herby saltiness—made me realise how easy it is to forget, when you're so angry, the things that you used to love.

Wayra looks at my arm for a long, terrifying moment. With the cooler air, her coat seems to puff up, making ridges that scour the lines of her muscles. We're surrounded by the aroma of musty hay and earth. Her pupils have shrunk to pinpricks, surprise written in them, black stars within a universe of yellow green. Around the edge of her eyes is that amber line, so familiar. An ink spot on wet paper. There's a new mark on her nose, almost heart-shaped, cut through with a scratch from whatever has hurt her, I don't know what. A spiky branch, or someone else's claw. I'll never know. She'll never be able to tell me.

"Wayra," I whisper.

I wait, not breathing. There is still the soft vibration of a growl. Her ears are still. She is barely breathing too.

Then suddenly she raises her head and leans forwards. It's a tiny movement, less than a centimetre. If she was the hand on a clock, it would be the click from 12:00 to 12:01. A very slight relaxing of her face, beginning with the widening of her eyes, the colour lightening ever so slightly to a soft shade of gold. It's the sign I've come to recognise. The sign that it's OK. I let out a breath and move my arm closer. She starts to lick, and the sound of her tongue against my skin is the most beautiful sound in the world. I am light-headed, blinking back tears, leaning forwards to touch my face to her neck. Relief squashes my ribs, then expands. The pull of her tongue is sharp and painful and wonderful. She smells of soil and a velvety wind, when it blows the branches of a tree at the lagoon. She's leaning closer, pressing against me with disbelief and joy. I can feel the fast pounding of her heart. My heart. Our chests touch, our bones, our breath. When I scratch the fluffy white patch behind her ear, she pushes her cheekbone into my hand and looks silently up into my face. Her nose is pushed against my palm, cold and wet. She's got her front paws on my boot, pulling me closer, and her head is cocked to one side.

"You can come over," I say quietly.

Dolf lets out a whimper, a kind of yelp. I hear the noise of the door, then the careful, excited thud of his footsteps. When he reaches us and crouches down, folding his long legs clumsily beneath him, I take his arm and nudge it gently in front of her. Without missing a beat, she sits up on her haunches, stares up into his face, looking at him from under her long eyelashes, no sign of haughtiness, of irritation, of frosty anger. She just gives a contented grumble and starts to lick.

"I love you, Wayra," I hear him say, just under his breath. An awed tear falls down my cheek. One falls down his too. I remember the first time she licked me. It felt like the world was turning to butter. There is a smile I've never seen on his face before, stretching from ear to ear. Clumps of his hair are sticking out at right angles, his pale, grey skin is no longer grey. He gazes at her, besotted. She licks and licks and at the end of it, just after I've treated her wounds, after I've cleaned them with the same stinging disinfectant that almost made me faint and yet she lets me do it, doesn't even question me, she gives an exhausted sigh, looks up into our faces, and meows.

Other pumas meow, all the time, when they're happy. They purr too. I've heard Wayra growl, grumble and hiss. I've heard her snarl. I've heard her be utterly silent. I have heard her purr, once, that first time she swam. This though . . . it sounds like the squeak of air being let out of a balloon. It sounds like she doesn't remember how to do it and it comes out higher pitched than she intended—I'm not even sure if she meant to make a noise at all—she looks surprised at herself, embarrassed.

"Wayra!" I feel an inflation in my heart, a feeling that I don't under-stand, that's so huge it suddenly makes me very afraid. It makes me want to cry and dance at the same time. I laugh quietly, reaching for her. She arches into my hand. I stroke her neck, which is downy soft. I feel the reverberations of her happy grumble through the layers of my skin. Then she lies her head tiredly down on my boot. I continue to stroke her as she closes her eyes. With her front paws on my leggings, her toes curled like a child on the edge of sleep, she finally lets herself relax and fall away. There is a tiny drop of snot stuck on her left nostril. All I can hear is the sound of her breathing and my heart thumping alongside it. The sun falls behind a layer of new cloud, casting our faces in dazzling yellow, and none of us moves for a very long time.

A few weeks later, I've just finished feeding Flighty and Bitey, the two toucans that live in the last cage in the aviary. Flighty has an orange beak, Bitey has a blue beak. Unless you're particularly good with birds, which I've discovered many people, including myself, are not, it's unwise to go into their cage unless you're wearing boots (preferably with a steel-toe cap) and some thick clothing to prevent your feet/legs/arms/hands from being sliced. Flighty, eager for more mango, hops off a branch and lands at my feet with a savage snap. Bitey joins her, making a loud rattle as he gyrates, which is very intimidating.

They've been here a long time, years, even longer than Agustino and Mila. Agustino tells me they originally lived in a hotel. In my imagination, they traumatised every one of the hotel's residents until they no longer seemed such abiding tourist attractions. I like them. Finding a last piece of mango, I split it in two and throw the pieces in the air. The toucans jump in perfect tandem, snapping the sticky orange flesh in their beaks before landing proudly on one of the branches that are stacked up the sides of the tall cage. I laugh when they rub their beaks together, purring a little, hoping for me to play some more.

"It's past all our bedtimes!" I try to insist, opening the doors to their night enclosures. Bitey hops in easily and settles on his perch.

"Thank you." I close his door.

But Flighty lets out a loud, dissatisfied croak and flies resolutely up to a very high branch, well out of my reach. I lean wearily on my broom handle as she cocks her head down at me. I look up into the twilight.

Behind the aviary, the canopy opens out a little. The sun has already disappeared but the trees are bloodshot, the sky deep-navy. I smile. I can just see the massive posts that mark the beginnings of our new aviary. It's going to be huge, almost triple the height of our current one. Birds like Lorenzo will be able to learn to fly by themselves.

"Speaking of . . . ," I mutter, peering through the layered fences. I can just see the little devil himself, terrorising Sammie and a young Scottish guy called Ned as they try to put Lorenzo to bed. Since he's been free, his personality has exploded, along with his desire to find a mate. Unfortunately, Sammie is his love interest of choice and he's turning out to be a jealous lover. Sammie reaches up to extract Lorenzo from a death grip on her head just as Ned reaches over to help. There's a loud scream.

I hear, "Lorenzo, come on!" and then a hefty sigh, and a lot of swearing. "You go, Ned," Sammie mutters. "I'll put him to bed." Footsteps, then the clang of the main aviary door. Low singing, the Grateful Dead, I think, and not long after, the soft shutting of Lorenzo's cage. More footsteps, the aviary falls silent. The navy-blue sky turns indigo. It'll be black soon. I switch on my head torch and balance it on the nearest platform, illuminating a silvery beam of fence and branches. I pull my beanie down around my ears. It's freezing tonight. In the last week, the cooling breeze has turned biting. It is an almost arctic cold. Utterly unprepared, we walk around with shocked expressions, bundled up in every single item of clothing we have stuffed in our backpacks. It makes for some strange-looking volunteers. I myself am wearing a huge fluffy mustard-yellow coat I found in the storage room over a pink eighties ski jacket. The beanie on my head is shaped like a frog. I hear Flighty rustle. A branch creaks, there's a low, contented croak. I sense her head cocking again, peering at me with one orange-rimmed eye. My eyes start to close. It's not even six. The days are getting shorter. I shiver, wrapping my coat around me. I've put hot water bottles in the birds' beds tonight.

When I see three lights bobbing down the path, coming from the direction of the river, I think I might call out but change my mind, preferring to keep the silence for as long as I can. I know they'll see my torch. Harry is in front, striding with his characteristically hunched gait. Tom is loping a few paces behind. Towering over both of them, Dolf. We still have a lot of volunteers, about fifty, but of those fifty only eight are male. Of those eight only five are here for longer than a month. There are a number of cats that have to have male volunteers. Either they hate girls—sexist—or they love girls too much. Ru is one such, and Dolf has been commandeered in the afternoons to join Tom and Harry on his walks.

Harry stops just before the animal kitchen, holding up Ru's empty, dirty meat bucket.

"Play for it?"

Rapid, torchlit arm movements. A game of rock, paper, scissors. Dolf's quiet "Fuck," Tom and Harry's laugh. Dolf takes the bucket and disappears into the animal kitchen to wash it. Harry and Tom, the winners, are about to head towards the comedor when Tom grabs Harry's arm. He points in my direction. He's seen my torch.

I hear Harry's audible curse as together, they start to plod around the front of the aviary, doing a wide circuit, before coming to a stop by me.

"Frodo." Harry leans against the fence.

"Harry. Tom."

Tom smiles. "Do you need some help?"

I grin, gazing up into the darkness. "She's up there."

Harry groans. "We should wait a bit. She might come down on her own." His voice is hopeful.

I nod. I'm happy to wait. Tom rests back against a tree, crossing his arms over his broad chest. Harry tilts his head, switching off his torch, and looks up at the first scattering of stars. He's wearing his Ru clothes. Boots, thick jeans, two thick shirts. Tom too. His clothes are just as battered. Just as dirty.

"How was Ru?" I ask.

Harry sighs. "I still don't think he's forgiven us for leaving." Then he hesitates, chewing the edges of his moustache. "Well, me. You could do anything, Tommy, and Ru would still be in love with you."

Tom laughs. "Not true. Dolf's his favourite now."

Harry looks at me sidelong and rolls his eyes.

I chuckle. Wayra and I are pretty enamoured with Dolf too.

"Ru's got good taste, then," I say.

"Sure," Harry snorts. "If sweet, sensitive, falls over his own feet more than you do is your type . . ."

I look between the two of them. "You think Ru'll ever forgive you?" I mean to say it lightly, but it doesn't come out right. When Harry's face falls, and Tom looks away awkwardly, I regret it. Neither of them reply for a long time.

It is Harry who finally mutters, "How could any of them forgive any of us?"

I try to laugh. It twists in my throat.

Harry turns so that he's facing me. When he speaks, his voice is savage. "Do you know how many logging trucks we counted on the road over lunch today?"

I hesitate, not sure if I want to know. Last time I counted, a few weeks ago, it was around four per hour. None of the new volunteers sit on the road. They look at us like we're nuts when we do.

"Fifteen."

My jaw clenches involuntarily. But I hear the rumble of their engines as I lie in bed at night. Agustino has made a guess that with the rains fully dried up, access to the jungle is easier. And they—whoever they are: governments, multinationals, rich cattle farmers—are taking full advantage. *Fifteen.* If you took a conservative average of seven trees per truck and did the numbers, that's two thousand five hundred and twenty trees a day. Just here. Just on this road.

Tom stares up into the sky. "There were people on the other side of the bank today," he murmurs.

I turn quickly. "From Ru's canoe?"

Harry nods angrily. The familiar blue vein on his forehead pops. "We think they're building something over there. A new road maybe, I don't know. We can hear the crash of trees being cut down."

I feel a sick sensation in my belly. It's like being squashed. Why shouldn't people build a road? There are communities out there, villages. But I also remember that riverbank. The wild wash of the waves, the warmth of that sheltering cacao, those two night monkeys snuggled in each other's arms . . . I have a sudden moment of panic. What's happened to those night monkeys? Finally I manage to speak again, but I struggle with the words. "How's Ru handling it?"

Harry shrugs, like it doesn't bother him. But I see the vein on his forehead. The tightness around his neck. The rips in his clothes. The bruises he comes back with nightly on his arms. "He hates it," he says quietly.

I nod, unsure how to reply. In the end, with nothing else to say, I start to talk about Wayra. "We're going to walk her tomorrow, did Dolf tell you? For the first time!" I can't help breaking into a ludicrous smile. Since we started going in the cage with her, she's been so much better. Calm, affectionate, not so listless. "She's started pacing a bit," I continue. "Looking down the trail. She's ready." I look at Harry, and then Tom, expecting to see my joy reflected in their faces. Tom's eyes are crinkling kindly, but when I see Harry's expression, my smile drops. I realise what he's thinking. I'm smiling when Ru has loggers yards from his riverbank and the jungle is being clear-cut for people like me who want to eat ice cream. I put my hands over my face. "Shit," I mutter. "I'm sorry. Wayra, Wayra. How self-absorbed am I?"

He just stares at me and then looks down at his boots. They're so old and familiar, it's like looking at an old friend. They were once blue, made of soft, cheap rubber. Now they're hard, a faded greyish black, stiff with use, and covered in so many slashes from Ru's overzealous playing that I don't think he'll be able to wear them for much longer. He shakes his head. "Self-absorbed is wanting a jaguar skin on your wall."

Tom nods, rubbing his curly red beard. "And it's expecting the world to shape itself around you. You don't do that, Lau. You couldn't be here if you did." His face seems particularly gentle. The muscles around his thick neck stand out in the pale moonlight. I am staring at him when Harry suddenly laughs. It makes me jump.

"Yeah, you're not self-absorbed, Frodo. You just love Wayra *way* too much."

I close my eyes briefly. How dare he say this thing out loud, in the presence of Tom, Flighty, the whole listening jungle? This thing I haven't even said to myself, even in the darkest times of night when I'm lying in bed alone, not able to sleep. Dolf said it so easily. I wish I could do that, be *easy* like that. I glare at Harry because I'm annoyed, more at myself than him but I try to kick him through the fence anyway, just to do something, to make a joke out of it.

"Like you both don't love Ru just as much!"

Neither of them argue with this. We listen as Flighty preens her feathers, somewhere high up in the cage. I'm glad she's getting to enjoy the night orchestra. Then Tom says, so quietly I almost don't hear him:

"You think she's got used to being back?"

The question makes me swallow a number of times. There are only two answers I can give, and both stick in my throat. If I say no, it means she's still miserable. And if I say yes . . . well, that's even worse. I put her collar back on about a week ago. The memory is seared into my brain. I'd gone out by myself. She'd raced up and down by the fence, over the moon to see me. Her face silly, her eyes googly. She's looking so much healthier. She's got flesh on her bones. She's eating almost two kilos of chicken a day, bones, organs, blood. Her coat looks thicker, her wounds have healed. She looks like . . . *her* again. But incredibly, a younger, more peaceful her.

I sat next to her, the cold still not quite set in yet, and we watched the sun move across the sky, shaded by the darkening canopy. A troop of howlers came to watch and they climbed playfully about the clearing, their fuzzy orange fur dark in the late afternoon. Wayra watched them too, pacing by the door, before slowly, almost reluctantly, coming back to me and letting her head fall into my lap. I slipped her new collar around her neck then, so easy. Like it was butter. Like it meant nothing. But it meant everything.

"Come on," I say, a timely rumble emerging from my stomach. "I'm hungry."

Harry grimaces. "Soup tonight?"

"It was soup last night!" Tom exclaims.

"Oh yeah, I forgot." It's soup every night. Harry laughs weakly. "You or me?"

"Oh, definitely you," Tom says seriously. "Your beard is so much more impressive than mine."

Harry sighs, stroking it for a moment. I roll my eyes. After a long pause, he finally pushes open the door.

"Hey, Flighty," he mumbles. "It's bedtime." He does try to purr, but just as he begins, Flighty bursts out of the darkness with an ear-splitting croak, beelining for his head, and he ducks wildly. I hear Tom chuckle from the other side of the fence as she lands on Harry's shoulder, sticking her beak into his beard, making a noise of perfect happiness. Beards are Flighty's cocaine. She loves them. Lives for them. It's her eternal misfortune that those who have beards don't want to share them. I guide Harry—his eyes wide with fear—towards her bed, trying not to laugh too hard.

"It's OK, Flighty," I reassure her. "It's not your fault. He's just a deeply selfish person, that's all."

"I hate you, Frodo," he mutters, whimpering slightly as Flighty gives his beard a last satisfied stroke before hopping cheerfully into her bed. Then he looks at me out of the corner of his eye and whispers, "Not a word to Ru about this, OK?"

I smile, patting him on the shoulder. "Not a word."

It's the next day, barely dawn, and the world is just turning from deep blue to a soft orange. I look around at the beach. I've cut back some of the largest prowlers, not too much, just enough so that there's a little bit of light. Today is the day that Dolf and I are going to take Wayra out on her first walk since she's been home. I stare at the winking lagoon. There are gold lines around the edges of the clouds sheeted across the sky, and the reflections in the water are fiery. It's going to be a beautiful day. Patiently waiting less than two hundred metres away is Wayra. Her face, flecked with more silvers, greys, whites and browns than there are colours on this beach, is pressed up patiently against the fence.

The sky now, though, only a few hours later, is dark tan. I was wrong. It's not a beautiful day. It's wild, and a storm is coming. Wayra looks not silver, grey, and gold, but a murky, flat bronze. We're as far away from the cage as we could possibly be. Wind whips the branches, whips my hair, whips the fur across her back. Wayra flattens herself against the ground. Her neck is angled unpleasantly, eyes storm-tossed, flashing fury. She spins, slaps her paw against a tree and growls. I stumble backwards. I remember my elation, only hours ago. I remember ten-foot flames crossing the firebreak. I remember the way she hissed at me the first day we met, and how it felt like she'd punched me. I remember the flash of grey as she attacked me in quarantine. And I try to breathe, to remind myself that I survived all that. That this is just Wayra and we're fine, we're going to be fine.

But her tail jolts and her claws rake jagged lines in the dirt. Dolf, a few yards in front, hesitates, worry crinkling his grey eyes.

"It's OK, Wayra," I try to say cheerfully. "We're OK." But I hear the break in my voice. I offered to take the rope, to walk behind, because I have much more experience than Dolf. But maybe this was a mistake. She knows me better. Maybe I should be in front. She flicks her head and snarls, saliva dribbling down her chin. She doesn't believe me, she doesn't think we're OK. She's on all four paws now, up and incensed, her long tail flapping violently, her fur dishevelled and confused, and the sound coming out of her belly is the angry prowl of a steam train. Suddenly she seizes the ropes in her teeth. We have two ropes now, Mila has insisted, for safety. They're both clipped to my belt, but if it gets bad, I can unattach one and give it to Dolf, so he can hold her off me. But this won't happen. Of course it won't! This is Wayra. We've walked together a thousand times . . .

A thousand times and I've never seen her as bad as this. She pulls back, lurching so fast into the murky forest of wild, head-high patuju that she almost takes me with her. I lurch back, grinding my boots into the scrabbly dirt, just managing to stabilise myself.

"Wayra," I plead.

I push the fear down. I don't let my hands shake. I don't scream, I don't run. I stay very still. But this is worse than when I hid from armed men in Colombia. This is worse than when I shat and vomited all over myself on a bus, a doctor swearing blind I had hepatitis B, when really it was just some river water parasite. It is so much worse than when I jumped from a roof in Ecuador to impress a boy, and dislodged my spine. I feel the pain of that accident now thunking into place, as it does when I'm nervous, and heat radiates outwards. Hot and scalding.

She knows I'm afraid. My hands tighten on the ropes, I can't stop them. And although I drop the ropes a split second later, holding up my hands, *I'm not touching the ropes, I swear,* it doesn't matter. She flinches as if I've slapped her. For a moment she fades, squeezes into a gap between the leaves, her bones contracting in terror. Then like a supernova, she attacks. She's in the air, claws and teeth and snarls. Its quarantine all over again but worse. She wants to run, she wants to be that cat who for a moment was able to run, but it's me who's stopping her. It's me who has these ropes, ropes that held her when she was a tiny, mewling puffed-up ball of fur, that tightened around her neck, that whipped her when she was sad, that took her mother and everything she knew away.

It's only a second. There's a rabid snarl, a tug, a horrifying ripping, a whir of grey and teeth, and then it's over. I don't really know what's happened. I think I've blacked out from the adrenaline, and when my head clears, she's back on the ground, her body small again, pulling away.

I don't have time to check myself. To see if I'm hurt. She wants to run. She's pulling hard, dragging me forwards, and so I run too. I have no choice. Dolf races ahead, looking back anxiously, but I've told him he has to stay in front. He has made a movement with his hand, as if to ask whether I want to give him the safety rope, but I shake my head. I don't want her to feel any more trapped. Adrenaline keeps me on my feet. The fallen rubber tree goes by, the rise with the yellow bushes that smell like vanilla, the mouldering termite mound, the mahogany with the face of a shocked old man. Finally she slows, and I have time to look down. I'm imagining another session in Agustino's clinic with that needle of horror, but there's no blood. My arm is screaming, I think it's going to bruise, but somehow even in her fit of panic, she knew how hard to bite, she didn't break my skin. And she didn't use her claws.

Emotions race through me, too quick to count. Gratitude, awe. She attacked me and she didn't hurt me. Blinding terror. Will she do it again? We've got a long walk left to go before we're back at the cage. Bamboo and branches and spikes entangle overhead until it could be dusk. There's a crack of thunder. She grumbles, her paws stumbling over the veined trail to get home, just get home.

"Lau, are you OK?" Dolf asks.

I nod wordlessly. She's staring at me from the bottom of a ditch. Patuju hangs, flopping soggily like old limbs. Dolf raises his hands, then drops them. They hang uselessly at his sides. He delivers pizzas in Copenhagen. During the winter, he toasts almonds on the streets. This is his first walk with Wayra.

She is lost. Her collar is skewed. She looks both ways, as if she doesn't remember how to get home. Her ears are still flat back against her head—that look, an angry seal, a terrified child. My lungs and heart thunder. Utterly without the permission of my brain, I crouch in the dirt above the ditch. I remember what Jane used to do every time Wayra was sad, without logic, without any sort of training, just blind trust. I fall to my knees and loosen my hold on the ropes. Her cheekbones tilt, the silver around her eyes hardens. There's a warning in her growl. The smudged line down her spine rises. I let go of the ropes entirely. She didn't hurt me. The ropes hang slack, connected to me only by my waist belt. Then I hold up my hands. I trust you, Wayra. Our eyes are on a level. I trust you.

A bright-green butterfly dislodges from its camouflage. Wayra jumps, then follows it with her eyes as it flutters unaware of the tension, or who knows—perhaps it does know. Her eyes soften as she watches it. When it flies away, she looks disappointed. It is lost in the murky greens of the quivering, wind-pitched trees. When she turns back to me, she hardens and becomes a vivid scathing jade, pupils shrunk to absolutely nothing. Did she come here, I think, when she was free? Did she chase butterflies? A troop of capuchin monkeys, which have been calling anxiously somewhere behind us, suddenly seem to disappear. And then the macaws I've been hearing, the toucans, the ants seething across the mulch in anticipation of a flash winter rain—they disappear too. The ticks, the caterpillars, the fungus. The whole jungle. The clouds go, the sky, the tan dirt under my knees. The world's broken, Wayra. But this forest is *yours*. I look around at it, at the veins of trails full of hope. I stand up slowly.

"Vamos, chica," I murmur. "Let's go home."

I don't even hear the snarl. But I feel the weight of her against my chest. She doesn't knock me down, but I stagger with the shock of it. I put my arms forwards to protect myself, then she's off. Again, it happens so fast. Dolf's lips are moving but I don't know what he's saying. Then she turns again and walks, swinging her head, stormy wild and flinching, as thunder shatters the sky, stopping every third step to turn, baulk at this person with the rope, at *me*, recover herself, snarl, lunge. Sometimes she doesn't come close enough to touch me, sometimes she does. But again, again and again, she doesn't hurt me. She rips my shirt, bats my legs, looks as if she will kill me. And in this way, in this awful, dreadful dance, we walk back to her cage. I can't hear anything but blood in my ears, the crack of the wind, and the lurching attacks of her hiss.

She runs for it when the cage finally looms before us like an apparition, or a nightmare, and I almost give myself a black eye on the corner of it in my rush to keep up. She just wants to be rid of me, and when I finally transfer her with shaking hands from my belt to the runner, she shoots away into the bushes without a backward glance, plonking down in a cave of patuju and beginning a fretful cleaning of herself. I sit shakily on a log by the door, Dolf by my side. We do not say anything. It feels like, as we watch her work her tongue desperately over every inch of her body, from paws to claws to tail to belly and back again, she would scrub herself clean of us too.

All the volunteers complain extensively about wet season, summer— November to March—but for me this winter feels like the longest of my life. It continues to be cold. What I wouldn't give to be a sweaty mess again. May, June, July . . . the months pass and Wayra continues to get no better or worse. On some walks, she doesn't attack once. On others, we barely get ten metres onto the trail before she loses it. Sometimes, she jumps twenty times. Others, only once. I never know when it will happen. I can't find a pattern to it. She'll be walking fine and then, suddenly, BAM. I never know if this time, my luck will run out and I'll come back broken.

It's as Harry said. It's in our heads. She doesn't hurt either me or Dolf, not enough to mean more encounters with Agustino and his sutures. But that somehow doesn't matter. The fear is no less. Somehow, it's worse. And the icy, unpredictable cold gets into my bones. Leaden grey clouds drown us in freezing rain, and there's no drying room in camp, no bath, no sauna, no hot shower, no way to get warm.

I'm back in Santa Cruz after spending the afternoon with Wayra, glacial in her cage. She didn't want to come out. I don't blame her. I've crept into Sammie's bed and we're huddled together, but even her warmth and the piles of blankets are unable to stop my shivering. Unfortunately, Faustino, a living hot water bottle, is already happily curled up with Tom on the bunk above. Tom is strumming notes on his guitar, Faustino in his lap, their identical red beards keeping their chins warm. I turn my face to Sammie.

"You still think the worst day here is better than the best day back home?"

She laughs. "I knew that would come back to bite me in the ass."

Through the wall, I hear shouting coming from the kitchen. Paddy's passionate encouragement, Harry's desperate yelling. They're making another cake, I think, snuggling down. Agustino bought an oven about a month ago. He was so proud of it, hauling it off the back of a truck. It's fuelled by massive gas tanks that are more likely to explode in your face rather than cook anything, and burns or undercooks everything that comes out of it. Doña Lucia refuses to touch it. But Paddy's taken it upon himself to raise wintry spirits. Harry is his unlikely assistant.

I'm almost drifting off, my eyes closing, when Sammie says, very quietly, "Yeah, I do."

I open my eyes.

"I mean . . ." She makes a movement under the blankets, which I take to be a shrug. "I keep thinking about Bobby, you know? Back in the States. Building kitchens for people who only care about how expensive their fucking fridge looks. I saw him when I was back there, did I tell you? Fuck, it was awful. It was like his spirit had just gone." She traces a cracked old termite trail that criss-crosses the wall. "I mean, I was just as bad."

I nod, watching her. "Do you think he'll be able to come back?"

There's another movement. Another shrug. "Don't know when. Once you dig in. Once you've got a job, a place to live, it gets harder. People look at you like you're nuts when you tell them about this. And when you tell them you want to go back?" She lets out a long breath. Shadows dance across her face. "Get a real job," she mimics. "Stop wasting your life! The environment? Pah! Go into marketing. That's where the money is." She looks at me sidelong. "I guess you've got that to look forward to. You haven't been back yet, hey?"

I shake my head.

"How long's it been?"

"Almost a year and a half," I say, my voice quiet. A year and a half. I look down at myself with a wry smile and trace the ridges of scars along my arms. Love bites, Mila calls them. Those first ones, from quarantine, were the worst, the only ones that needed stitches. The rest are just scratches, some barely even leaving a mark.

"Do you think you'll keep coming back?" I say softly.

"I don't know." She turns to look at me, the notes of Eric Clapton's "Tears in Heaven" drifting down from Tom's bunk as he quietly plays his guitar. Paddy and Harry have gone silent. I can smell the scent of warm cake wafting through the window. Sammie smiles at me. "I had a pretty good life before, you know?" She laughs. "I was prom queen in high school, can you believe that? That was a really big deal back in Florida. Look at me now!" I look at her. Her hair has started to form dreadlocks, it's so matted. Her nose, just poking out of the covers, is grey with dirt. "I was on track to a decent job. I was going to live by the beach. I had a boyfriend! My parents were over the moon. Shit. Now they think I've lost my mind. Maybe I have. That's what it felt like when I was back there. But when I'm here? It feels like I've never been saner. You know?"

I nod. That's exactly what it does feel like. Despite how much I miss my family. Despite the cold. The sweat. The bugs. The long drops. Despite the awful, awful fear and worse—*failure*—I feel every day when

Dolf and I turn down the track between the two witches, my arms burning with a canvas of barely healing bites and scratches. Despite all of that. Sammie grimaces. She doesn't say anything, but she doesn't have to. She understands. Every single person in this room understands, every person in camp.

I turn over, shuffling down into the pillow, when I jump, feeling something moving in the bottom of the bed. Suddenly Morocha's wild head of black hair pokes out from beneath the blanket. Her pink face gleams. She knows she's not allowed in here! Morocha uses Santa Cruz as her own private toilet. She's meant to be learning about being outside. But Sammie just grins guiltily, and Morocha gives a soft, pitiful chirp, wrapping her long gangly arms around my neck.

It's late July when the cold finally ends, and the heat comes back with a vengeance. It's so hot, my bones feel like they're baking. I wear tank tops over thin cotton leggings. These slowly migrate down my thighs because, without noticing, I'm thinner than I was. My body has more angles, more bones. I've emerged out of winter, a bear rubbing her eyes in the sun, and it feels like there's a whole world to play for.

"¡Vamos!" Mila exclaims, one particularly hot, heavy Saturday. "Let us go camping, no? A la laguna. ¿Con el sol y amigos perfectos y Wayrita y Vanesso y todo los gatitos, no? We bring all the cats, no?" She giggles like a girl, a rare, precious moment where she seems to have no cares in the world. We laugh back, me and Sammie and some of the other girls who've lasted the winter. Ilsa and René, two tough, hard-working yet particularly filthy Australians, Ally, chain-smoking and swearing her way down the road as she drags her tent and backpack behind her. Of course we do not take the cats, but maybe we do . . . sometimes I think Mila takes them everywhere.

We head south, over the river, towards a far-away place called the Laguna Corazón. We don't make it there of course. Everyone but Mila and Sammie are extremely unfit. Cats like to sleep. Most of us spend all day on our butts, waiting for them to get up, and the most energetic thing we do is shovel pasta into our mouths.

As the sun gets lower and Mila reluctantly admits defeat, finally letting us pitch our tents in a patch of brambly scree, she takes us down one last trail. When the trees part, Sammie reaches out and grabs my hand. Rocks. Rocks! Giants, at least as tall as the canopy. Taller. Five of them, ten, I'm not sure.

"Fuck me!" Ally mutters.

I brush one of the rocks with my palm. I feel soft, sandy skin. I don't know how long this rock has been here. Since the dinosaurs? Facing the other rocks, as if from a conference that happened millennia ago, and in the dying light, they all shimmer gold from the inside out. Somewhere there's the faint tinkle of waterfalls.

Mila goes first, scrambling up the side. The rest of us follow soon after, trainers desperately scrabbling against rock.

At the top, none of us speak. We find ourselves on a ledge, thirty, forty metres above the ground. The other rocks are turned to face us, dotted through a canopy that stretches as far as I can see. The sun drops, and streaks of what was pink become red. There is a haze, turning darker by the minute, that looks like smoke. A forest floor goes on and on and on. Somewhere, I know, there's the road. The headlights of trucks crawling along it. Somewhere is the village, where the generators will be turning on. I imagine I can hear the tinny chords of Doña Lucia's eighties pop CD, still the only one she owns. I imagine too that I can hear Iskra calling. I can see Sama, asleep with his old white chin on his paws. Wayra pacing, the others spread out through the bobbled, mottled mist. Closing their eyes, pressing up against their fences as wild cats weave past outside. Claimed by and claiming this land, land that once, when this rock first formed, was free.

I don't know what that word means anymore.

Free is a green that stretches forever with no ending. Free no longer exists.

I think about Sama. About him trapped in his small box, and Sama now, not with real space, as he could have had, but with more space than the people who knew him ever thought possible. The sun on his face, the *pride* in his eyes.

We sit in a row, the tops of our arms knocking, the scent of our sweat and the syrupy mould on our skin intermingling with the gritty, dry earth. What are the others thinking about? Home. Work. The jungle. Their friends and families, so far away. This family. The animals. Sammie, with Vanesso. Is Ilsa thinking about Leoncio? The puma she's been working with since 2006 and will continue to work with until both of them grow old. Is René thinking about Juan and Carlos, the two baby pumas? She met them a few months ago, and they'll be her best friends until Juan dies of a parasite, and then it'll be just her and Carlos. For Ally, it's Amira. One of our female jaguars, who arrived while I was away. Ally, like me, came thinking she would stay a few weeks. Now she's changed all her plans. She will change her life, leaving her home, her family, her job, her boyfriends, just so she can be here, so she can take Amira out of her enclosure, so Amira can be wild for a few hours each day.

We are starting to feel it, in the way our faces won't stop turning towards them, the way our hearts beat when they are near. The rock is rough and cold, and we are silent, church silent.

"Mila," I whisper. I don't know who Mila is thinking about. All of them, perhaps. Everyone. I stand by what I said to Tom, what feels like ages ago now. That all of it, all of them, is so much to hold in your head. Too much. But then . . . what is the alternative? The world out there feels completely blank. Everything is flattened, two-dimensional, and can't compete with this, can it? Where everything is in technicolour. The jungle that used to horrify me? When I walked down a trail I didn't know, I felt like the blood of my brain was seeping out of my ears, popping like a machine gun, the unfathomable number of heartbeats rewiring and undoing my body. Now, as I look out from these old rocks, it is the opposite. My body is being remade.

Mila turns her face towards mine. The evening shadows light her up, a gleaming golden bronze. I could never suggest building Wayra a bigger enclosure, not to Mila. There are too many others who need it first, who need it more, who have homes that are so much smaller, who can't even come out of their enclosures at all. The birds. Iskra. Juan and Carlos, still in quarantine. We haven't finished Yuma's yet. Rupi's enclosure floods every wet season so that he has to walk around it on a system of platforms if he wants dry feet. His paws bloom with fungus for months on end. Vanesso . . . his cage is about to fall down around his ears. Sammie is organising a fundraiser for it right now. But if Wayra can't have an enclosure . . . and if she's going to keep on going round and round and round on the same trails . . . I stare out over the mottled green.

"We have to cut her a new trail."

Mila looks at me, sharp eyes tracing the lines of my face. A face that, when I look in the mirror now, I struggle to recognise. When she speaks, the gentleness in her tone is hard to stomach.

"She will get too scared, Laurita."

I stick out my chin. "She's scared now! She needs something. Some kind of freedom, even if it's not the kind she deserves."

Mila is quiet. "Say you do this for her," she finally says. "And she likes this new trail. What will happen when you leave? What will happen during next wet season, when we have no volunteers again and she wants to go on this new trail, but her volunteers are not able to take her?"

"I won't leave!" I say quickly, too quickly.

Mila laughs bitterly and doesn't answer.

In the end, I just say hopelessly, "Can we try? Please." Wayra has the shortest trails of any puma in the parque. I have to give her something. The sun starts to melt across the horizon.

Mila sighs. "Who will cut your new trail, Laurita? Me?"

"I will!" I hiss. We're doing construction every day. We're trying to finish Iskra's enclosure, Yuma's, something for Darwin, Morocha, a place for the four tejones who have turned up, maybe for Teanji too since he seems hell-bent on injuring a hapless volunteer in flip-flops. We need to get the fire trail up to scratch, who knows if there'll be fires again this year, and when will we get going on the aviary? "I swear, I'll get up early. Dolf will help."

"I will too!" Sammie pipes up, listening from the other side.

"And me!" Ilsa, René, the rest of the girls. I feel a flush of warmth.

"Shit!" Ally exclaims, squeezing my hand. "I'm in. But only"—she holds up her finger warningly—"if you swear not to let Dolf use a machete anywhere near Mila." Ally pokes Mila in the side, and she laughs. Mila's face relaxes as she shakes her head despairingly. Last time Dolf used a machete, it flew out of his hand and wedged itself in a tree, inches from Mila's ear.

Later, when we've climbed down off the rocks and the sun has disappeared entirely, leaving just a canopy of stars and blackness, I go to sleep in my tent with Sammie. I can't quite bring myself to smile. Not after what Mila has said. What I see her saying silently to all of us volunteers when she looks into our faces. *You're going to leave. I can never forget it, and neither can you.* Sometimes accusingly, but mostly just . . . true. Even after I fall asleep, I think that her words, spoken and unspoken, stay in my mind for a long time, long into my dreams.

It takes a few weeks but the first chance I get, I'm out there with Dolf and the girls. Osito and Germáncito come too, excited for the challenge, and their wicked machete skills halve the work. Dolf optimistically calls the new trail, once it's done, spreading before us gleaming and glorious, the Paradise Expressway. We all share a celebratory snack of fresh motoyoé fruit, picked by the boys. The fruit is tart and lemony, and as we hang our legs over a tree at the lagoon, everyone laughing, Osito trying to hit Dolf with old, rotten fruit, I try not to be anxious. I try not to imagine being stuck out there, a long, long way now from the cage, and I try not to let Mila's caution dampen things. The trail is beautiful. We've added more than a mile. It's new jungle for us, for her. Maybe she went there when she was free, north of her cage and runner, but not with us. Never with us.

The next day I'm walking in front of Wayra, Dolf with the ropes behind, and when I veer off, onto the start of the Paradise Expressway—new, strange, uncertain—my heart beats wildly. I see her eyes cloud and—for a second—I hesitate. Fear flickers over her face. She looks tawny, ochre with a yellowing sun. Confusion. Then the rest. Excitement, incredulity. A flash of stubbornness, but it's only a flash. It's overtaken by something that jams into my stomach and makes me feel as if I'm flying. Trust. Broken and built between us so many times. She raises her head, meeting my gaze. And then we walk. She doesn't grumble or growl. She is silent, she is awed.

About halfway round, we reach a sunlit tree, massive and old and fallen along the right bank of the trail, and she lurches up it, scampering, almost pulling Dolf off his feet. I realise I'm laughing. I realise the tension has melted off me, just as it has her. She's relaxed, lying across the tree, her paws hanging, her eyes wide and raised to the gorgeous beauty of the shards of sky. I see Dolf out of the corner of my eye, a daft grin on his face too. The salty taste of sweat and happiness sticks on my lips. She turns, turns again, casting a pose that sends a long shadow across the ground. Not a princess. A queen. Her silvery fur glistens, the light catching patches of her, criss-crossed with shadows.

"I love you," I say quietly, my voice breaking.

Her neck arches into the sun, catching a sweep of gold. We both watch an eagle soar across a patch of sky. I can't believe it's taken me this long to say it out loud. She turns to me and flicks her tail mildly, agreeing. *I knew you loved me, ages ago.* She puts her cheek on both her paws and gazes at me. There's a marvelling look in her eyes. A questioning look. Far away, the eagle disappears, lost within the clouds.

There's a full moon just coming up, its face swollen and pale, hard as a penny. It's so light on the road we don't need torches and when Sammie stops walking, the lines of her face are stark, almost blue. I can hear the frogs. The nightly chirp of the crickets. The soft touch of a breeze. The dark blackness of the trees on both sides is solid, unflinching. A shape, not too far away, slithers out of the shadows. A snake perhaps, or a lizard. Sucking up the last heat still caught in the tarmac. Sammie's turned away though, so she doesn't see it. She's turned away from me too. For a moment, she's very still. Then she bursts into tears. She's weeping, inconsolable—loud, ugly tears spilling down her face. The curve of her cheeks, pale now in the darkness, gleams. Her thick hair shakes as she cries, her strong shoulders shuddering. I gaze at her. I don't know what to do. It looks like her heart is breaking.

"They're going to shut him back in that shitty aviary!" She sobs, choking. "They want to take away his freedom! They're going to do it, aren't they?"

I press my teeth together hard enough that pain reverberates up my jaw. A group of volunteers have organised themselves into something called VAPTOL. It stands for Volunteers Against the Preferential Treatment of Lorenzo. They've been campaigning for a few weeks, but it finally reached its peak tonight when Lorenzo almost took the lead member's ear off, just because he tried to help Sammie off with her boot. It would make me laugh, if I didn't want to scream instead.

Sammie bends her knees, then collapses into the grass. It's wet, a little bit dewy. I pass her a cigarette, but she just holds it in her shaking fingers. "Are they *right*?"

I sit down slowly across from her, brushing my hand over the tarmac, checking for more snakes. I find none, but it's warm and reassuring, and I curl my fingers around the loose gravel until the tiny flakes dig into my palm. I used to be afraid of Sammie. And now, she might be the closest friend I've ever had. I stare at her, at the ugly tears running down her muddy face, a crumpled wet mess on the grass. I probably have Wayra to thank for this friendship. Over and over, she's taught me that maybe it does hurt to get close to someone. But also, maybe, it's worth it. A million times, it's worth it.

Is it worth it for Lorenzo? I picture him flying ecstatically around the tallest trees. His wings pump like bellows, a gleeful squawk shattering the beautiful blue. I picture him curled up in Sammie's shirt, right by her heart. Warm and cosy after a day on his own scavenging palm nuts and his favourite fruits. Refereeing a game of volleyball, twirling impatiently from high up on a branch, his pupils contracting at each throw of the ball. Chasing Sammie down the road, shrieking unstoppably, almost sailing into the side of a logging truck, and the hours of work we have had to waste trying to get him into bed every night. The rest of the macaws desperately sharpening their beaks on the aviary fence. Crazy Eyes dancing for attention, for even a hint of the life Lolo's got. Finally I see Sammie getting on a plane and Lorenzo, lost and alone, searching for his beloved mate amongst the empty faces on the patio.

Is it worth it? Is it *right*?

I don't know.

The next morning when I wake up, I hear a yell coming from the direction of the aviary. When I get there, still pulling on my boots, I stop short. There is a small crowd of people standing as I am, speechless. Mila is inside, tears running down her cheeks. She's in the cage at the furthest corner, near the back. Cage five. It's where Dontdothat lives with a trio of tiny sweet-natured parrots called Pica, Pico and Picky. I see Big Red peering blindly through the fence, cocking his head from side to side, dancing anxiously. Romeo and Juliet stare in too, very still. Lorenzo watches from outside, his expression unfathomable.

"What . . . ," I begin, but don't finish. I can see that cage five is empty. I can also see that there's a hole in the side of the fence, towards the back near their night enclosures. It's not a hole made by an animal. It's straight, rectangular. It's been cut. Cut by a person. My hand goes to my mouth as comprehension dawns. This is where the aviary backs onto the jungle. It's the point where someone would come in, using our trails. Fishermen, poachers, illegal loggers. Someone who knows our land. We've been finding empty shotgun cartridges on some of the trails for months now. Cigarette butts by the lagoons. Empty beer cans by Vanesso's cage. I look at Mila wildly. Her hair is a mess, her face pale. Agustino is standing very still with his hand gripping Osito's shoulder. Both of them look like they're going to be sick. I think I'm going to be sick.

We search the market. We search the village and we search the town. We search the streets for any sign of Dontdothat, Pica, Pico and Picky. Mila and Agustino suspect they've already been sold and we will not get them back, but over the next days, weeks, months—every time I turn a corner in town, I expect to hear the jibbing shriek, "Don't do that!" or see the soft little wings of three perfectly green Amazonian parrots, one with a V-shaped blue tuft around his neck. But there's nothing. Mila and Agustino are right. There's no sign of them at all.

We've just come back from Porn Bar in Santa María and we're desperate for cake. The moon shines down on the comedor, illuminating patches of bone-almost-blue brick across the floor. The rafters hang darkly above our heads, full of rats and cockroaches and Teanji, most likely. Cascades of giggles erupt out of the kitchen. Tom and I look at each other, the single candle flickering on the wobbly back table between us, casting shadows across his beard, which seems to have somehow grown even redder in the last months, perhaps by proximity to Faustino. My mouth tastes of rum and too many cigarettes, my feet are aching from the long walk home, but I am blissfully, drunkenly happy.

Harry races too fast out of the kitchen and trips over one of the benches, catapulting to the floor, taking Sammie with him. The two of them lie on top of each other, laughing hysterically. I roll my eyes, and Tom chuckles. He's wearing Bobby's "SMILE" T-shirt, not ironically, and his freckles stand out across his strong forearms, his skin still so glaringly pale. But as I stare at him, I see that his eyes are glistening. Without thinking I reach over, putting my hand on his. His skin is warm.

"You OK?" I whisper, slurring only slightly.

He nods, wiping his eyes. With effort, he manages to focus his face. He gives me a brave attempt at a smile. I manage to smile back, although now I'm feeling slightly sick inside. I remember I'm still touching his hand, and I pull back quickly, but not before I register with a kind of dawning sadness how nice his hand feels.

"Did you get it?" he murmurs, and for a moment I'm not sure who he's talking to.

Sammie giggles breathlessly, climbing to her feet and pulling Harry with her. As they collapse onto the benches next to us, she slams something down on the table.

"Ta-dah!"

"*Cake,*" I murmur.

Harry leaps back up, raising his arms, and shouts with triumph, "Cake!"

"Shhh!" Tom and I hiss, pulling him back down. I look around anxiously, but the rest of camp stays dark. The only light is ours, our single fluttering candle.

"Do you think he'll notice?" I stare in wonderment at the slab of fluffy peach, papaya and peanut butter sponge they've liberated from

Paddy's lockbox, which is a bucket with bricks on top of it. Teanji safe. Rat safe. Not Harry and Sammie safe.

"No way." Sammie hands out a spoon each, reverently. "We only took, like, half of it." She explodes into giggles again, holding up her spoon. "It's for Tommy anyways, right? In honour of his last night."

Tom winces. "Salud, amigos," he says very quietly.

We raise our spoons. They clink above the cake.

"Salud," I whisper.

"Salud," Sammie echoes.

Harry bursts into tears.

A while later, cake crumbs are spread across the table. Harry and Sammie are fast asleep, their heads cradled in each other's arms. Tom stares at the last piece of cake. Then he looks sadly at Harry.

"You think he'll be OK?" he whispers.

I shake my head. "You're his best friend."

"He's still got you and Sammie. And Ru."

I'm afraid that I can feel my own tears starting, and so I look down hard at the lonely cake crumbs and try to swallow.

"How will you cope? Back in England," I finally whisper, when I've got myself under control. "There won't be any cats there!" I try to laugh, but it comes out mangled.

He doesn't look at me. He stares at his hands. "There'll be cats."

"Not big ones!"

"No. Not big ones." He gazes up into the rafters, where the names of the cats have been inscribed. Earlier tonight, Harry took out his penknife and carved our names up there too. "I'll be a vet though," Tom murmurs, trying to be jovial. Then he laughs, putting his big head in his hands. "In five years or so."

I gaze very hard at one of the constellations of freckles on his left arm. It's the shape of a puppy, I think. Or an old tree.

"You'll be a good vet," I say quietly.

He is silent for a long time. "You know," he finally whispers, a faint flush on his cheeks, not quite looking at me. "I'll be not too far from you. When you get home, that is."

I look up. He looks at me. And for a while, we just stare at each other. I think it's the longest I've ever looked at him before. His eyes are the most curious shade of blue. Almost grey, but not quite. I gulp, feeling heat rising in my stomach, a strange tingling in the backs of my ears, a sort of dizziness. I feel myself leaning forwards, tilting almost, and for a moment, we are so close to each other, I can feel the heat off his skin, the smell of him, heady, slightly monkeyish, like Faustino's fur when he's too hot. I feel hot all over. I lean forwards a little more.

"I'm never leaving!"

Both of us pull back sharply. I laugh to cover the flush that's staining my cheeks and put my hands over my face. When I sneak a look back at Tom, I see that his cheeks are bright too. Harry grabs my arm, oblivious, barely able to lift his head off the table, and repeats what he's said, slurring badly. "I'm never leaving, you know that, right?"

I grin, patting his hand.

"We know, buddy," Tom whispers.

"You have to leave at some point." Sammie snorts, rubbing her bloodshot eyes. "That's just life."

"Nope." Harry looks dreamily off into the middle distance, towards where I know he is imagining Ru to be, even though he's got the direction completely wrong and he's actually looking towards the baños. "Never. Never again. Nu-uh. Can't. Not doing it."

"You'd really stay here forever?" I gaze at him. "Truly?"

Harry lays his cheek affectionately on Tom's shoulder, their dirty beards touching. "This is my home," he murmurs. His lips tighten, just for a moment, and in that moment I think about the Harry he is outside of here, who has a family in Australia he doesn't talk about, a place he grew up in that none of us know about. I cannot think about leaving. The idea is too huge, too awful. But it is also inevitable.

"But what about . . ." I wave my hand vaguely.

"What?" he snaps. "Out there? Fuck out there."

"I don't know if I could stay forever," Sammie says quietly. "I don't know if I'm strong enough. Mentally."

Harry shrugs. "I don't think I'm mentally strong enough to leave."

Sammie stares around at all of us. Tom just places his head on Harry's, and Sammie takes Tom's hand, and I take his other one. There are tears now on his cheeks, proper tears. I watch them fall silently into his beard. His tough calloused fingers entwine with mine. Eventually the candle splutters, then goes out. We continue to sit there, none of us wanting it to end, as the moonlight darkens, and then also goes out.

The sky is duck-egg blue, the clouds all blown to nothing. I let myself float, as if I'm weightless. A wide orb framed by a ragged crown of green. My ears are under the water and I can hear nothing but the muffled thumps of my heart. The milky lagoon settles. I take a deep breath. I smell the scent of lavender and the sun beats down on my face. Wayra is swimming. I can feel the strong surge of her legs, her paws making waves underwater. We've strung an eighty-metre runner across the lagoon so that she can swim on her own. She likes it, I think. Another touch of freedom. If I turn my head, I'll see her. Not far, ten metres or more. Her eyes bright, clear, green, concentrating on nothing but the rhythmic pulse of her swim. She'll be bobbing, snorting as she tries to keep her nose above water, one dark line running from the top of her head all the way down to the tip of her tail. She is smooth and graceful as a sea snake. Doggedly angling her face to the opposite bank. I have no idea what it is she hopes to reach. Perhaps nothing. Perhaps she just likes the hypnotic drag of an unknown, unchanging shore.

I don't turn my head though. It's enough to know that she's there. Just for now, I let the water hold me and the bright blue of the sky fill my eyes. Absently, I scratch an itch on my leg that Agustino says might be scabies. And I think back to the beginning, when my onion layers cleaved to my bones. I remember those layers falling away like old skin, as the seasons turned and the months passed, as the jungle rose and fell, expanded and contracted, lived and died. I turn on my side. She's a swollen, distorted shape puffing in a coffee-brown sea. The surrounding forest is a fairy crown. I feel naked. The sky is pulling me under. When I lie in bed at night, I think about this look that Wayra gives me now. When I stand in front of her, she gazes up at me. It's not like when she's curled in a ball. She doesn't look small. She has filled out her body. She looks around at her jungle, and then she looks back at me. And she *sees* me.

Wayra and I are swimming in a wild lagoon that has been in this place for thousands of years. Millions perhaps. And maybe it will continue to be here, millions of years after we're gone. Maybe it won't, I don't know. All I know is that I wish I could travel back in time. I'd give anything to be able to go through the acres of jungle, through the seasons, through the wind, the rain and the sun. I'd go to the moment that changed everything. The moment the hunter shot his gun. I'd stop him, of course. The hunter who came for Wayra's mother. If it meant I'd never have met Wayra, even if it meant none of this would have ever happened, I'd change it all in a second if it meant it didn't have to be like this for her.

But I can't. I can't change anything. And I feel that she knows this, when she looks at me now. Maybe she always knew it. It just took me a while to catch up.

It's a month after Tom leaves that the fires start. The air is too dry and crisp for them not to come ripping through fields that are slashed and burnt and broken. Everything else goes out of our heads. It's worse than last year. There are more fields, more farmers—Mennonites, Colombians, settlers moving in from elsewhere. The government looks away, a socialist government with a hatred of American consumerism but a heady desire for progress. Slashing and burning is illegal, but not controlled. So the new farmers set new fires, even when the old ones are put out. And we've got more animals. Our firebreak is there, so that's good, we don't have to cut it anew, but where last year it was Wayra, Katie and Sama at risk . . . now we have Iskra, her new enclosure built merely two hundred metres from the break. Amira the jaguar, somewhere between Wayra and Iskra. Leoncio, the male puma, not too far from Sama. Perhaps it was stupid to build on that side of the road, but even though we've got almost a thousand hectares of land, most of the land behind camp floods more than waist high in wet season. So what do you do? Where do you put the cages? The feeling of being squeezed, the panic of it, the horrible feeling of not being able to breathe . . .

We push through, keep going, buy a few more machetes and wheelbarrows. Nobody we know dies, none of our animals have to be moved. But other people's homes are destroyed. Hectares of forests are devastated. The fires rage on, across the Amazon, but they leave us behind.

Not unscathed though. Never unscathed. Agustino has a blank look on his face for a long time afterwards, not even grief. I think he's past grief. He walks aimlessly through the charred remains, searching for injured animals to treat. He doesn't find many. Only corpses. So many corpses.

When I try to speak to him about it, he just looks at me with eyes purple with shadows.

"Estoy cansado, Laurita," he says, shaking his head, a tiny dead lizard in his hands. Its skin is cracked, its body empty. I am so tired, Laurita.

Mila. She's just angry. All the time.

And soon, we don't talk about the corpses. Nobody has asked for Lorenzo to be caged for many weeks. VAPTOL is long gone. We don't talk about Dontdothat, or the rest. We get back to our animals, to our work. We don't talk about the fires, but I see them on people's faces. I see the question no one wants to ask, the one that I hear now at night, with the scratching of branches on the roof. With the knowledge that wet season is coming on the back of the fires, fast and unstoppable like a high-speed train. With heavy bruised clouds, the smell of rain in the air. As the dry heat melts, no less hot but different, a wet heat that seems to drip from every atom. As half our volunteers leave. As we drop down to sixteen, then twelve the following week. As I imagine the jungle filling with water, oozing into every brown, ravaged pore, green with moss and water lilies, with an urgency that makes me tingle. As tarantulas emerge from their holes and coat the road in a seething, downy black.

The question I cannot get rid of is this: Will it be like this every year? Will the fires get worse every year? And if they do, how will we survive?

The light, a high swinging bulb, seems particularly harsh tonight, sputtering every few seconds. Doña Lucia's eighties music plays on repeat, right now it's Kate Bush, "Hounds of Love." Scores of insects are flying, brought in by the rain, some scattered dead around my feet. Their fragile tissue-paper wings crumple. The hum of the generator gives a low rhythm to the patter, to the rise and fall of laughter, and to the song of the frogs in the grass outside. My jaw cracks as I dislodge a wad of coca and spit it into my hand. It's starting to disintegrate and I can feel green saliva running unattractively down my chin. With a sigh, I take a fresh handful of leaves from a bag on the table. I'm chewing them peacefully when suddenly, Sammie and Ally come up behind me and slam their beers down on the table, tipping half of them into my lap.

I've been in the parque, since I came back, for almost eight months.

"You're ready, sugar?" Sammie demands, her southern drawl thick when she drinks.

I sigh. "Where's Mila?"

Ally, her shaggy hair swaying down her back, is already waving to Mila. Mila is talking to Paddy, her arm tight around him as if reluctant to let go. But when Ally signals, they both saunter over. I place my leg on the table and we all peer down at it. Just above my right knee is a red lump the size of a walnut, a tiny black hole at its centre. Stu, a new volunteer, cranes over my shoulder.

"What's that?"

Ally rubs her hands together gleefully. "Boro boro."

"Es grande." Mila nods. Then she looks at Stu and enunciates seriously. "Very large."

Stu pales. "What is boro boro?"

"It's a worm," I say. "From a botfly."

His cheeks go white.

"See that hole?" Paddy points, grinning. "That's how he breathes."

"And Frodo here is going to birth him." Sammie looks to Mila. "Sí?"

I've named my worm Harold. He's been growing inside me for about a month. I've conflicted feelings about him. Mostly he sleeps. Only when I disturb him does he start burrowing, finding somewhere deeper, a softer, fleshier cocoon. Harold is a stabbing, urgent pain that keeps me awake at night, but he's also become part of me.

Mila nods her assent.

"Can I do it?" Ally's smoking a cigarette and has a wad of coca in her cheek so big it looks like a growth. "Squeeze, squeeze, squeeze!"

I anxiously pull my own wad away from my raw cheek with one dirty finger. "But . . ." I look plaintively at Mila. Mila's excellent at squeezing stuff. But Mila is shrugging, and she and Paddy are retreating back to their corner laughing. I sigh, glaring at Ally. "Fine! But be respectful. Harold's my friend."

She's already leaping up, a manic expression on her face, returning mere seconds later with Sammie's backpack, from which she pulls out a roll of industrial duct tape. When I raise my eyebrows at Sammie, she just shrugs. "Always be prepared."

"Come on." Ally taps my knee and I straighten it reluctantly. "Ready to say your last words?"

"I'm sorry," I whisper towards my knee as she unrolls one of her cigarettes and makes a little pile of tobacco on top of Harold's breathing hole. Then she slaps three lines of tape over it and presses down.

"Don't move."

"What's happening now?" Stu asks.

"Harold's being asphyxiated."

The room spins a little. I would have let poor Harold pop out by himself if he hadn't started chomping on my flesh. I don't know how much time passes, but when Sammie plops onto the bench next to me, I open my eyes. She straightens her filthy flannel shirt and passes me a lukewarm beer. I see Stu's eyes moving around, taking in the bugs. The filth on our clothes, on me. The unforgiving concrete. The locals gossiping around the pool table. The massive pile of corn that has been laid out in one corner to dry. The overwhelming, unstoppable darkness outside. My leg. Harold. The look of horror on his face makes me think of England. Stu is from England. And I think of the bars there. With no pigs outside. Where it isn't appropriate to wear gumboots and a T-shirt that hasn't been washed in months and could technically be classed as a nightie. Where it's frowned upon to eat peanut butter for dinner from the jar, and fall asleep on the floor. Where there are so many people and it's so loud, I would drown. Where there are only humans and human noise and no parasites to keep you up at night, only men who stalk you around the dance floor and try to touch your breasts.

I shake my head, suddenly laughing. Sammie looks at me like I've gone nuts.

"Samwise," I say to her, leaning back against the wall. "Do you ever think that it's not this place that's mad. It's the rest of the world?" I came to Bolivia wanting to transform. I wanted to be a butterfly. Maybe I should have been hoping for something else. A botfly, perhaps, like little Harold. That's more what I feel like now anyway. Last month, around mid-November, when the rains truly started in earnest, I shaved my head. I sold my hair at an auction to raise money for a new enclosure for Amira. I also had head lice the size of raisins. I've lost so much weight that for the first time in my life, my bras are too big. My collarbones stand out across my chest, and my neck is thin like a giraffe. I've spent my life praying to be thin and now I am, and yet I realise that wasn't what I was praying for at all. I was just praying to feel comfortable in my own skin.

Sammie stares at me. "I think we're all mad. Every single one of us. Here, there, everywhere." And she laughs too, looking down at herself and whispering, "I was prom queen, did I ever tell you?"

"Yeah." I grin. "I think you might have done."

She winks, puts two fingers to her lips, and lets out a long, piercing whistle. Ally clambers onto a table and claps her hands, yelling loud enough to deafen us all.

"Oi! Any of you dirty pricks want to watch Harold being squeezed out of Laura?"

Doña Lucia sets out candles, the generator turns off. Sammie switches on her head torch and Ally tells me to brace myself. Then, everyone holding their breath, she rips off the tape. I grit my teeth on a yelp. She's taken the tobacco and half my leg hair with it. People ooh and aah. I stare into the fathomless black hole, wondering if he's still breathing. Sammie calls for silence. I can hear the trucks rumbling past on the road, the cicadas rattling. The crush of two different worlds. I think the rain has finally stopped. I can just see the edges of the stars. Ally leans in, a lit cigarette between her lips, and puts both her thumbs on either side of the hole. Then she squeezes. I do squeal now, but she keeps going. I see pus, bubbling blood, and then suddenly, with a cry of release, something sails out of my knee in a miraculous spray of white liquid, right into the sea of waiting faces.

"Where is he?" Sammie yells, looking around. "Nobody move!"

There's chaos until Stu weakly holds out his beer. His face and glasses have been splattered with what is probably pus, and there, floating in his drink, is Harold. Stu thrusts his glass at me. He sprints through the back of the bar, out into Doña Lucia's garden, presumably to vomit, as I reach my finger in to pull my worm to dry land. We all stare at his forlorn, lifeless body. He's about the length of half my pinkie finger. He looks like a translucent tadpole with spines along his tail.

"He's so tiny," Ally murmurs, staring at him.

I nod. A little bit sad, a little bit proud. And then I burst into tears.

I wake up the next morning to a long, ungentle shaking.

"Laura!" Dolf hisses. "Come on!"

I start up, rubbing my face. It's pitch dark outside. Dolf's eyes are gleaming in the eerie blood-red light of his head torch.

"What's happening? What time is it?"

"Five! Come on!"

I stare at him for a moment, and then I remember. Volunteer numbers are so dire, ten at last count, that I've been assigned three extra work areas. I'm back with Sama, which I love. Then the puma sisters, Inti, Wara and Yassi, and Leoncio, alternating afternoons. Spending all day with Wayra is a luxury long passed. In order to fit my new cats in, Mila says Wayra will either have to drop down to every other day or . . . a reprieve . . . we can try and walk her before breakfast. Most cats would be too energetic so early, and too playful. But maybe Wayra will be different. We don't know because we've never tried. We're going to try today.

The air is grainy by the time we get to her cage. The jungle is weightless. Silent. I hesitate just before we reach the top of the bank where her cage is, pressing my hand against the fallen strangler and unconsciously stroking the furry threads that I've been watching expand over the last eight months.

"Ready?" Dolf whispers.

I nod.

"¡Hola, mi amor!" I exclaim, as if I haven't seen her in weeks. "Wayra, princesa. Gorgeous girl, I've missed you!"

There's silence and then, I hear something. It sounds like the air being let out of a balloon.

I grab Dolf's arm.

"*Meow!*" I copy tentatively.

She meows back. Then I'm running and when I burst into the clearing, she's racing up and down. Her eyes are gleaming in the dawn light, her tail jerking. I collapse next to her.

"That's the first time she's ever meowed at me!" I exclaim. Not counting that one time in the cage. I push my arms through and she grinds her face against me, starting to purr, resting her chin in my palms. I lean my face close, telling her how much I love her. I can't stop saying it now. She listens. I rub the backs of her ears, taking off fresh blood from nightly mosquito bites. I rub her eyes, getting the sleep out of the sides, I massage her cheeks, feeling the hard bones underneath and the smooth give of her skin. She yields, savouring the feeling of being touched, and when she looks up, she has a dazed, hopeful expression.

What are you doing here so early? She yawns. *I wasn't asleep, you know.*

She looks different in this light. In this time of magic, between day and night. More real. This is the time for wild creatures. Her time.

We're on the trail in seconds.

"Come on, gorgeous girl," I whisper.

We walk at a quick trot, the soft, cool granular air brushing us, the only sounds the shriek of the crickets, the hum of the forest waking, the muted beat of our footsteps. Shadows float through the limbs of the surrounding trees, making the whole world look like it's made of liquid. She's liquid too. She gazes around, standing very still in the centre of a little clearing, patuju on all sides with the red blush of flowers, spindly bamboo stalks and vines tethered above our heads. Her pupils are night swollen. She can slide in between shadows. The sun isn't beating yet, the mosquitoes and the bugs are still asleep. Even the leaves under our feet are soft, wet with dew and soundless. The smells are new, freshly grown, and she's filling herself up with them. She swings her head left, right, up, down, around, down again, her ears gyrating, the tip of her tail trembling, her whiskers going wild. Her mouth is open, her eyes googly. She's a kitten who's just discovered feathers.

There's a whirling burst of birdsong, high and sonorous, and she freezes, one paw raised off the ground, her tail caught mid-jerk, her face angled towards the bamboo. The world is lightening by the second, a soft grey filtering through the leaves. Dolf and I look at each other, and I am too happy to smile. I'm too happy to even breathe. I feel a swell of incredible love right at the centre of my chest. Wayra's anxiety can feel like waves in the air, pulsing and filling an entire world. But now there's nothing. Only peace.

We walk until Wayra wants to stop, and when she does, settling happily on her fallen sunlit tree, Dolf pulls a thermos of coffee and two swollen mangoes—each the size of two fists—out of his backpack, their bruised skins already slick with juice. I stare at him, not quite believing he's had the foresight to bring breakfast. Quietly, he just hands me a mug, steaming with black coffee, and one of the mangoes.

"Salud." He raises his mango in the air, and I touch it wonderingly with mine.

Mango juice runs down my arms. I can't believe any of this. Last year, I thought she was happy. But this . . . meowing when we come to see her, purring into my hands? How did this happen? The ephemeral feeling of the dawn has almost gone but there's still a shadow of it around the hazy edges of her whiskers, the mottled tresses of leaves.

I don't look at Dolf and I don't look at Wayra. I can't. I look down at my boots, my familiar, wonderful no-longer-white gumboots that I've worn every day for more than half a year, with the orange football socks pulled up to my knees. I wrinkle up my nose, trying not to cry again.

"Are you OK?" Dolf whispers.

I look at him. His shape, his tall familiarity, his tenderness. His pale balding hair pokes out under his wide-brimmed sun hat. There's a streak of mud across his cheek. I shake my head, and then he's next to me, wrapping his arm around my shoulders. I feel tears cascading down my cheeks and Wayra going very still.

I'm so tired. I'm not even twenty-six years old, and I've got scabies and a parasite that's been making me shit yellow water for months. And I'm sad. Just . . . sad. When I see the aviary, I see Dontdothat squealing for help and none of us hearing. When I look at the road, I don't see the road that I adored anymore. I see a cattle field, a slashed and burnt farm, a multinational carving up a land that is beautiful and sacred, that has been taken from its peoples, and that is *home*. When I watch a young man pass by on a motorbike, a gun slung over his back, I don't see his family. I don't see the possibilities of what might happen if we were able to stop him, speak to him, learn from him. I see only the ghosts of the creatures he's killed. The jaguars, the pumas, the pigs. I am angry, so angry. When I look at the forest, I feel my fingers curling around the hot metal handle of a machete. And when I look up at the sky, I don't see the bright shining blue. I just see the smoke lines of planes.

I remember when Jane told me she was ready to leave. I didn't understand it then. I wasn't ready. I wasn't ready at all.

I gulp painfully. Now, I think, I am.

"I'm ready to go," I say.

Dolf stares at me, his eyes very wide. And then he hiccups, and he is crying too. Convulsing heaves hit my chest and his wet sobs dribble hot down the back of my neck.

"Was Harold too much?" he finally chokes, trying to laugh.

I laugh too, but it's lost. I don't know what to say. The truth is, I can't even believe I've said this out loud. He's shaking his head but I'm nodding, I can't believe I'm nodding, and thinking about those planes I've been watching, casting their harsh white streaks across the sky. The tragedy of the birds, the fires, those planes that I will get on, my body, crumbling bit by bit, my empty bank account that I'll have to beg my parents to supplement until I start earning money again. And they will, because I'm lucky. Privileged.

When Wayra's ready, when the bugs start to annoy her and the sun gets too bright, she leaps soundlessly off her tree and leads us back to the runner.

I gaze tenderly at her as she cleans her butt, nestled safe in her garden of patuju that fills the centre of her runner. I love her so much. It's like a parasite, I think with a panicky laugh, rubbing my wet hands over my damp scalp, maybe that's why I have to visit the long drop ten times a day. I'm just trying to empty out all this emotion. But I can't. Deep down, I don't *want* to get rid of it. Part of me wants to feel like this every day of my life.

Wayra and I . . . we've gone through so many different versions of ourselves. We've learnt to trust each other, and broken that trust, again and again. Each time we do it, I think it will break me. But I think it has made us stronger. Each time we do it, it makes me love her a little bit more. How can I walk away from this? I don't think I dared hope that something like this could exist.

Dolf picks up a palm leaf and trails it along the edge of the clearing. Wayra stares at it, her pupils swelling, and then she's up and they're running back and forth, the leaf gyrating and Wayra pouncing, hiding, delirious with a joy that is just another layer I never knew was there before Dolf tried to play with her, and that—like everything that we've tried to do this year—has pushed the grief back, just a little bit. The clearing, its tangled trees, its familiar bamboo, its lemon tree that drips yellow to the ground, its sentinel . . . they've all been watching, I think. And if they are watching now . . . what they see is a puma and two strange, filthy, happy, entangled humans. The puma leaps for the curling spines of a leaf and her eyes shine with an impossible green. Her fur gleams silver and in this moment, it's hard to see any tragedy at all.

I don't leave. Not for a while. But it's there, in the back of my mind. When Faustino stares up at me, making kissing actions with his lips from my pillow. It's there when Paddy and I spend an entire Saturday, finally, if ineptly, fixing the lock on the aviary door. And it's there when I go into town and open my email to find another message from Tom, making me laugh with stories about sheep, and cows' bottoms, and tiny cats that fall in love with his beard. I miss him, more than I expected. And I think, perhaps, I might see him when I go back.

"Laurita," Mila calls one day across the patio. She is smiling, her hair shining, her cowboy hat crooked on her head. "¿Puedes ayudar con los pìos?"

It's not yet six, the dawn just breaking. I brush the mosquitoes away from my face. There's a thick haze of smoke emerging from the animal kitchen. We have to burn egg cartons now to chase away the bugs. I thought I knew what mosquitoes meant. I didn't. Nowhere close. Yesterday, the record for one palm slap on someone's forehead was eighty-six. In the jungle they flock in black clouds. I can brush my hands through them. The whine is incessant. It is a drone that sends us loopy, cats and people and monkeys all. The only place anyone is safe is under a mosquito net, and even then not really. I spend hours every night shining my torch into the crevasses, searching desperately for stragglers. I have my head net in my pocket now, but there's already too many around for me to put it on safely, without trapping at least a dozen inside. I chew hard on my coca, the only thing that's keeping me upright, and pull my collar up to my neck despite the reams of sweat. There are aubergine-coloured clouds. It'll rain again soon, I think with a shudder.

Faustino is on the roof. I look up at him, expecting to see him on his own. But Morocha is curled up closer to him than is usual, balanced on the metal roof, her long tail wrapped loosely around herself. Darwin is in her lap, almost too big to ride on her back now. In between breaths, I catch Faustino looking dubiously at the two monkeys sidelong, as he puffs up his shoulders, straightens his neck, leans forwards on his hands to let out another howl. His howls are so loud they bounce off the trees and back again, hitting the roof. Darwin crouches, trying to muster his own emulating cough that one day, I think, will be a howl. When Faustino finally settles himself back with a grunt, he sneaks another sly look at the others. They're gazing at him, their eyes full and admiring. Faustino looks away quickly but not without a small self-satisfied huff that makes me smile for him as I wallow through ankle-deep sludge towards the animal kitchen.

Inside, Ally stands at the high table chopping papaya as smoke billows around her boots. It looks like she's on fire. Her eyes are watering, a hacking cough in her lungs as she chops, her fingers red, swollen, bloody sausages, black from the swarming mosquitoes. She waves me off when I try to help, sending me out again towards the pìos' enclosure. I go happily, patting her gently on the shoulder, to which she just grimaces, her face a mask of horror. I think back to the first time we met, the tough-talking Kiwi who toppled Dolf so easily, gold hot pants in hand, and I think about Amira, that jaguar that she is so in love with. Since I've been here, she's returned to New Zealand and come back again, sporting a full-sleeve tattoo of Amira's face. But even her enthusiasm cannot withstand these conditions. I laugh a little to myself as I head back out towards the pìos. The water is calf deep now. I've got a nasty fungal rash spreading between my toes, my skin peeling off like old apples, leaving raw scarlet flesh behind, and I wince as the flood fills my boots.

"Lau, we going?" Dolf calls from the path, Wayra's meat bucket swinging at his side. I grin. Wayra has been meowing every day. She is sprinting round her trails. She is swimming every day. Playing most days. Even though she only gets a few hours, at most, outside of her cage, they are a good few hours. Even Mila is impressed. Walking her in the early morning, before the world wakes up, has agreed with her.

"I'm just going to help with the pìos," I call to him, waving. "Be with you in a sec!"

I increase my speed. I see quickly that the overflowing food bucket has been abandoned just outside their enclosure and Matt Damon is blocking the doorway, his long neck curved, his scraggly, flightless wings poised, his butt out. A few months ago, the other Matt, or Damon, died from a parasite. Nobody knows how old he was. They live for about a decade, and Agustino claims that both Matt and Damon have been here since he arrived—more than five years ago. But there's only one Matt Damon now. I cannot tell if he misses his friend, but he hisses dramatically as I pick up the food and push my way past, wincing as I sink up to my knees in dirty brown water.

"It's OK, bud," I say, touching him gently on the side. "Here's your breakfast, OK?" Quickly I put it down and call out, "¡Comida!" At this, the rest of his friends race out from the trees, swaying from side to side. A posse of drunken, feathered giraffes, making a ragged bee-line for their breakfast. Wading behind them, a shell-shocked expression on her face, is one of the new volunteers who arrived yesterday. Her forehead is a ravaged mess of swollen bites, her clothing—not meant for the jungle, new lightweight travelling gear—is caked in mud from where she's obviously fallen over. She hasn't managed to find any decent gumboots, so she's got an ill-matched pair, one red and one black. Petunia is following hard on her heels, peering malevolently over her shoulder. I can see the girl is already missing a few buttons.

I smile. "You're Laura Dos? I'm Laura too. Laura Uno." I reach out my hand for her to shake. She acquiesces gingerly, trying to smile. "Are you OK?" I ask.

"I'm fine!" she exclaims, casting an anxious glance back at Petunia.

"Come on," I say with a grin. "I'll show you how to clean the cage. Did anyone give you a spade?"

She nods, holding up a rusty spade with no handle. I stare at her, at the terrified expression on her face, her ruffled hair, her red swollen forehead, and I try not to laugh, wondering vaguely who Mila is planning to assign her to, whether she's assigned her to a cat already. I'm about to ask her how long she's staying, when Petunia stretches out her wings and lets out an explosion of sloppy purple poo over my boots. Big Red, up on his perch in the aviary, lets out a delighted shriek of laughter. And I think I hear Lolo, high above Big Red's cage, cackle in reply.

A few days later I sit on the earth outside of Sama's enclosure. It's the afternoon, and the two o'clock rains have just finished. The sky is still brown, but I think it will clear soon and turn blue. I can still hear the patter of the last raindrops as they fall through the leaves, like fingertips on a piano. I'm cross-legged, watching as a tiny mushroom pushes its way out of the mud. It's the size of my little fingernail. Snow white. Sama's been looking at it too, lying flat on the other side of the fence, his belly slick with mud. But he's bored now and saunters away to clean himself off, back in a patch of patuju. I stay though, the low flat clouds drifting, and watch.

The mushroom starts as just a tiny thread. I crouch, pressing my cheek through my head net into the wet earth. The mosquitoes make a high-pitched whine, and I desperately rub the tops of my ears to dislodge them. The scents of mould, damp and fungal spores draw into my lungs. By the time evening comes, Sama is next to me again, amiably cleaning his paws. The first stars are starting to pop, the clouds blown away, and the mushroom is half a foot high with streaks of pink across its cap. I cannot tell where it's come from, but I imagine fibres spreading out, talking. Thinking together. Going far, far away. All the way through this enclosure, under the road and back to camp, even further—to the village, to Ru's canoe at the river, to the mountain and the place where Alfredo lives with his dogs.

I rub my nose and continue staring at the little mushroom long after the sky turns black and the moon rises. I know I should go back to camp, but I can't bring myself to. Not yet. I've realised something while I've been out here. With my cheek pressed into the dirt and the spores.

The knots that've been growing inside me, ever since Harold popped out and I started ridiculously and unfathomably to cry in front of everyone, have dropped away. Sammie said it to me a long time ago, but I think perhaps I didn't believe it. Not till now. I'm not the same person who got off that bus almost two years ago. She's there, and I can still be tender with her, while also being someone else as well. A person who'll blissfully spend a whole day with her cheek in the dirt, watching a single mushroom grow, as a jaguar lies by her side. And here's the thing. I like this new person! I trust her. It's a strange feeling. I never trusted myself before.

I watch the mushroom. The pink of its cap is turned towards the moon. I was so set on what I thought I had to do that I didn't see what I was missing. Of course I don't have to go into marketing and buy a glamourous fridge. I don't have to marry a man who tosses back sambuca shots with the boys on weekends, I don't have to marry a man at all. I don't have to have kids. I can go back to England and I can hold on to this new person, this person I'm just starting to get to know, tentatively, carefully. I'm transformed, but I'm not a butterfly. I'm a botfly. A dirty, glorious, disgusting, complex botfly.

This place and these people are my family, my kin. Mila, Agustino and the kids. Wayra, Sama, Faustino, Matt Damon, these mushrooms.

Part of me is desperate to stay with them forever. But the other part knows I won't. Can't. Not blindly, not now that I know there are other animals—pumas just like Wayra—and communities of people, of trees, of rivers and lakes and mountains, who are dying inside and out. I watch new animals arriving in droves, watch our animals being taken, knowing that the zoo is less than eight hours away, while I run through trails, groom Wayra, swim with her, make my whole glorious purpose *her*. As the jungle is being taken to bits, the flooding and fires intensify, and more and more roads are built.

Leaving isn't a failure. Not if I choose to do something I'm proud of every day. And I'm so lucky to be able to choose. This is the gift of my privilege. Wayra has no choice at all. So, mushroom friend, I choose to question what I thought was unbreakable. Marriage, the meaning of success. Sexism, racism, capitalism, speciesism . . . the other isms. The things that have made this destruction possible. All the things that have made me into a person who was scared of herself and her desires. All the things that have hurt so many people, so many homes and so many creatures. I choose to question them and to help fight them.

If I don't, how can I ever look Wayra in the face again?

She's lying in her garden of patuju, halfway up the runner, front legs crossed daintily and resolutely under her chin. She opens one eye, assesses the situation, and squeezes them shut again until they're just hooded lines, angled like the eyes of an Egyptian cat goddess.

She yawns and irritably swats a particularly annoying mosquito away with the end of her tail, leaving a smear of blood across her nose. They're sort of beautiful, the mosquitoes. There are a lot of common ones around us now, black with white underbellies and spots along their legs. Their whine is low and insistent. But there are others too. White ones. Big ones, with golden spun-sugar wings. Their sting is savage.

Ones with sapphire-blue feet that hover shyly. Ones with emerald legs that drone louder than the rest, and lighter green ones too, limbs like gossamer lace.

Wayra watches me out of the corner of her eye when I start to edge forwards. As I get close, her eyes soften. I come down onto my knees, reaching out my arm. She nudges it away, stretches her neck and tries to lick my face. Laughing, I push her away and offer her my arm again. With a sigh she looks once more at my face, covered in sweat and dirt, before settling down to my arm. I roll up my sleeves, pushing my many layered shirts up to my elbows, and let her have at it. She licks with abandon, competing with the mosquitoes for space. I press my nose into the fur along her spine. She smells of earth. Air whipped up by a heavy wind. Damp, and jungle leaves. I close my eyes. I feel her chest rising. Her heart is going thump, thump, thump. She nuzzles in and I whisper snatches of endearments, rubbing her ears, her eyes, her cheeks. She's hot and velvety, and a low grumble rises out of her stomach.

I pull away. I stare at her, almost blindsided. I'm not afraid of her anymore. The canopy hangs over us darkly, drawing in, the leaves thick, slick leather, but I know it so well it's a comfort. It's home. Being here with her, like this, is normal. Normal is not getting into my car and getting stuck in a traffic jam at eight every morning. Normal is not going to a club bursting at the seams, wearing high heels and too little clothing, and drinking my body weight in tequila. Normal is not sitting in my bedroom with no one but my anxious spiralling thoughts and Saturday-night TV for company. Normal is not having a force field around yourself so strong that you don't let anyone in, ever. This is normal. *This.* I pull this into my chest, this feeling that I know I'm going to hold on to forever.

I'm leaving on the night bus. I've got a flight in two days' time, I'll land in Heathrow, my mum will pick me up. Just in time for Christmas.

Wayra's grumble gets louder and I inch backwards until I'm leaning against the trunk of the sentinel tree. Its silver bark is warm. She watches me for a while, her eyes hooded, before starting to roll back and forth, rubbing her face in the clammy dirt. When she settles, I think she goes to sleep. I keep watching, memorising the lines of her as she lies so perfectly.

I don't know how long I keep vigil for. Dusk is beginning to deepen and she's still stretched out. Suddenly she stands, and I ease myself to my knees. She's wearing her silly face, the face that I love more than anything, that makes her look like she's four months old and she could play with a football made out of vines for hours. Before I can stand, she ducks her head and springs, knocking me to the ground. But she's gentle and when I push her off, she bounds away to hide, crouching down in a patch of patuju.

"Wayra," I say quickly, standing up. "I can see you!"

She cocks her head. She looks up at the darkening sky, at the dark leaves rustling above her head. Then she looks back at me, relaxes her face, and plods over to our sentinel. I crouch back down and she leans her body against the tree, her ears swivelling. Both of us listen to the evening sounds, the eerie hoots of owls, the bullish rasps of frogs, the rise and fall of a wave, our heartbeats, and I reach out to give her a stroke. She shifts and plonks herself, heavy as a sack of potatoes, in my lap. When I ease her off with a laugh, she hangs on to my boots for a short, heart-stopping minute, before falling still. Then, very gently, she takes my hand in her mouth and starts to nibble the dirt out from underneath my fingernails. For a moment I think I should pull my hand away, but I let it be, lying easily in her mouth as she uses her teeth, gnawing at the dirt, making the same low *num-num-num* noise of concentration she makes when she's grooming herself. Every day, I think, shaking my head with a barely muffled sob crawling up my throat. Every day. Another layer.

When she finishes, satisfied, I assume, she rests her head gently against my chest. With a gulping panicky sensation, I realise I've run out of time and I never want this to end. Despite the mozzies and the rotting of my feet, the crippling heat and endless physical pain, this can't be over. All that stuff I said, about being too tired, about being ready to go? Bullshit! I run my palm along the curve of her neck. Over her ears, the slight tear in the right one, the raised scars on the left, the tiny white line of fur along the tips. I know her body better than I know my own. I rub the thick white fur under her chin, clean out the gunk from the sides of her eyes. I check for ticks. I find a few, big ones, swollen and brown with blood, and she snatches them from my hand before I can stop her. She eats them, rolling their bodies around on her tongue until they pop satisfyingly.

"That's disgusting," I tell her, smoothing the grey fur along her spine that grows in the wrong direction, then I lean my cheek against hers. She turns her head. Her rough tongue scrapes my nose. Her whiskers tickle and I brush them away. As I do, she rolls off and I roll with her until we're lying side by side. Her eyes, green as the tops of the fresh wet grass, are soft. She could rip open my throat. Instead, she lifts her front paws and places them on my arm, pulling me closer. A tear falls down my cheek. I trust this cat, this cat that could rip me to shreds, that has ripped me to shreds, with everything I've got.

Somehow I have to get up. I have to say goodbye. I raise my head and we look at each other. And then she pushes me away and launches off, sprinting back to the other side of the runner and hiding in the patuju. Will I ever see you again? I don't know.

"I'm leaving, love." Tears fall over my nose and make a little puddle in the mud. "I have to go." I'm leaving.

I love lying in the dirt with Wayra. I love it more than I've ever loved anything in my life. She's changed the world for me, opened a window and pulled me through in such a way that I can never go back.

It's dark and I swipe angrily at the mosquitoes. I put on my head torch. Her eyes reflect back at me, two pale disks floating in a sea of black. She's excited. Her tomorrow will be the same as today, just without me. I can't even think about my tomorrow. She's perched in her garden of leaves. She's been happy for a really long time. I have made her happy. I don't know if it will last. But it'll be up to someone else. It won't be up to me anymore.

When I walk over to the door, she knows. After a moment's hesitation, as if making it clear that this is her idea, not mine, she saunters past with a dignified shake of her head. A perfunctory hiss in my face and then she's in. I sit down and unclip her. She stays next to me for a while, uninterested in the meat that I've already put out on her throne. My hands shake as I stroke her through the fence. Then she gives me a last hiss and is gone. All I can see are her eyes, gleaming like fairy lights, as she waits for me to go.

Very slowly I turn, and then I'm walking away.

"Bye, Wayra," I choke, my hands over my mouth. I'm crying properly now, tears flowing unchecked down my cheeks. By the time I reach the bank, the strangler fig with its net of musty hair, I'm crying so hard, I can't see. My hands are shaking, my legs giving way. There are stars somewhere above me, I know, and a rising full moon. But for a long time, I don't see anything at all. Just Wayra, the scent of her, and her eyes. Gleaming so brightly, surrounded by a single rim of amber like the line on a heart monitor. It's all I see for a very long time.

PART THREE

I stand behind the truck and gaze sadly at the four sacks lying on the blue flatbed. It is 2017. The heads inside are starting to bake, giving off a questionable odour. Dark runnels of blood are oozing through the hessian and down over the side, dripping onto the left back wheel. I move my foot to avoid the blood, looking up at the sky. It's blue and heavy, grey clouds on the horizon full of rain. For the tenth time, I check my phone. Still no signal. I lean my cheek against the hot metal of the truck and watch motorbikes swerve over potholes and kick dust into the air. I'm parked just outside the mercado, the town's covered market. Inside, people come together to share stews and meat on sticks. Around the food are stalls that sell anything from monkey wrenches to princess crowns to knock-off electronics to watermelons. Along one side of the market, next to the food tables, are the butchers, where flies congregate and blood and the smell of old meat drips off hanging carcasses. Doña Bernita, our meat lady, is second on the right. It's from her that I picked up the cows' heads, hanging from hooks above her white tiled table. We respectfully stuffed them into sacks before I lugged them, horns and all, into the truck.

"¿Hay campo?"

I raise my head. An old man, his face so lined I almost can't see his eyes, is behind me, managing to look both hopeful and resigned. He's looking for a lift back to the village. He has a sack of rice over one shoulder, as big as he is. He's wearing jeans, sandals made from old tyres, and a Real Madrid shirt. I smile. Osito's dad.

"Hola, Don Antonio."

He grins and holds up his sack. I help him put it in the back, and as he gazes at the blood impassively, my phone rings. I jump, startled, despite the fact I've been waiting over an hour for this.

"Lo siento," I whisper, trying quickly to clear away some of the debris from the dashboard as I balance the phone in the crook of my shoulder.

Don Antonio smiles. "Por nada," he says while gingerly removing an empty packet of Doritos from the front passenger seat. Spread out among various crumbs is also an almost-empty family-sized bottle of Coke and a huge bag of coca. This is the sum of my breakfast and lunch, and my hands are starting to shake. I left camp at seven this morning, wanting to get into town early, pick up the shopping, collect the heads, make my call and leave. Impatience churns my stomach.

"Hello?" Perse, the director of the arts charity I founded five years ago, crackles through. I put her on speaker and balance the phone against the wheel. It sounds as if she's in an ocean. Or I am. I imagine her at her leafy desk, my cushion with the beaded puma on the front propping her up, a hot tea in her hands. Thinking about artists and exhibitions, funding applications about climate change, education, extinction, pollution . . . I wince, rubbing sweat off my forehead.

"Hey," I say.

"Hello! How are you?"

I think about this. "Fine, thank you."

"Sure?"

"Yup." I think a little harder. "I got another worm out of my arm yesterday. I found a triple-X tick in my vagina and I've shat nine times today, and it's only . . ."—I check my watch—"one p.m."

"OK. So, you're on speakerphone . . ."

I close my eyes.

"Hi, Laura!" A chorus of voices appears.

"A *tick in your*—"

"Hello, everybody." I try to make my tone professional.

"Can you tell us where you are?" Perse again, trying to steer the conversation somewhere less controversial. "Are you surrounded by toucans and jaguars?"

"Sure . . ." I look over at Don Antonio, who is staring at me and grinning. I can smell the dead cows in the back. My thighs are sticking to the seat and I'm getting more concerned by the minute that I'm going to need the toilet yet again, very soon. I had to beg for six months' leave when I made the decision to come out to Bolivia, again, leaving behind my job, again, in the care of Perse. Another six months, another stint, this time filling in for the role of parque director. We hadn't been able to find anyone else to take it on more permanently. We've been looking for someone local—someone from Bolivia, but we haven't found anyone. There are so many animals and plummeting volunteer numbers. Now the best we can hope for is twenty volunteers during dry season, maybe at a high, thirty. We used to top one hundred.

"OK!" Perse says chirpily. "Let's start the meeting, then, shall we?"

"Great idea!"

"You get me anything?"

Charlie is standing on the road, his hands on his hips. Bruce, our camp dog, is at his side. I pull into the driveway, inexpertly negotiating Osito's sporadically and spectacularly stupidly placed wooden boards, which cover the permanent deep trench between road and garage. Bruce barks happily, wagging his tail.

"Nope," I say as I jump out, spitting an old wad of coca into the bushes. The garage, opposite the fumador, was built a few years ago. It's a huge roofed shed where we keep the truck, gas, welding tools, old fencing, old wood, volleyball net, and construction materials. "Just these cow heads."

He gazes at the bloody sacks. "That's no Frappuccino," he mutters as Bruce leaps up with a sigh of relief and starts to make a little nest in the back of the truck. The truck belongs to him, really. He is a leggy dog, white with a brown spot. He is now stained red from all the blood. I wrinkle my nose. Charlie is in his work clothes, sodden up to his chest. He's been walking cats since dawn. We went out together, with one of the ocelots, at five. Since then, while I've been in town, he's been out to walk Rupi and feed at least four others. He shoves his hands into the pockets of his jeans. He's tall and pale, and his too-long hair—which hasn't been cut since he arrived at the park a year ago and is wrapped into a man bun—coupled with a chest-length auburn beard, wouldn't look out of place in a hipster coffee shop in Melbourne.

"How was your meeting?"

"Fine." I nod. "Far away. Any dramas here?"

He begins hauling the sacks out onto the ground, Bruce watching him with suspicion. Bruce turned up in the fumador a few months back, stick-thin with wounds and cancerous lumps. We treated him and now he's on probation. In order to stay, he has to get over his unfortunate tendency of biting people. Charlie opens one of the sacks, swings back rapidly and holds his nose.

"Jesus."

Charlie looks exhausted, his face grey in strange places. Charlie is our cat coordinator—a job that pretty much does what it says on the tin. He coordinates the cats and their volunteers. Makes sure everyone is trained properly, routines are upheld, animals and people are safe, happy, looked after. It used to be Mila and Agustino who did that and, basically, everything else. Jobs that we now aim to divide between two cat coordinators, an administrator, a volunteer coordinator, two cooks, a construction coordinator, a construction team, small-animal coordinators, one, two or even three vets, and a parque director.

Mila and Agustino both left the parque about six years ago. Not easily. It was long, drawn out and painful. They suffered from undiagnosed PTSD, grief, stress on top of stress on top of stress. They have other jobs now, other families, in other parts of Bolivia, and I hope they are happy. In the years since, despite their roles being portioned off in an attempt to make the running of this place more sustainable, it isn't sustainable. This isn't a conventional job. We need local staff, but local staff are hard to find. The pay is low, the conditions difficult. We continue to depend on foreigners and volunteers that might leave at the drop of a hat—or that might stay, but who knows? We ask people to give up their lives and often their mental and physical health for little money. People have been doing this same thing for decades, in grassroots organisations and NGOs across the world, because there's always the next disaster to deal with, right, and too little support? But every year, it seems to get harder, particularly for the people who stay. Friends leave, volunteers don't extend their trips anymore. The world is uncertain, jobs are harder to secure. Travellers stick to their schedules. They travel to a plan and it's rare that they'll change it, even for something as magical as peeling away your onion layers and losing all your body weight and probably your hair just to make the jungle happy.

Currently we have eleven great volunteers and twenty-three cats, plus the birds, monkeys, tejones, pìos, peccaries, tapirs and twenty or so animals in quarantine. Our staff includes two cooks, the stalwart Doña Lucia and a younger, sweet woman called Doña Clara. Osito—Oso—is our construction coordinator. He's no longer a chubby eleven-year-old. He gets mad if I call him Osito, because he's a strapping twenty-one-year-old now with twin baby girls. He is one of the most amazing, resilient young men. He's the only one of the kids, who were in the parque when I first arrived, who's still here year-round. Our construction team is made up of him, and Jhonny. Like Oso, Jhonny grew up round here, although not in the parque. His family used to hunt. Through their work with us, though, they've become activists. Jhonny is one of about eight brothers, at least four of which have been working at the parque, and our two other sanctuaries, for years. Monkey experts, construction experts, cat experts. They are all insanely handsome. Jhonny is perhaps the most handsome of all and can carry more cement through the swamp than anyone I know.

Alongside Oso, Jhonny, Doña Lucia and Doña Clara, there's Charlie and Ally. Ally is our volunteer coordinator. She's exactly the same as she was a decade ago, except for a few more lines on her face and a few more tattoos of Amira. Our only vet left last week and our new one should arrive next week. But until that happens, Ally and I are the closest we've got to "vets." We are not vets, but we do enjoy giving volunteers vitamin injections in their butts if they're particularly hungover.

I gaze at Charlie. He looks even more grey than usual.

"Did something happen?" I ask warily.

"Teanji escaped again. Jhonny had to catch him in the laundry basket. ¿Verdad, Jhonny?" Charlie raises his voice.

Jhonny is welding fence posts on the other side of the garage. His T-shirt is tight across his burly chest and his dark hair is slung stylishly across his glistening golden-brown forehead. He looks over at us, cupping his hand over his ear and switching off the machine.

"¿Qué?"

Charlie does a complicated mime to indicate catching a tejón in a laundry basket. Jhonny giggles, nodding enthusiastically. I shake my head in desperation. Jhonny is surprisingly good at catching things in laundry baskets. He goes back to his welding.

"A lot of volunteers barricaded themselves in their rooms," Charlie says. "You might have to do some damage control."

I sigh. "Did he hurt anyone?"

"Nah. Not this time."

I nod. Desperately relieved. I remember Mila and Agustino's blind belief that Coco had the right to be free, more than a person had the right not to be bitten. Gradually, though, over the years, as those animals who were our friends back then died, new animals that arrived—along with new staff members, and new policies on safety—weren't given the same kinds of freedom. It was for the best, probably. Lorenzo . . . he disappeared, in 2011. We don't know what happened to him. One day he was flying about the patio, flapping his bright wings at Sammie flirtatiously, and the next he was just gone. Hit by a logging truck, stolen and sold as a pet, caught and eaten by an animal. Nobody knows. And Faustino. Oh, Faustino. He was hit by a car in 2009 on the same road that took Coco two years before.

Teanji is our last survivor. He was still free until the beginning of this year, when Oso and Jhonny finally completed a brand new "tejón garden," a huge enclosure for him to live in. He is safe there, as are volunteers who still insist on wearing flip-flops. Teanji is blind and senile, but he still manages to escape, sometimes climbing into Oso's bed for a cuddle, and sometimes robbing the breakfast rolls out of the comedor.

"Everyone was panicking." Charlie leans against the truck, crossing his arms. Bruce sidles over, sticking his snout affectionately into Charlie's ear. "He ran out of the bushes and I'm not joking, that guy moves so fast, he's like a tiny orange roadrunner. He launched right at my nuts, I squealed so loud. I blocked him with a broom, and Jhonny was just giggling, watching, but then he picked up the laundry basket, cool as a cucumber, and caught Teanji mid-air like some kind of superhero."

I'm laughing so hard, I'm choking on my coca leaves.

"I swear, I almost lost it."

We sit there for a bit, my green bag of coca between us, stuffing leaves into our cheeks and listening to the sounds of volunteers playing volleyball on the patio, the crackling reggaeton music from Jhonny's radio propped next to him on the bench as he works. Finally, when my cheek is full and Bruce has started to snore, his chin on Charlie's shoulder, I pat Charlie on the arm.

"Come on, then," I say.

"Let's crack some skulls?"

"I guess so. Have you got the axe?" I touch the heads softly and say a short thank-you. Their dark eyes gaze back at me. They're huge, each weighing about thirty kilos, with horns that curl majestically and sadly from their soft hay-coloured foreheads. I haven't eaten anything cow-related in years, but cats will be cats. We start splitting the heads in half, ready to be divided up amongst the jaguars.

I spent a long time, after I left in 2008, trying to process what had happened to me. I stayed with my mum because all I wanted to do was earn enough money to get back to the parque. I tried to be normal, to put it out of my mind, to get back to "reality." Tom helped a lot. I did go and see him, and we started dating. We were together for about three years. It didn't work out. Tom was at university studying to be a vet, I was all over the place. We both missed the parque with a fury that kept us up at night, but he had something else, other than Bolivia. A purpose. He was going to be a vet. He never wavered from it, and in the end he met someone else. Someone also training to be a vet. I didn't blame him, not really. I'd made my commitment, and it wasn't to him. I kept trying to fool both of us every year—I swear, this is the last time, this is the last time I'm going to go back to Bolivia, I'll move in with you next year, I swear . . . but I never did, and it never was the last time.

I wrote a lot. Drew pictures of Wayra. Made sculptures. Tried desperately, oh so desperately, to find a way to talk about her without people eventually drifting away like I was crazy, with a blank *Oh, that must have been cool, I guess, a puma, huh?* expression on their faces.

I walk across the patio, covered in blood and cow brains. I've got a hessian sack containing one head, destined for Ru, slung over my shoulder. It's difficult to walk. A cow head is heavy, and I am slow. Charlie's laughing at me, trotting behind, carrying his two heads with ease. One of his is whole, going to Amira, the other is split in half for Rupi. A jaguar who can't bear to eat anything that looks remotely like an animal. Give him a whole cow head, with two liquid eyes to stare at him, and he'll hide under his bed and won't come out until it's been removed.

Sammie is waving, her wild honey hair, dyed darker than it has ever been, caught up in a huge ponytail. She's wearing a dirty old flannel shirt and jeans, another shirt thrown over her shoulders to protect her from the mozzies, which she has always hated but seems to hate even more with age. She's an attorney now, fighting for the rights of immigrants in the US. She's able to come for only two weeks every year, has a massive student debt and is in her mid-thirties with a serious job, a house cat, and a wardrobe of trouser suits. She's still one of my closest human friends, even though we're lucky if we see each other every few years. We try to cross paths here, and occasionally she's managed to come see me in the UK, or I've gone to her on my layovers in the States.

"Frodo!" she exclaims, her waving getting more dramatic.

"Yeah, Samwise?" But even as I say it, I see who is behind her, talking emphatically to Oso, and my sack drops to the floor with a thunk. "Fuck," I whisper.

Sammie dances on the toes of her boots. Oso beams, his cheeks just as round as they were when I first saw him on the patio, eleven years old, carrying Teanji in his arms.

"Harry," I murmur.

Harry turns to me, his face flushed. "Hey, Frodo."

"Are you real?" I exclaim, breathless.

"¡Sí!" Oso exclaims, gripping Harry's biceps, barely able to contain himself. Last time we saw Harry, Oso came up to his chest. Now, Oso is the taller one. Oso squeezes Harry's unimpressive arm muscles with delight. I shake my head, shake my head again.

"Frodo," Harry repeats, stepping forwards to hug me, so awkward that we miss and knock heads. We both laugh. His voice is familiar and strange. He's wearing a T-shirt and jeans. He smells—clean. His beard is trimmed, his hair short under his baseball cap. He's got lines around his eyes, but other than that, he looks . . . healthy. Normal. He looks like a normal person. "You're covered in swamp," he says dryly.

I put on a low drawl. "Well, ya know. You don't really know yourself until you've spent months in the swamp."

He looks at me for a long moment, and then chuckles.

I feel light-headed, giddy. "But it's not swamp," I clarify. "It's cow brains."

"Oh." He looks around. Then he laughs again and prods my cheek. His fingers are suspiciously clean too. "Still chewing, I see?"

I touch my wad of leaves with my tongue and shrug. "Are you . . ." I pull down his head, staring at the hair poking out from under his cap. "Are you going grey?"

He pushes me away.

"¡Sí!" Oso giggles. "¿Viejo, no? So old." He grins cheerfully. "Y un poco gordo." He pokes Harry in the stomach.

"Yeah, alright!" Harry jumps away, holding his cap firmly on his head with one hand, the other over his stomach, which is definitely larger than it was. "Maybe! That's what happens when you approach your forties."

I nod wearily. "Sammie and I at least won't be the oldest people in camp anymore."

Harry looks pointedly at Charlie. "So it's true. The volunteers are getting younger."

Charlie grins, raising his eyebrows. Charlie is barely twenty-three, and very proud of it.

"No," I say, rolling my eyes. "We're just getting older."

After I left in 2008, Harry stayed. Not forever, but for a while. But like Mila and Agustino, in the end, he lost his mind. PTSD. Overwork. Too many parasites. Too few vitamins. Too little sunlight. There are some of us—me and Sammie, Ally, Bobby, Ilsa, René—who've spent the last decade booking return flights every year. Not quite able to assimilate but not quite able to let go either. There are others who did that for a while, but eventually settled for a stable life. A house, kids. Oscar, Bryan. Paddy, Tom, Dolf. Once that happened . . . each year they might say, *Yeah, next year for sure. Next year I'll definitely come back.* But then next year would come, and there'd be another bill to pay, another deadline, or just something else, another project to visit, another chance at changing the world, or it just became less easy to justify flying halfway across the planet. Jane. She did a PhD in illegal logging and is a researcher now. We talk, sometimes. She always likes to hear how Wayra is. But it is vague for her. Distant. Like hearing about a person she once knew a long time ago.

And Harry. After he burnt out, none of us heard from him. It was like he'd dropped off the map. I haven't seen him in over six years.

And now. *Here.*

I raise my sack. "I'm just on my way to take this to Ru." I eye Harry, not quite sure what to say. "Do you want to come?"

He looks at me for a few seconds, and I cannot read what he is thinking. But then he looks away, down at the ground.

"No," he murmurs. "Not yet."

I nod. "I'll see you when I get back, then?"

He raises his gaze, and his blue eyes are as blue as they always were. "You can count on it."

In 2012, I opened an art gallery. It's called ONCA. *Panthera onca.* Jaguar. With a lot of help, it became a charity. The idea was that it would be

My hand-drawn map of the parque.

Teanji, a rescued coati (tejón in Bolivia), patrolling camp in 2007.

Faustino, a howler monkey, on his favourite seat above the dorms in 2007. (Photo by Sarah M. Hanners)

The road outside camp after a rainstorm in 2007.

Panchita, a rescued semi-wild peccary (chancho in Bolivia), taking a well-deserved nap outside the aviary in 2007.

My drawings of Coco and Faustino, camp's resident howler monkeys, rescued from life in the pet trade.

Lorenzo, a rescued blue-and-yellow macaw, enjoying time outside the aviary in 2007.

Matt Damon, a rescued rhea (pìo in Bolivia), enjoying a stroll around his enclosure in 2018. (Photo by Nicole Marquez Aguirre)

Wayra on her "throne," watching us arrive at her cage, in 2007.

Me and Wayra in 2017. (Photo by Lucas Ring)

My drawings of Wayra, one of the many pumas rescued from the illegal pet trade, living at Sanctuary Ambue Ari.

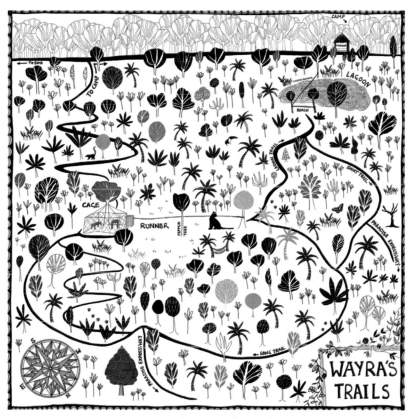

My map of Wayra's walking trails.

Jaguarupi was rescued as a baby. Here he is enjoying one of his many jungle walks. (Photo by Robert Heazlewood)

Jaguaru, once a pet, now cared for at Ambue Ari, taking a nap on his canoe on the Río San Pablo in 2009. (Photo by David Magrane)

Vanesso, an ocelot, was rescued as a baby from the city. Here he is on his laguna walking trail at Ambue Ari. (Photo by Sarah M. Hanners)

My drawing of Sama, a rescued jaguar and a friend.

Sama in 2008, enjoying the freedom of a large enclosure that was built for him in 2007.

Wayra taking a swim with me in her laguna in 2009.

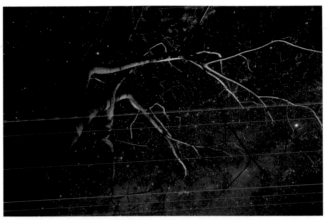

Stars above camp. (Photo by Jean-Philippe Miller)

A sunrise picnic on the rocks in Santa María. (Photo by Scott Fletcher)

Fires spreading across Ambue Ari. (Photo by Benjamin Portal)

Coco and Faustino, living semi-wild in camp, howling at dawn in 2007. (Photo by Sarah M. Hanners)

My drawing of Big Red, a blind elderly macaw rescued from being a pet. He lived in the aviary for many years before dying peacefully in 2019.

My drawing of Bitey, a white-throated toucan, another long-term resident of the aviary.

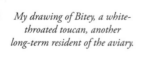

My drawing of Teanji on his favourite branch. He lived semi-wild in camp before moving to a huge enclosure in 2018.

Camp in 2019. Looking out to the road, past the office, the showers, and my old mural of Coco. (Photo by Scott Fletcher)

Wilber "Osito" Antonio and Morocha the spider monkey in 2008.

Layered footprints on Wayra's trails.

Wayra using my leg as a pillow in 2019.

Wayra relaxing in her sunny spot at her laguna in 2008.

Wayra's first day in her new enclosure in 2017. (Photo by Antoine Mellon)

Wayra, perfect in every way.

a place where people might come to share stories, take part in stories, listen to stories—through painting, performance, writing, music, puppetry, whatever—about the issues that were important to them. The kinds of things that affected animals like Wayra, and the people that I met in the parque. The kinds of stories that I was so desperate now to tell but for which I couldn't quite find the words. The forests across the Amazon were disappearing. Cattle farming and soybean production were increasing, multinationals were stripping communities and lands of their identity. Fires continued, flooding got worse. Climate change was still a side note, barely covered in the news in the UK, but in the parque—it felt real. It was real. We saw record numbers of wild jaguars, not because they were doing well, but because their territories were decreasing so sharply. Because of deforestation rates and the increase in slash-and-burn agriculture, the increase of temperatures, the loss of food sources.

You wouldn't believe how many people said to me: *Er, are you sure? Art about the* environment? *Why don't you just start a normal gallery? Otherwise you'll never make any money.* But ONCA was the first arts space in the UK that was dedicated to environmental justice. Environmental justice cannot be separated from social justice. The two are deeply intertwined. Over the years, I've learnt this. I've learnt that the stories that affect Wayra are similar, and connected, to the stories that affect a lot of people, a lot of different species, and a lot of places. Health, for example, and happiness. Loss and homelessness, soil and waste, food, water, work, isolation and otherness.

Now ONCA has two spaces—a city-centre gallery and an old floating barge. We work with many people—young climate activists, people suffering from cancer, people wanting to connect across generations, and ways of living . . . We explore transformative sci-fi that envisions future worlds, we try to admit our failures, and question—and challenge—the cultures that we find ourselves in. We discuss extractivism, surveillance, the extinctions of peoples and species. We provide space for queer make-up tutorials, Deaf poetry nights, and—as thinker Donna Haraway advises—we try to "stay with the trouble" of climate grief. I don't know if art can change the world. I don't think there is just one world to change, there are thousands, millions of worlds, and of worldviews. But I do think that art can change people, just as Wayra, Coco, Mila and all their stories changed me.

I will never forget my realisation in the forest, about my choices, and my privileges. I can't take everyone I know to Bolivia. I can't introduce Wayra, and the parque, to everyone. But they opened my eyes. They gave me a gift. They changed my world and because of them, I set up ONCA in an effort to repay that gift, just a little bit. To create a space where Wayra and the parque, and the multitude of worlds they are entangled with, might change other people's stories too.

"Hey, buddy," I croon softly.

Ru stares at me, his eyes wide as I start walking around the fence. The hexagonal-shaped enclosure seems to go on and on, the jungle exploding around and inside it, vibrant green with red and orange lobster-claw petals. Trees shoot upwards, mahoganies and gringo trees, strangler figs, spiky ochoo trees, striped bamboo, walking and huicungo palms, banana plants, lemon and mandarin trees, spreading carpets of flat and bulbous spicy seeds across the swamp. The whine of mosquitoes is unreal, the temperature scalding. It smells sweet, wafting on bursts of heat. I follow a path about six metres wide around the outside of the fence. Ru's lying down, his handsome, strong head pressed against the side. He's thinking about pawing the ground again, trying to dig his way out. It's never far from his mind. But when I start to move, he watches with half an amber eye. It's only when I reach the first corner and I'm almost out of sight that he gets up. I feel rather than hear his muscles bunching.

"Come on, Ru!" I break into a sprint. In no time he catches me and we run, he on one side of the fence, taking corners like a pro skater, me on the other, scrabbling to stay upright, stumbling on roots, falling into holes. We manage two laps, each almost two hundred metres, before we both collapse, me with my hands on my knees, panting for breath, Ru a little way in, in a patch of shade underneath some curling silvery-yellow vines. He's flat out on the ground, his sides labouring, his tongue lolling. Even though the sun has already gone down, if my clothes weren't already soaked from the swim through the swamp to get out here, they would have been just as wet from the amount I'm sweating. It's mid-March and we're in the throes of one of the worst and longest wet seasons I've ever seen.

Finally, when I'm able to speak again, I raise my head. Ru's still panting.

I laugh. "You're getting old, bud!"

He just looks at me as if he couldn't care less what I think.

In 2009, Ru started injuring people. Not badly, but bad enough. He was playing hard, growing up, getting more boisterous, more difficult to control. There was more noise over the river. More people, more construction, more logging. It was during a dry season when there were a lot of volunteers, and yet nobody really knew Ru. Harry wasn't there. I remember it like it was yesterday. Ru's volunteers standing there wide-eyed, one guy with his chin raised, stubborn, determined, the others just pale, terrified. One with a claw mark too close to his eye. Agustino was blank and frail. Osito, his face uncertain. Germáncito, lost. López, his throat working, his dark eyes confused. Mila—flushed and blotchy, angry, desperate. We stood in a circle in the clinic.

"¿Deberíamos dejar de caminar Jaguaru?" Agustino asked. He tried to make his voice strong, but it came out little more than a whisper. Should Ru continue to be allowed to walk? We went round our little circle, one by one, giving our answers. If we said no, then Jaguaru would never come out of his enclosure again. He would never go down to his canoe. He would never watch his river again. If we said yes, Ru would still have his freedom. But at what risk? Was it worth it this time?

We said no.

That was eight years ago. I think, if I'm honest with what I believe, that's what broke Agustino. Really and truly. The light left his eyes and didn't come back. Mila lasted a little longer. But after that decision, after we voted for common sense over trust, logic over love, something in Agustino died. Maybe that's what did it for Harry too. I'm not sure. I never saw him again to ask.

Ru gets bored a lot. He's smarter than I am. He is always testing, always probing, frustrated, sad. He's not like Sama. All Sama had were bad memories. Ru had mostly good ones. But he hasn't hurt anyone else. So . . . I don't know. I don't know how I would answer Agustino's question now, if I could take the vote all over again.

I look at my watch. It's after six and the shadows are deepening.

"Best give you your treat, right, Jaguaru?"

Ru, seeing me look at my watch, looks up at the sky, as if to check the position of the sun. When he looks back at me, I wonder if he will remember Harry. I don't really doubt it. I sometimes see him gazing towards his old trails, overgrown now, and his riverbank, in the direction of his canoe. Where they used to sit together, side by side, so many years ago. I hope it isn't too painful, when Harry does come. I hope it doesn't make Ru even sadder.

"Alright, buddy," I say once I've tied his cow head to a tree in the centre of his enclosure. I've put him in his small management cage, but after I've left him his cow treat I let him out, once I'm safely outside again, and then all I hear is the raucous crash, the crunch of branches, and the thud as he single-mindedly wrestles the head to the ground. He'll be busy with it all night long.

I pick up my things and steel myself for the long walk home. I hate wearing a head net with the cats, hate it when they can't see my eyes, but I put it on now, brushing at the hundred or so mosquitoes stuck to my face. Then I forge into the growing grainy darkness, half-blind and almost incapacitated by my net. The layers of heavy, wet clothing, the mud that sucks at my boots, the swamp now up to my knees, thighs, waist . . . the sweat in my eyes and the deafening whine of the bugs. I'm as exhausted and physically ravaged as I've ever been and yet . . .

The black dappled water threads and makes lakes out of fields of emerald patuju. At dusk, it drips with rain and shadows. I can just hear the reverberating call of howler monkeys and, as I always do, I imagine that it might be Darwin—leader of his own semi-wild troop now. He lives in the jungle. His howl is an impressive boom that always makes me smile, he had the best teacher after all.

Thousands of yellow moths congregate on fragrant branches. Sapphire butterflies, their wings the size of my hands, flutter around my shoulders. Impossible fungi wave their caps. Jelly-like snails' eggs, pink, purple and cream, float in grids across the water. Algae blooms. Frogs and flat, weightless spiders hover. Rainbowed snakes hide in tree knots and hummingbirds' wings move faster than thought. I imagine pumas skulking. Anacondas curling under the water. Lizards closing their eyes, sloths slowly climbing and night-time bats starting to wake up. The shadows growing grainier by the second. The trail winds, the swamp knee high, crotch high, chest high, the worst bits neck high . . . I wade past a bulbous tree covered in a thousand caterpillars. Their heads are facing each other, as if gathered for a community meeting. They make the bark purple and quivering.

It's nearly dark. This tree is the halfway marker. Even in daylight it's difficult to see where the path goes, easy to get confused in the vast spread of passages. Familiar shapes become other things entirely. My heart thumps with the thrill of balancing so delicately on the edge of *lost*. I don't have any ridiculous notions of invincibility, but I do feel . . . tingly. Acutely alive. More than just the nominally present feeling I have when I'm in bars with friends, at work, standing in a shop with Visa in hand, staring at the latest Instagram posts . . . the feeling I've never quite got rid of, as if I'm staring at life through a plastic sheet. This, when I'm here, *here* in this rot-inducing, kidney-disease-causing, anaconda-infested swamp, there's no sheet. Not even a whiff of it. All I can smell is mud, thick and cloying, heady algae, moisture, creation and decay.

Harry used to say the swamp teaches people who they are. I thought it was macho bullshit, and it was, but he was also a little bit right. For me, it was only when I started to trust the swamp, really, not to *not* kill me, because it will, it will totally kill me, but just to let me be who I am. A frail, strange human in a frail, strange, composting, muddy world. Once I'd fallen in love with the swamp, as I'd fallen in love with Wayra, I think that's when I fell in love with my life.

The landmarks are friends: the caterpillar tree a reminder of the root that trips me up every time, the hole that almost catches my ankle around the next bend, the bat tree on its floating island. If I take off my net and listen, I will hear them chittering, I will feel the brush of their wings over my face. My head torch is starting to fade and I shiver, the cold seeping up my bones, deliciously cool.

I fall, my toe catching on an unseen root. I'm scrabbling for purchase, chin deep in water now, squealing and laughing, when I understand, for no reason I know, that something, someone, is watching. I whip up my net, getting my footing, and turn my head. My torch catches two eyes high off the ground, about a metre up, wide enough apart to belong to something sufficiently large to make me stop laughing immediately, my heart shooting so fast up into my brain that for a moment I see white spots. Bright yellow in the rapidly fading torch beam, batteries about to run out, the eyes like stars. The rest of the jungle is still, the little creatures suddenly silent. I don't move. I can't run, not through the swamp. I gaze across the gloom and the creature gazes back at me. I taste sour bile. I can see now, my eyes adjusting, the bulk. Pale with black rosettes.

I have a blunt knife in my backpack, that's it. I don't have a machete, and I stink of blood and dead cow. There haven't been sightings of wild jaguars for over a year, not in person and not on our camera traps. We saw a lot between 2009 and 2015 as the forests around us disappeared and jaguar territories shrunk, but with no sightings in the parque for the last two years, David, our researcher, has been worried that the corridor of jungle connecting our land with the protected areas in the north and to the south of us, the corridor that's one of the key jaguar migration routes in the Amazon, may be gone too.

This jaguar is small, smaller than Ru. Is this the one that used to hound his cage whenever she went into heat? David calls her Cersei. Perhaps, I think with a flash of horror, she's been following me. She's sitting on her haunches. Jaguars are pro swimmers. I am not a pro swimmer. I can barely doggy-paddle. I keep my torch on her eyes but I can't hear anything apart from terror, and it is deafening. A canal of black water separates us. I've encountered wild jaguars before, the end of a tail, the flash of an eye, but never like this. Never yards away, never alone, never in the swamp at night. I give a little desperate laugh. This serves me right, all that bullshit about trusting the bloody swamp! Should I feel small, I think, like prey? I feel huge, I feel like my brains are flying out of my nose. My synapses are firing, pop, pop, pop—pops of panic as my lungs struggle and fail to normalise.

It's an eon in a split second, and then I remember that I'm me, and as I have trained myself to do—what began as a coping mechanism for anxiety turned into something useful, something that helped me over a decade of working with animals who smell fear as sharply as bullies do—I take my fear and I swallow it. I push it into my belly, where it sits, hidden, until later, when I'll look at it again and it'll be valuable, useful and precious. Something to learn from. And I reach round very carefully, take my metal water bottle and one of the empty meat buckets from my backpack. The jaguar's muscles tense, and then, my muscles tensing too, I open my mouth. I bang my bottle against my bucket and sing "Purple Rain" as loudly as I can. My voice explodes across the darkness, punctuated with the thundering slap of metal on plastic, and the next time I look, she's gone. There's no one there at all.

"I saw a jaguar!"

"What?"

"I saw a fucking jaguar!" I grip Charlie's arm, panting hard.

"Yeah, so did I. I actually walked one today. He was called Rupi."

"No!" I try to glare at him but I'm panting too much. "I was stalked by a jaguar."

"Sure, sure." Charlie laughs. "Was it Ru?"

"David!" I yell, spinning, brushing at the cloud of mosquitoes that have followed me out of the jungle. After the jaguar fled, I flailed, splashed and swam at my top speed back to camp.

"Yeah, what?" David pokes his head out of the office. It's pitch dark now but the electricity generator (finally installed in 2012) is still on, the hum whirring in the background, our tiny, box-like office glowing with sharp electric light, illuminating my old, faded seven-foot painting of Coco, gripping a branch with his toes, on the wall of the shower block.

"I saw Cersei!" I exclaim.

David has a wad of coca in his cheek and an unlit cigarette in his mouth, a scar down his face from a recent bout of flesh-eating bacteria.

"You're fucking with me."

"No! I swear. It was like out of a film or something. She was a supreme being! She was just watching me across the swamp. I could have died tonight!"

"Sure." Charlie laughs again and I kick him, and he just kicks me back. David has already gone back into the office, talking to himself and shaking his head excitedly. I can just see Oso in there too, plotting construction budgets or something. He should be home already. Back in Santa María with his girlfriend and one-year-old twins. I should go in and finish the accounts. The finances no longer depend on a wet notebook and an old powdered-milk tin stuffed full with bolivianos, kept underneath Agustino's bed. We have a safe now, which I can never manage to open, and a computer, which has to live in a box of rice to stave off the humidity lest it die. But I need to get out of my wet clothes, I need to shower, I need to dry my feet, I need to eat, I need to sleep . . . I need to find Sammie and Harry!

It's past seven thirty. "Birds in bed?" I ask Charlie hopefully.

He shakes his head. "Big Red's being difficult."

I sigh as we both start towards the aviary. Our boots, full of water, make sucking noises. The comedor shines on my left and I catch the delicious smells of dinner, making my stomach rumble. I can hear Big Red laughing maniacally, and I see a crowd of volunteers around the fence looking worried. One of them shoves a long stick at Charlie.

"That bird is crazy," I hear her mutter as she passes me. "He bit a hole in my fucking boot!"

The rest of them shuffle after her. I sigh as I put my head torch away, batteries entirely gone now, and pull my phone out of its dry bag. Using its torch, I peer into the pìos' enclosure.

"Matt Damon's still out," I say. Charlie grunts, already half into Big Red's cage, so I open the door to the pìos, listening as Charlie starts singing. He's got a good voice, so good he routinely uses it to convince gullible volunteers that he reached the finals of *Australia's Got Talent* 2015. I listen with half an ear to his upbeat version of "No Woman, No Cry" while Matt Damon skulks awkwardly in the trees.

"Hey, Matty D."

He stares at me with beady, baleful eyes. The pìos' ranks have risen and fallen in a soft undulating volunteer-terrorising wave. Some were able to be released, some died. We gained about four new ones and gradually people forgot who was who. Now there's just Matt Damon, the lone survivor, and most likely not the original Matt or Damon.

We're hoping to release him next summer. There's a reserve for free-roaming pìos to the north of town, managed by a friend of ours, and we're hoping Matty D can find a home there.

"Time for bed, buddy."

Matt Damon draws out his wings, curls his long neck and hisses. I coo gently, walking slowly past and making for his house. Sneaking a glance over my shoulder, I grin. He's following close behind. He makes a big fuss, but I have a suspicion he just really enjoys the palaver. When I push open his wooden door, he stops at the entrance to shit explosively on my boots before trotting by semi-belligerently and lying down in a soft pile of hay.

"Hey, Bitey," I murmur, entering the toucan's cage next. I can just see the eerie lines of the massive black posts that are still waiting outside—ready for the new aviary that never happened. Bitey swoops down with a rattle, his curved black beak, neon-blue stripe across the base, snapping. The moon has started to come up, giving everything a soft blue glow. He feints at my boot, then hops up onto a branch so that he's at head level, still snapping. "OK, friend," I laugh. I hold up a stick. Bitey looks at it for a long moment before rubbing his beak, hopping on and letting me carry him to his little night house. I stare at him as he croaks haughtily from his perch. I just see him cocking his head, his blue-rimmed eye expanding in the darkness. Flighty died four years ago. Since then, like Matty D, Bitey's been alone. He must be at least fifteen, his feathers bedraggled. We're an old people's home, I think sadly, hearing the jar of Big Red's agitated laugh.

I lock Bitey's cage and circle back round.

"How you doing?" I lean against Big Red's fence.

Charlie gazes out at me, a pained look on his face. "You want to try? He's not digging Bob Marley tonight."

I nod. Pulling out my phone again, I scroll through my music. When I find what I'm looking for, I turn up the volume. "Bridge over Troubled Water" is usually a winner. Entering the dark cage, I go to stand by his bed.

"Come on, friend."

Big Red waddles towards the music, but the moment he comes within inches of me, he sets off in the opposite direction, until he's underneath a leaf, where he stays, rocking back and forth. Charlie and I gaze at each other, smacking at the increasingly infuriating bugs. If by the time I get to the shower there's no water left, I will kill someone.

"Don't move . . ." I slap Charlie's sweaty, dirty forehead, which is seething with black, blood-swollen mozzies. "Shine the light, will you?"

Charlie angles his phone onto my upturned palm and we begin to count.

"Fifty-two!" I exclaim, wiping the blood and the broken bodies off on my leggings. "That's a good slap."

"Look!" Charlie points as he crouches down, and holds out his hands. Big Red waddles into his palms and rubs his beak miserably across Charlie's fingers. Charlie gazes up at me, wide-eyed. It's only in the last weeks that Big Red has started letting Charlie pick him up. Charlie carefully lifts the blind, senile macaw up into his night cage, slides him inside and closes the door. I pull the curtain over.

"How much battery you got?" I whisper. "I'm almost out."

Charlie peers at his phone. "Yeah, I'm OK." He chooses some music and sets it on repeat, something to help Big Red get to sleep. When we're outside, I immediately start to feel jubilant again, imagining all the joys this evening still holds.

"I'm going to shower!" I clap my hands. "Or maybe I'll eat first. Oh, I can't decide! What are you going to do?"

"Eat." We're at the water tap in the middle of the patio. The comedor is shining brightly to our right, the showers—almost begging me to enter—to our left.

I bite my lip. "Do you know where Harry and Sammie are?"

Charlie grins. "Ah, you oldies. Probably in bed. Reminiscing about the crazy old days over some hot cocoa."

I laugh, then set off at a run. The comedor, the showers—they can wait. Charlie is wrong. I know exactly where Harry and Sammie will be.

When I get to the road, the moon is bright, almost full, a hanging silver penny. There's a group of volunteers in the fumador, but no Harry and Sammie, so I cast left, then right, and am about to go back in when I see two shapes a few hundred metres down the tarmac. I wave wildly and am about to set off when I see them getting up off the ground and coming back towards me.

"This road sucks," Harry snaps as they fall level with the fumador. He casts a suspicious look inside, at the volunteers almost half his age. Sammie gives me a twisted, slightly pained expression, and I cock my head, imagining how they've spent the afternoon. Harry looks deeply unhappy. A truck zooms past us too fast, and all three of us jump into the verge, shielding our eyes from the rocks that fly out from under the tires. The truck is closely followed by another, and then another.

Harry yells over the noise of the traffic, "I see you never got the speed bumps Mila was fighting for!"

I wonder if Sammie has told him that the government is trying to expand the road. They have already clear-cut five metres on both sides for the electricity pylons now lining the banks. They want to increase this five to thirty, making this into a double-lane highway and the comedor into a roadside café. We're fighting it, but . . .

I choose not to say anything. Harry is staring at the rowdy group of volunteers, as if dazed. Sammie just shrugs, and silently we walk side by side back through camp, lighting the way with the last of my phone battery.

"I see everyone's got phones now," he mutters.

I look down at the incongruous piece of plastic and minerals in my hand, and nod.

"When?"

I shrug. "About five years ago, people started bringing laptops and watching films in their dorms rather than hanging out in the comedor. We got phone signal three years back, then data. Anyone who's got a Bolivian SIM and a smartphone can get patchy internet now."

Sammie tries to smile, nudging Harry in the side. "I hated it at first too, but it's world-changing. No one gets lost in the jungle anymore. No more cooees!"

Harry just snorts. We're passing the office.

"And you've got a fucking office? And electricity?"

"Not quite electricity," I say quietly. "Not properly. They put in the power lines, and every month Oso goes into town to ask them to hook us up. Santa María has it but we're still on a generator. It only powers the office, the clinic and the fridge. There's no light switches in the dorms . . . not yet anyway."

"You've got a fridge?" he exclaims. "I'm going home."

"I know." I laugh. "No more rotting meat. And vegetables. We eat so much salad now! And oh my goodness, the fruit! Here." I push open the door to the comedor, stepping into the yellow candlelight and the low chatter of the few volunteers not in the fumador or already under their mosquito nets. Oso seems to have gone home, back to Santa María on his motorbike, Jhonny also. "Have you eaten?"

"Yeah." Harry's looking distractedly up into the crumbling rafters, still covered in faded graffiti and termites. If you look hard, you can still see our names. "I can't believe this place is still standing."

I grin, ladling a portion of dinner, thick and steaming pumpkin soup, into an old plastic container, closing the lid and sliding it into my backpack.

"Come on."

Harry follows dumbly. Sammie trails after.

"Did you get a bed?" I ask.

"Yeah. Ally put me in one of the new dorms with that guy Charlie?"

"Oh good. Charlie's filthy, you'll get on great."

"I wanted to go in Santa Cruz."

I keep on walking, not looking at him. But I see his jaw tighten, out of the corner of my eye.

"There's tiles on the floor in there now." Sammie laughs, trying to make a joke. "So it's not the same. I miss the old mud soup between my toes."

I laugh too, but what I don't say is that I don't go in Santa Cruz now. Not if I can avoid it. It is too painful. Too quiet. Too empty.

We go past the showers, past the new dorms in their own little courtyard surrounded by mango trees. Past the new, shiny eco-baños.

Harry suddenly grabs my arm. "What happened to Faustino?" His eyes are wide, the light of the moon just barely slipping through the canopy. I sigh and hold my phone awkwardly against my leg so as not to blind him.

"A car." I hesitate. "I wasn't here. You were, though, right?" I look at Sammie.

She nods. "It was a few years after Coco. Faustino . . . you remember. He was so sad. He just kept sitting on the road, like he was waiting for it. And then, eventually . . ." She doesn't finish her sentence.

We stopped letting animals live free in camp after that. People expected more . . . more health and safety. More normality, more control. Social media changed things. People uploading photos of monkeys in bed? Pretty soon that became unthinkable. Sammie starts walking quickly again, down the trail to quarantine. After Mila left, Sammie took over for a while. A few years. Before she started her law degree. Before she realised that she couldn't live here forever but that she had to do something that would make her feel useful. Somewhat powerful. Or she would lose her mind for real. I shine my torch forwards, down the dark winding slip and slide. Its grey cloying mud is still above boot height. I look back to check that Harry is wearing boots. He isn't. He's trying to leap over the worst patches as best as he can.

"There's a dry trail," I call back, "to the left up here."

"Where are we going?" he mutters.

"To my house."

A screech owl calls, an eerie *oo oo oo* bouncing between the dark boughs of the canopy. I skirt over a little bridge made of wobbly, rotten planks, covering a little swamp, and then left again. From that fork, it's only a few hundred metres until the house comes into view, its metal roof shining silver in the moonlight.

"You have your own house?" Harry exclaims.

"More a hut. Sammie's staying with me while she's here." I grin, staring around the tiny dark clearing. "It was built for René, she was in charge, after Mila, after you." I nudge Sammie, grinning. "An incentive to get directors to stay. It's . . ." I shake my head, trying to find the words to explain what it means to have a house, an aging thirty-something with a bad back and arthritic hips, ancient in a camp of teenagers, even if it's just one brick room with a tin roof. But there are tiles on the floor, which are always cold. There's a double bed with a real mattress. There are shelves, a chair, hooks on the walls for my things. There's a couch made of folded-over foam. There's a family of rats in the roof and a porcupine that visits at three a.m. to eat the brick. There's a tiny spot between bushes, just off the path, which I use as a toilet, with dung beetles that clear away any mess. "I love it," I whisper.

Sammie looks up at the hut wryly. "It's no mud soup."

I roll my eyes, pushing open the door. Sammie goes in first, then Harry. I follow, lighting two candles balanced in glass bottles which throw out a flickering yellow glow.

"You can sit on the couch, Harry." I smile.

Harry laughs ridiculously, shaking his head. "So much space."

They both plonk themselves down as I start peeling off my work clothes, layer by sodden layer.

"Mind if I shower?"

They shake their heads. Harry leans back, closing his eyes. Sammie takes out a cigarette and twirls it between her fingers.

"Still smoking?" Harry murmurs.

"Just when I'm here," Sammie says. "I get two weeks off a year. I choose to come to this mosquito-infested hell-hole. Let me enjoy what I can." But she doesn't light her cigarette. I laugh at her pained expression. Knowing she's joking but also, not. Her job is gruelling. The fact that still she comes down here, in whatever rare moment she can, just so she can see her elderly, ailing Vanesso. Just once more. Every year we think it's the last time. Just to say thank you, and I love you, one last time.

A decade. Neither of us has had any kind of functional romantic relationship with anyone—man, woman, or person—apart from me with Tom. This is our relationship, with Wayra, with Vanesso, with each other, and with the parque. And we wouldn't give it up for the world.

I wrap my towel around me, shaking it first, dislodging a black spider, who scuttles under the bed. Then I slide my swollen feet into flip-flops and beat my way around the back through vines, patuju and palms. Looking up, I see stars, pinpricks scattered across an indigo-black sky. It's still hot, sweat trickling into the small of my back. I tread carefully, keeping my eyes peeled for bushmasters and coral snakes, the kind that will kill me, bleeding from my eyeballs, in twenty minutes. I can hear trucks lumbering by on the road, less than a hundred metres to my left. To my right there's a rustling, a pig perhaps, or an armadillo. I feel a faint shiver, a thud of fear as I think about Cersei. Then, why she was here at all. The same reason we see the prints of wild jaguars on the patio some mornings. I close my eyes. There is so little wild anymore. I think of Wayra, still in her old cage. No longer walking her trails. Mila was right, in the end. The happiness that I left Wayra with in 2008 didn't last. Every time I came back, it seemed she had found a new thing to be scared of. The trails would be overgrown, the lagoon unused. The Paradise Expressway just took her too far away, ultimately, from safety. I closed all her trails in 2014, three years ago. We cut her a series of runners instead that take her in a loop from her cage all the way to her lagoon. She likes them. She's happier, I think. More stable than she was when she was walking her trails. Less free. But also . . . less stressed. She doesn't have to be connected to anyone on a rope. And I think that's a good thing now.

Frogs sing in the grass and crickets chirp, mosquitoes whine and trees creak. When I reach my private outdoor shower, I hang my towel on a tree branch and, with an expectant sigh, reach up and spin the tap, which brings cold water down the pipes from camp. When the first drops hit my face, I let out a moan. It is ecstasy.

I sit in my pyjamas on the tiles. Sammie and Harry are next to each other on the couch, close but not too close, still slightly awkward. I lather my poor rotten feet in baby powder to dry them out. Only when I'm done do I let myself open my dinner. With no more coca to keep me wired, I'm getting more tired and hungry by the second, and the smell of the now cold soup makes me groan. I hold it out to the others, but they just shake their heads and watch as I shovel food into my mouth.

"Wow." I shake my head finally, grinning. "You look so clean!"

"People out there don't talk to you if you're not." Harry smiles but it doesn't reach his eyes.

"True story!" Sammie mutters.

I try to smile too, but it doesn't quite work either. The initial joy of seeing Harry has twisted into confusion. I eat with even greater vigour, just for something to do.

"So," I mumble between mouthfuls, "how weirded out are you?"

"I'm feeling very weird right now," Sammie exclaims.

Harry laughs and it sounds like a real laugh, but then he takes off his baseball cap and runs his hands through his hair. When he looks back at us, his eyes are stretched wide and red around the edges.

"It's all the same. But . . ."

"It's different?" I nod. "It's like that every time."

"How's Wayra?"

"Perfect."

He raises his eyebrows.

"She's always perfect," I say stubbornly.

"You haven't built her a bigger enclosure? I thought you might."

I shake my head. "It always seems there's other animals who need it more," I say quietly, not looking at him. "The birds are still in the same aviary."

Harry doesn't say anything.

"There was a time," I continue, "when we went up to thirty cats. Did you know that? We had to stop taking them. People turned up with cats and we had to say no. Now we've got the space again, so many have died, but we don't have the people. There's four jaguars in the zoo they want us to take. But volunteer numbers . . . last year during high season we went down to five. Five volunteers!"

Harry just looks at me, so I keep on talking.

"Sama died at the beginning of this year. All the macaws are gone, Lorenzo as well, all apart from Big Red and Romeo. Juliet, she died last year, Romeo's heart is broken. At first he stopped moving, staring at an empty spot on the floor. Then he started pulling out his feathers and hitting his head. It was when he started provoking fights with Big Red, they almost killed each other, that we moved him to quarantine, where he is now, alone. We hoped that this year we might raise money to finally rebuild the aviary. Then we might be able to take some new macaws, and Romeo might find another Juliet. But we just don't have the money." I take a gulping breath. "Inti, she died of cancer. They're all riddled with tumours, leukaemia, bone disease. Babies fed on rotten pasta and crisps. No one deserves to go through what they go through! The cats die, the monkeys too, the vet opens them up, and they see their insides are broken. We just don't know." I sniff, holding tightly to my bowl. "Wayra's fourteen, did you know that? Fourteen. They're all *old*."

"Like us," Harry mutters.

There is a long silence.

Finally, Sammie says very quietly, "Was it Ru? Why you didn't come back?"

I stand and go over to the window to put my unfinished dinner on the ledge. I don't want it anymore. Harry looks at Sammie, his legs curled up beneath him, the grey patches in his hair and wrinkles around his eyes illuminated cruelly in the candlelight.

"Yeah," he finally whispers. "It was too hard. I couldn't see him trapped like that."

I rub my eyes, leaning back against my bed.

"He would have liked to see you." Sammie stares down at her hands.

He doesn't reply. There is nothing to say.

"How long are you staying?" I whisper.

He gazes at the flickering candle. "Two weeks. That's all the time I could get off work."

I nod.

"Will I be able to see him?" His voice cracks painfully.

It takes me a moment before I can speak. "Of course. Whenever you want."

We all listen to the noises for a while. The hoot of an owl. The rustle of the night-time porcupine. Finally, he says so quietly I almost don't hear him, "I got a job I liked. Then I got a girlfriend, and a house, and a year turned into two, then five. I was broken. My body was so fucked, my head too, and . . . I was . . . happy."

Sammie snorts, grinning weakly. "Happy? You?"

Harry flushes, and then suddenly the tension just seems to disappear. He laughs. "Yeah, shocker!" He hesitates. "Are you guys happy?"

"Fuck no!" But she is smiling.

We are quiet again. Then he says, "You ever hear from Tom?"

"No," I say. "Not since we broke up."

He nods.

"But I think he's happy. Working with sheep somewhere, I'd guess."

Harry chucks one of my old socks at me, and I catch it. "I suppose not even Tom could compete with Wayra."

"Nope. Not a chance." I laugh. "I think about her every day. I wake up in cold sweats that she's not OK." I shake my head. "But when I get back here and I walk down her path and she remembers, with that meow! This place . . . it fills me up." I look at Sammie because I know she feels the same. "We manage to convince ourselves that it's worth it, right? That it's OK to keep flying, to keep on coming, to live in this in-between just to make sure they're OK, to be a body here, to remind whatever volunteers they have how to keep them safe. But the problems out there, the problems here. There's no difference anymore. No here and there." I sigh, chucking the sock back at him. It lands in his lap. "Why are you here now?"

He stays very still. "I kept dreaming about Ru. And around him the Amazon was burning, the climate was going to shit, the world was falling apart . . ."

Sammie takes his hand. He looks down dumbly. We are all silent. We listen to the rats in the roof, to the distant rumble of the road, to the soft breaking waves of the jungle. Finally Harry laughs.

"My family think I'm nuts."

I stare across at the dark mosquito-netted window. I can see the bugs beating up against it, drawn by the dance of the candle-flame.

"It's hard to explain," I say quietly. But then I smile. My mum came with me last year. She fell in love with all the broken creatures. She spent days with Big Red and Bitey. She made friends with Doña Lucia and Doña Clara, helping them chop vegetables in our rat-infested kitchen. And she loved Wayra. It was love at first sight. She knew I wasn't nuts, right from the beginning. I didn't need to explain it to her after all.

Harry runs his fingers across the edge of the couch's dirty coverlet. Eventually he leans his head back and closes his eyes. I think he falls asleep, but then he murmurs, "Is Sama's enclosure empty?"

I stiffen. Sama died of old age, his many ailments finally getting the better of him. "Yes," I say tightly.

"Are you thinking about moving Wayra there?"

I don't reply for a long time. Of course I've thought about it, but I've also spent ten years getting my head around the fact Wayra's life is as it is. There's nothing more I can do to change it.

"It's Nena's call," I say finally. Nena, the president of the organisation. She's based at another sanctuary, Parque Machía, in the cloud forest to the west of here. She's in love with spider monkeys, some of whom she's looked after for over twenty-five years. When she was about twenty, studying biology in La Paz, she rescued her first spider monkey, and that monkey changed her life, just like Wayra changed mine. She gave up her studies, and travelled to the jungle, where she set up Machía so that that spider monkey had somewhere safe to live, in the trees rather than in the city. Nena and I are friends now, I hope, although I had little to do with her in my first years at the parque. I've spent time with her, over in Machía, helping out where I was needed. And Nena comes here when she can. She deals with the worst of it, with the exhaustion, fires, deaths, floods, avalanches, government corruption, volunteers leaving year after year . . . But she doesn't leave. I'm not sure if she can.

The candle stutters, then falls down the neck of the bottle, fizzing into darkness.

"Then call Nena." Harry opens his eyes. "Don't tell me it hasn't crossed your mind. No more ropes."

I take a long, shaky breath. Wayra's runner system works. I've come to believe that it truly is the best we can do for her. Over the years, I've watched her love her walks and I've watched her hate them. She changes according to the season, the weather, the individual volunteers, the number of mosquitoes, the level of diligent path-raking, the light, the dark, the sounds, the noise . . . our other walking cats thrive on the excitement. Not Wayra. She's exponentially happier on these runners, where she doesn't have to have someone walking behind her. But . . . she's still Wayra. She still hisses and grumbles every day. She is still terrified. She still wants to sleep next to you, her head on your boots, then the next minute snarl savagely at what looks like nothing. But to her, it's the opposite of nothing. She still can't bear to be in her cage, yet can't bear to be outside of it.

I don't answer Harry. An empty enclosure, the size of Sama's, is like gold dust. There's a long list of cats who might benefit from it, who might be a better fit than Wayra. There are so many unknowns. Maybe such a big change would terrify her. Maybe it would be the worst thing I could do for her. But then, maybe she would love it. I can barely imagine what it would be like. She'd be able to run, for more than ten metres at a time, without a rope on her neck. She would have space. Space! I would be able to take her collar off.

Harry closes his eyes. Sammie picks up her unlit cigarette and starts again to twirl it between her fingers. After a while, I fall asleep to the sound of her fingers, and to the rats, who are rustling in the rafters.

The next evening we go into the village to play football. The place has swollen over the years, increased by traffic and development, but things—at the same time—have gotten worse. With the weather more extreme, crops have been failing, the shop shelves emptier. On the surface, there's a glow of electricity and investment. They have a cancha, an impressive outdoor sports court. Teenagers flock to play football there and we join them once a week, led by Oso and Jhonny. Despite Oso and Jhonny's skill level, which is high, we always lose. Oso watches now from the goal, his head in his hands, as volunteers flail uselessly

Anoka County
LIBRARY

Ideas, Information, Inspiration

Northtown Library

Items that you checked out

Title: The puma years : a memoir
ID: 32085036694993
Due: Thursday, May 23, 2024

Total items: 1
Account balance: $0.00
Checked out: 1
Overdue: 0
Ready for pickup: 0
5/2/2024 2:18 PM

ANOKA COUNTY LIBRARY
Find us on social media

Thank you for using the Anoka County Library

about the pitch. I sit in the benches, happily eating an ice lolly that I'm sure is one percent mango, ten percent ice, eighty-nine percent sugar. It makes my teeth hurt.

"You're not playing?" Charlie collapses down, taking a break from the game, shaking his hair like a wet dog and covering me with beads of sweat.

"I have no desire to sweat any more than I am already, thank you."

He flashes a winning smile at the local eight-year-olds behind me, busy plaiting my hair. The girls all put their hands over their mouths, giggling wildly.

"Did you give them full disclosure before they touched you?" he asks, turning back to the game. "This may contain lice, grease, hasn't been washed . . ."

"Hey! I washed my hair yesterday."

He raises his eyebrows.

"Or maybe the day before . . ." I grin, passing him the end of my ice lolly. "Are we winning?"

"No. I think Oso's head is about to explode."

I nod. "How was Ru today?"

"You mean how was Harry? He held it together."

"Good. And Ru was . . ."

"Yeah. He was OK! Happy to see Harry, definitely."

I cannot help but smile with relief.

"Harry told me lots of stories, about the old days." Charlie grins. "About Ru?"

"Yeah, sounded amazing, walking him. I wish I'd been here."

"You were still in nappies then."

"Yeah." He miserably takes a big bite, getting mango all over his beard.

I stare at the teenagers running rings around our team. Finally, after a long pause, I say, "Do you think Wayra should move into Sama's cage?"

Charlie looks at me with surprise. "Do you?"

I gaze at my feet. Finally, I just say, "If Nena says yes, would you help?"

He puts my sticky ice lolly back into my hand. "If I said no, would you still be my friend?"

I laugh, tension releasing in my chest. "No."

"Then I'll help." He turns, winking at the girls and eliciting another peal of giggles. Then he nods towards the court and stands up, stretching and extending his hand to pull me up off the benches. "Come on, it's over. Look, Oso's about to cry."

I stand on the road by myself, the moon just a thin sliver of a single edge. At first the stars fill up everything, the Southern Cross, Orion's Belt, a gazillion flickers I can't name, which make up the Milky Way. Here it's called Willka Mayu, or the Sacred River. Some of the stars move, shooting into the darkness trillions of miles away. Oso has told me that Quechuans animate the dark shapes behind the stars. They see animals, in the absence of light. And these dark-space animals live in the Sacred River, watching over their living, breathing animal counterparts below. Oso told me that this world, the one that lives and breathes, the one that he and I stand on, is represented by the puma. This makes a strange kind of sense to me, as do those dark-space animals. I never used to see anything behind the stars. Just blackness. Now I see Mach'acuay, the Serpent, with their undulating shadow. I see Urcuchillay, the Llama, and Atoq, the Fox at the Llama's feet. I see Hanp'atu, the Toad.

I listen to the toads and frogs now, conducting their nocturnal symphony. Mila used to say that the louder they get, the more likely it is to rain. I don't doubt it. There's a light breeze now that smells of rain, pulling my braided hair off the back of my neck. I brush away the mosquitoes who homed in the moment I got here, like wasps to a bright mango ice lolly. I pace and wave my hands desperately, slapping at the wobbly backs of my thighs. It doesn't do much good, but it helps me from losing my shit. I stare at my phone for a long time, and then I pull up her number.

"¿Hola?" The line crackles, reception terrible anywhere but some indiscriminate place on the road that seems to change every day.

"Hola, Nena," I say, shoving my hands underneath my T-shirt and clasping the phone in the crook of my shoulder.

"¡Laurita!" Nena exclaims. She's probably still out in the jungle, her spider monkeys, dark as those shapes in the sky, curled up in the branches of the trees. Morocha too. She's there now, in those trees, with other monkeys just like her. Nena's face, her black hair caught up in a brightly coloured scarf, gleaming in the starlight, the phone cradled in her hand.

"Nena, ¿todo bien?"

"Sí. Y tú, ¿cómo estás?"

"Bien. Todo bien aquí. Pero . . ." I hesitate, not sure how to get this right. I feel the heavy weight of the dark spaces between the stars watching me. I can almost feel their breath on the back of my neck. "¿Podemos hablar de la jaula de Sama?"

There is a long pause, and then I hear her nod. "Sí."

"Entonces." I take a deep breath. "¿Qué piensas de esto . . . ?"

Charlie and I stare up at the sky. It's a groaning, freezing cold. Four months have passed since that phone call with Nena, and I'm a month short of my leaving date, a date that can't be extended, not this time.

"Are you sure tomorrow's the day?" Charlie asks, bouncing up and down on his toes.

I gulp. "We can't wait anymore."

"It might rain."

"It might." I look at him, my eyes stinging. And I grin, so wide my cheeks hurt. Tomorrow, if all goes well, we will walk Wayra into Sama's old enclosure. It will be the first time in over two years that she will walk with a person on a rope. Charlie and I separate, waving to each other, as I head down her trail. And as I round the corner, moving a little faster, skidding down the bank, I call out:

"Hola, Wayra!" There's a familiar swelling in my heart. She squeaks at my approach. She has two volunteers who take her out on her runners every day. My routine is too erratic to be with her permanently, I need to be in the office or training volunteers on other animals. But I try to see her a few times a week, even if it is just to feed her. She is always happy to see me.

"Hola, sweet pea," I murmur, kneeling down by the fence. I push my hands inside and she squashes them in her excitement, making me wince. Her face has become more ruffled as the years have gone by, her bones more fragile, her fur less well groomed. But she is always perfect. She meows again and I meow back, rubbing her chin. I let her lick my fingertips and nibble at the dirt under my nails, before she races off with a half-hearted hiss and waits, swishing her tail by the door. Her head is all over the place. Up, down, left, right. She hasn't been out today. Her volunteers have been busy with their rakes and machetes, cleaning the trail on the other side of the lagoon, the one that will take us all the way to Sama's.

As I let her out, I try to work out in my head how many times I have walked down the trail to this cage, how many times I've clipped her onto this first runner. A thousand. Two thousand, I don't know. I try to remember every detail, holding each one. The grass-green excitement in her eyes as she tracks me coming. The twitch of her pink nose. The massive sweep of the silvery-grey branches of the mapajo tree, right in the centre of this huge new runner area that stretches over seventy metres and is almost fifteen metres wide. There's a lake-type pond underneath the tree, which she sometimes likes to lie in, chest deep in mud, her white chin brown with swamp, simple happiness in the lines of her muscles. It's getting shadowy, the clouds lowering, and I think she might want to play. Her head is still bobbing, her eyes a little silly, her mouth a little open, her tongue lolling. Instead of picking up a palm leaf, though, which would have been the signal that it's playtime, I go to her instead and crouch just inside the cave of patuju that she has settled in. She immediately leans forwards and begins to lick me, pulling at my arm with her sandpaper tongue. When she is done with one, she switches to the other. When she is done with that, she starts on my hands, and then back to my fingers, and then my fingernails, which are her favourites. As she licks, I run my other hand over her back, her ears, her throat, neck, chin, searching for ticks. I find one, a swollen purple one under her lip. It takes a few tries and a few hisses, but eventually I get a good grip and twist him off, his little legs flailing. The moment he's off, Wayra's searching my hands. I hold the tick obediently on my palm and Wayra takes him in her teeth, chewing. After swilling the little creature around on her tongue, I see her swallow. Then she looks at me, satisfied.

"That's so disgusting, chica." She's the only princess—the only puma—I know who insists on eating ticks.

She doesn't care. She goes back to licking my hands. When she's done, I leave her to complete the process on herself. First her front paws, then her chest, then her white belly, grumbling a low contented moan. I walk to the sentinel tree. Last year, it started leaking a gelatinous orange ooze, seeping into mounds around the roots. When I prod it, it wobbles like brains. Oso told me, when I asked him to come and look, worried that the tree was dying, that the jelly can cure cancer. I touch the bark, warm and silky under my fingers. I've known this tree for over a decade.

"Hey, love," I whisper, turning back, wiping my eyes with frustration. Stop fucking crying! I laugh at myself. Wayra has stopped licking, half on her back, her tail in her mouth, and is watching me suspiciously. I walk back quickly and sit down next to her. We are in a patch of fallen seeds here, bright-red and black ones, and the earth is still slightly damp, seeping into my jeans. The moment I am still, she goes back to her licking.

"Wayra," I say quietly. "Tomorrow, you're going to a new enclosure."
She ignores me.

"You'll never come back here."
She continues to ignore me.

"I need you to be brave, OK?" Wayra gives a low grumble and spits out her tail. Her eyes are huge, pupils tiny pinpricks. Then she yawns and sniffs some wet leaves above her head.

After I've put her back in and she's happily gnawing on some chicken, I go to the lagoon, just for a few moments, and sit at the top of the ridge to watch the colours turn. It's getting dark later again. I love that about wet season. The long days, the early mornings. Dry season is nearly over. We're meant to be in fire season. There are fires every year, but recently the bad years have been falling in cycles. One year on, one off. Last year was terrible. With no rain and no swamp at all, massive swathes of jungle were crackling by mid-June.

Pachamama, the Andean earth mother, is important in Bolivia. About sixty percent of the population identifies as Indigenous, belonging to thirty-six recognised ethnic groups. In 2011, Evo Morales—Bolivia's social-ist, Indigenous, longest-serving president—and his government created the Law of Mother Earth, controversially giving legal rights to all nature, equal with humans. Morales is outspoken in his criticism of industrialised countries and their failure to adequately tackle climate change. However, despite grounding Pachamama at the heart of his politics, industrialisa-tion continues apace. His government has offered the parque barely any financial support, while still relying on us to take many unwanted animals who would find no homes otherwise. And worldwide, in just one decade, a conservative estimate is that corporations have destroyed over fifty mil-lion hectares of forest, largely in the production and use of palm oil, soya, meat and dairy for profit. More of the Amazon is sold off, and the world becomes hotter, drier, wetter, sadder and stormier.

We wouldn't have survived last year if it hadn't been for teams of local volunteer fire fighters—los bomberos—who poured in to help.

This year, though, with one of the worst wet seasons in this area in living memory, most of the jungle never having dried out, swamp still up to our waists, there have been no fires. Not here.

I pick up a handful of sandy toffee-coloured dirt and sieve it through my fingers. The familiar capuchin troop, babies all grown up, sits on the big tree across the water. A pair of night monkeys, eyes huge, are hiding in the bamboo above my head, I can hear them rustling. I watch the black shape of a caiman glide past and laugh, the noise startling me a little. The amount of time I've spent in that water is certifiably insane. Hours, hours which have probably added up to days, weeks of my life, trying to convince Wayra to go swimming. But she hasn't been in in years. Maybe she's finally decided that she doesn't want to get her legs bitten off. I don't know. I still go in. And she just gazes at me from the bank, quietly judging, head on her crossed paws.

She'll never come back here. And I wonder if I'll ever come back, sit on this bank, touch the dirt, watch the monkeys, watch the caimans, watch the family of turtles sunning themselves on their log. The edges of the beach have changed over the years, it's larger than it used to be, the vines and bamboo tamed, we've cut down a few dead trees and there is more space to see the sky. Will I come back and will it feel small? Will it feel like a happy place or just a place where she was stuck, where we were all stuck? The sky is red now. I pick up a dark stone, split down the middle, the inside the colour of caramel and melted milk chocolate, and hold it in my palm, feeling its trapped warmth. Then I throw it, with a heavy plop, into the water, and watch the ripples spread outwards.

By the time I get back to camp, the red sky has faded to black.

"You OK, Frodo?" Sammie eyes me carefully as I step into the fumador. She has come back, just for this. She'll only stay a week. But

I'm grateful she's here. So very grateful. A candle is going on the ledge, fluttering gently.

I nod, wiping streams of tears off my cheeks.

Charlie turns to Ally. "Do you think she's going to start crying before the walk tomorrow, or during?"

Ally makes a face. "I'd say both."

"Fuck you! This is very emotional!" I sniff, laughing. "Moving home is one of the most stressful things anyone can do." I look at Charlie. "Are you ready?"

He jumps up, rubbing his hands together. "I'm an empty vessel. Fill me with knowledge."

"Ropes?"

He holds up the ropes that I made earlier, two ropes five metres long, one thin, one thick, attached together at one end with an automatic-locking carabiner, copies of her old walking ropes. I hold them for a moment, remembering the feel. Then I take them both and clip the ends to my belt.

"Who's going to be Wayra?"

"Oh me! Me!" Ally jumps up and grabs the carabiner.

The four of us troop onto the path.

Ally, on hands and knees, leaps at Charlie, hissing and spitting. She catches him off guard and manages to topple him to the ground.

"No más, Wayra!" Charlie yells, legs flailing.

"Guys!" I snap. "This is serious."

They both stand up, grinning, sheepish.

"Alright, Charlie, go in front. Wayra always has someone walking in front."

"What?" Charlie, rubbing his shin, looks around for confirmation. "Always? That's nuts. None of the other cats—"

"That's Wayra." I shrug.

"OK, cool. But am I going to get fucked up?" He looks at Ally pointedly.

I look down at the ropes. "If anyone's going to get hurt, it'll prob-ably be me." I take a long, shuddery breath, feeling the emotion bub-bling inside me together with everything that has passed between me and Wayra over the past ten years. Quietly I touch the raised scars along my arms. It's been two years, two long years since Wayra and I walked together. By rights, I should go in front. She knows me better, doesn't know Charlie at all. But . . . this will be her last-ever walk. I never thought she would get to walk again. And this is my mission. I can't ask someone else to take the ropes. "This"—I nod to Charlie, indicat-ing that he should start walking—"is how you walk with Wayra . . ."

Charlie and I meet on the patio at five. It's still dark, but I want to walk the trails one last time, to do a final rake of any last leaves, covering the scents of any wild animals that may have prowled during the night. There's no one else up as we set out, just Bruce, keeping an eye on us from the back of the truck in case we're planning on giving him any unsolicited attention. I have my backpack, full of snacks and water in case Wayra decides to lie down in protest. I have my head torch, I have the ropes slung over my shoulder, I have an extra-thick shirt, in case things go badly. We walk in silence. It isn't raining but the clouds are hanging low and dark, blocking out the stars. The frogs are quiet but I can hear the crickets in the grass and the occasional hoot of an owl. The tall white trees sway on both sides of us.

"You remember what to do?" I ask, nervousness and excitement twisting in my stomach when we get to the witch trees.

"Sure. I just laugh when she hisses, stumble a lot because she likes clumsy people, and tell her she's a sweet princess and it's all going to be fine?"

I chuckle, despite myself. "Exactly."

He nods again. "Cool."

"Hola, princess!"

"Hola, darlin'."

I close my eyes briefly. *"Darling?"*

"What?" Charlie crosses his arms. "What's wrong with *darlin*?"

"I don't think she's a darlin'. She's not from North Carolina in the fifties."

"Oh and *sweet pea* suits her so much better?"

We both glare at each other, until we hear Wayra squeak.

"Meow," I squeak back, nudging Charlie. "You do it too."

"That's a ridiculous noise."

"Just do it!"

"Meow!"

Wayra squeaks again and, when we round the corner, she is waiting by the fence. We both crouch and put our arms in. Her face is a beautiful soft grey, chalky in the early golden light. She immediately goes to Charlie and presses her face into his hands. He grins irritatingly. I snort.

"She's a flirt."

"She loves me! Don't you, darlin'?"

Finally when she's done with him, she gives me a cursory lick before running into the doorway, where she lies down and starts avidly licking her belly.

"Alright." I stare at her for a moment.

"Alright," Charlie repeats, his hands in his pockets. "You got this?"

I take a deep, steadying breath. "I've got this."

"Where should I stand?"

"Just where you are. When I let her out, go down the human trail a bit and start calling her." I thread the end of the ropes with her carabiner through the gap in the door. Wayra watches me out of the corner of her eye, her ears back, but she doesn't do anything. She just grumbles as I fumble with the lock, but then it's on and she's up, clipped on, and waiting.

"Alright sweet pea. We've got this, right?"

She turns her head, ever so slightly, and gazes peaceably into my eyes, before hissing so savagely I start backwards a little.

"OK," I laugh. Charlie laughs too, although for the first time a little nervously. I swing open the door, and the grey shadows of dawn still cling to the clearing. Wayra springs out, over the moon to be out so early. She goes like clockwork to the sentinel tree, where she noses around a bit before squatting to pee. It takes her a while, her legs stiff. After she's peed, she thinks for a moment and then turns in a few slow circles. My heart is thudding so loudly, I am sure she'll hear it.

"OK, Wayra," I finally say, taking a deep breath. "We're going to walk."

Charlie agrees, at the start of the trail. "This way, Wayra!" He rustles some palm leaves, trying to catch her interest.

Wayra looks askance at me. She is frozen, unsure what's going on, caught half between wanting to go onto her long runner, as she is used to, and curiosity about what the hell is happening. *Please, Wayra*, I pray. If we can't do it like this, we'll have to sedate you. Sedation in older cats is so dangerous, particularly here in the jungle. They can die from it.

I watch her. Maybe, I think, bracing myself for disappointment, maybe today isn't the day. We'll just have to try again tomorrow, and the next day. If a week passes and she still hasn't done it . . .

"¡Vamos, chica!" I call. She looks at me once more, then races towards me, and I feel my heart jump, but she swerves at the last moment and leaps onto her runner platform, a new one we built last year, where she sits, craning her neck to see what's making all this noise.

"Has she moved?" Charlie calls.

"She's on her platform," I call back. "Keep doing what you're doing."

"Vamos, darlin'!" It sounds as if he's picked up a palm leaf and is waving it at head height through some bracken. Wayra's ears prick up. Steeling myself, I walk in front of her, holding out my hands. Then I unclip her from the runner and put her onto my belt. Her eyes turn black with utter horror and outrage. *What are you* doing? She snarls.

It's been a long time since I've been attached to her like this and I have to gulp, grounding my boot heels into the dirt so that I don't see stars.

"Come on, love," I beg. "We're walking."

She swipes the ropes.

"You can do this, I know it. If I can do it, you can do it."

"¡Vamos, Wayra!" Charlie shouts.

Her head snaps towards the sound of Charlie's voice.

"You can do it," I repeat, in a whisper.

Her eyes grow and then, suddenly, she's off. It takes my brain a few moments to understand and by the time it does, I'm running. We speed past Charlie, I just have time to register his startled face before he's gone. I think she's so shocked to be out, to be down the trail she's seen people arrive from for the thirteen years that she's been in this cage, that she just runs, and once she starts, she doesn't stop. I am so unfit I can't breathe, but I keep going. Over our immaculately clean trails, past the lime tree, past the pink-flowering bush, we are almost at the fork to Amira before she slows. I hear Charlie close behind. Wayra spins, perhaps realising she doesn't know where she is. I jump to the side.

"Go in front," I choke out and Charlie does, skirting past her without hesitating. She watches, her ears back. Remembering this after all these years. Remembering her bodyguard.

"It's OK, darlin'," he soothes. "It's OK."

She doesn't hiss. She just starts walking again, slower now but still at a good trot. She is silent. She doesn't question the fork, she just follows, her eyes wide, her ears going in every direction. Charlie looks back at me over his shoulder.

"Are you crying?"

"No!" I sniffle, wiping away a tear, grinning so much I can't quite see properly.

"You're the worst runner in the world."

"I think I might puke." I laugh, gripping my side.

"Please don't."

"Look at her!" I whisper. "She's so brave."

She keeps on walking, not looking left or right, just forwards. We're approaching the opening to the road now, and here she falters. This is the most dangerous bit. The trail intersects with the road for about five metres before swinging back into the jungle again. This is the place where, once upon a time, I stood before a pile of rocks next to a disgruntled Bryan, having no idea that the enclosure we hadn't even started building would one day lead me here.

"Go forwards," I instruct Charlie. "Go past the road."

Wayra sniffs the air, testing it, scared now, and turns her head back to me uncertainly.

"It's OK," I whisper. "It's OK."

She almost breaks into a run again after Charlie, doesn't even look at the road, just a quick fearful dart of her head, and then we are past the danger, back into the jungle. I'm crying again but it doesn't matter, she just keeps going at a fast trot, totally silent, not even a single hiss or a grumble. This is a good walk. This is a perfect walk. The sun is just coming up, peeking over the canopy, giving the lagoon to our left a pinkish glow.

"We're almost there!" Charlie croons as the trees part and the fence of her new home comes into sight. Then she does stop and I stumble backwards so as not to tread on her tail. We are on the long north edge, and in order to reach the doors we have to skirt left, around the corner of the high fence. I think this might be difficult, but when Charlie goes left, she hisses, just once, at the fence, before following him. I truly think she is just so shocked at being somewhere she doesn't know, that it hasn't quite registered in her brain yet.

"That's right, love," I whisper as she goes around the edge, following Charlie through the open doors. I follow right behind her. Charlie hangs back, I hear him closing the doors behind us and then I'm fumbling with the carabiner at her collar, she is still walking, not sure where she is, I pull the carabiner up and round, and then before she even knows it, she's off.

She stands uncertainly, looking around. The enclosure spreads all around us, left, right and in front. We've cleared this first section a bit, about the size of her old runner area, and there's a raised wooden bed filled with fresh hay, a tepee we've made out of palm leaves, some logs for scratching. Other than this, outside of this open clearing, the patuju plants start, thronging first and then thickening, turning everything dark grassy green. There is a knotted patch of bamboo on our left, a clump of massive palms in front of us, ferns, fanned and silvery, thin red trees next to them, a huge bronze mapajo tree, more patuju . . .

I reach behind me, reaching for Charlie's arm, and grip it hard, thinking I might fall over if I don't.

"Are you OK?"

She spins. She gazes at us. She sees us, she sees *me*, further back than I should be if I was still attached to the ropes, if she was still attached. I watch her calculating the distance, her limbs strangely, doubtfully angled, I watch her understanding, her green eyes widening, turning black, then her pupils falling to pinpricks.

Then she's running. In no particular direction, she just runs. My hand flies to my mouth. The jungle rustles and then she's gone.

We hear her, hear the forest collapsing under the burst of her paws, her body, her muscles, but we don't see her again for many minutes. Slowly the two of us inch backwards and sit on a big log by the doors.

"How long did that take?" I finally whisper.

He lets out a long breath and I see his throat working as he tries to swallow.

"Ten minutes," he says very quietly. "Just ten minutes."

I half laugh, half sob, half I don't know what. It could have taken all day to get here. More than that. "She did it."

"She did!"

"After all that."

"And I thought I was going to see you get fucked up!" he exclaims, laughing, sounding extremely relieved.

"She didn't even hiss."

"She . . ." He hesitates, just as she bursts out of the patuju in a blur. She runs so fast, for a split second I don't quite understand. She's running differently, she looks different, she's . . . Then I get it. She's running without ropes. She's running without ropes and without a fence cutting her off at the corner. She's just running. I remember the first time I ever saw her, and how she'd looked squashed. Outside of the cage, on the trail, she'd looked huge. Expanded. This is like that, only a thousand times more. I watch her, my mouth open, unable to move, unable to process, but Charlie is grabbing my arm, pulling me up. She's sprinting towards us. Her eyes are wide, disbelieving, thrilled. My heart thuds with adrenaline, a free puma coming straight at us, but a few metres away she slows, then she's headbutting my legs. I put my arms down to block in case she's planning on jumping, but she just starts licking. I immediately sit down again, and she pushes herself into my chest, licking, licking my arms and hands. Then she begins to purr. Normally whenever I've heard her purr, she cuts off quickly after a few moments, after she remembers that the world isn't so great. But now she just keeps going, reverberating through the top layer of my chest and into my heart.

"Oh my . . . *goodness!*" The words come out kind of garbled.

She moves on to Charlie and licks him too. She continues to purr, purr and purr and purr. She stays with us for another few minutes, precious minutes, before leaping away, disappearing again. She goes, comes back, goes, comes back. After a while, her sides heaving, exhausted, she sniffs the fence, licks some branches, scratches a tree log, before lying down in some wet leaves a few yards away from us and putting her head on her paws, leaning a little to the side, her cheek just touching the damp earth. And she just continues to purr.

"I've never heard her do that," I finally say, not quite believing that this is real, this is actually happening, she is lying in front of us not on a rope, with more than half an acre of jungle that is now hers.

"Is she . . ." Charlie hesitates, as if he doesn't dare say it.

"Saying thank you?" I whisper.

"Yeah."

I just stare at her. I stare and stare, unable to speak, unable to even think past the fact that she's done it, we've done it, it's over, we're here.

"This . . . ," Charlie finally says, searching for words, "is amazing."

"Yes," I agree, laughing dizzily. She falls silent and eventually falls asleep in the sun. The two of us sit on the broken log. Finally I pull out my phone and dial.

"¿Hola? ¿Laurita?"

"Nena," I whisper.

"¿Sí, todo bien?" Nena's tone is strained, stressed. "¿Qué pasó?"

I put my head in my hands. "Nena. Wayrita está en la nueva jaula."

"¿En serio?" Nena exclaims, the phone crackling.

"Sí." I nod, my legs starting to shake.

"Oh, Laurita," Nena whispers. "¿Ella es feliz?"

"Sí." Relief, shock, pride, disbelief. It clamours so loudly I can barely hear anything. I can barely hear my own words. She is happy. *Happy.* "Wayra es feliz." And then we both burst into tears.

EPILOGUE

It is early 2019. There's a tree in her enclosure. It's right in the middle, in the places I never went to with Sama, the places I never saw. We walk there, Wayra and I.

She purred every day, in the beginning. For months, she played every day too. She was blissfully, gorgeously happy. Recently, the world has started to leak in again, I think, and her pain is coming back. Sometimes she hisses at nothing, sometimes she growls. But it's sometimes. It's not always. It's not like it was. She's not like she was.

She limps as we walk, favouring her front right paw, trying not to put weight on her back legs. Stiff in the musty wet of another dying summer. The cold will be here again soon, bringing the winds that rock trees out of their root systems, that make us pull on our beanies and fleece jackets. Then the fires will come again, nightmarish, the dread of smoke on the breeze across Brazil, Bolivia, Paraguay . . .

Now, though, it's still wet hot. There's an underlayer to the air that smells autumnal. Falling leaves scatter the earth around our feet with bruised purple. Wayra and I walk down the paths she's made for herself, she is inches behind me, which is how she likes it still. She wears no ropes, or collar. I feel a slight tingling between my shoulder blades, the whisper of a puma stepping on my shadow, but it's no more than that. Mostly, it feels like walking with a friend.

When we reach the middle, I look up into the branches. I don't know the tree's name, but I know its canopy spreads like a weeping willow's, knotting a thousand times and enclosing this tiny clearing with its carpet of violet and gold. I can hear the high *ee ee, ee ee* of a bird, the resonant shriek of another, piercing the morning with its car alarm. The tree's bark is the colour of honey. The limbs are thick, sturdy, wrapped in mossy spots and whorls that are rough when I touch them. There are still scratch marks from Sama around the trunk. The leaves are dark green, almost black on the bottom, and they feel like wet paper when I hold one in my hand.

Wayra, who's standing by my side, so close I can feel the heat of her fur on my thigh, the thump of her excited heartbeat, is looking upwards too. I know that soon I'll have to bring Oso out here with his machete, and we'll have to cut some of these branches down. It's not safe for her to be climbing, not good for her arthritis, but . . . not yet. Not now. Now her eyes are swollen with the early light, the sky still pink. I can smell citrus. Her nose is wet, her ears, dipped in charcoal, turned towards the noise of the birds. The monkeys will be coming soon, capuchins, squirrel monkeys. I feel a rush of heat, a tingling up my spine, a sense of just being gloriously, luckily, wildly here. With her.

Suddenly her tail quivers and she's up. She's in the top branches, the tree rattling, five metres above my head, ten, and I step back so that I can watch her. I'm here because she says it's OK. My heart thuds with alarm—*Please don't fall*—and respect as she leaps blindly, perfectly, through the canopy. She's covered Sama's scratch marks with her own, over and over like a language, like a claiming. I've touched them too, pressing my fingers into the scars.

She stands, poised between tree branches, her tail juddering, her mouth wide, indescribably content, her eyes and mine pulling upwards into a pale pinkish-gold sky that is just starting to rain, pattering against our faces and the leaves that are papery thin, dark bottle-green like glass.

I wish I could end this book here.

I want to tell you that the parque is thriving. That we're inundated with eager volunteers. That all our staff are from the local communities, and that those strong links have balanced out our work, making it long-lasting, sustainable and hopeful. That all the animals are healthy, in fact that nobody gives us animals anymore at all, because the trade in illegal pets has plummeted. That I don't fly anymore. That deforestation is over, climate change isn't happening, Australia hasn't been on fire, the Amazon and communities across the Global South aren't being destroyed by mining companies looking for minerals for mobile phones, oil companies aren't setting up new pipelines, multinationals and governments aren't turning the forests into monocrops . . .

Inti Wara Yassi means "sun," "star," and "moon" in Quechua, Aymara and Chiriguano-Guaraní. "The parque," as I call it here, is Sanctuary Ambue Ari, one of three sanctuaries run by Comunidad Inti Wara Yassi (CIWY), a Bolivian NGO, founded in 1992. Back then, Bolivian volunteers started working with miners' families in La Paz, up in the country's highlands. They hoped to give the young people in those families a sense of purpose, teaching them life skills while also showing them the beauty of their country. Along the way, the volunteers and the young people encountered deforestation, slash-and-burn agriculture, and wild animals in cages. So together they set up the first-ever sanctuary for rescued wild animals in Bolivia. That sanctuary was called Machía and it's where Nena, one of CIWY's founders, now lives with her spider monkey friends.

It has been a bad year—for CIWY, for Bolivia and for the world. By September 2019, Bolivia will have lost nearly 2.4 million hectares of forest and savanna due to wildfires. This is the same amount of rainforest destroyed as in Brazil, despite Bolivia being one-eighth the size. On top of this, and perhaps in part because of this, Bolivia's president Evo Morales (stalwartly holding on to power since 2006) got caught engaging in election fraud and went into exile in Mexico. There were riots and fighting across the country between the collas—Evo's diehard supporters, the coca farmers, Indigenous groups from the altiplano—and the cambas: the richer, lowland communities, accusing Evo of corruption, trickery and election rigging.

Machía is a sanctuary that a decade ago used to depend on fifty to eighty volunteers during high season, but this year, there have been months where Machía didn't have a single volunteer. Ambue Ari, during Christmas 2018, had three volunteers. Our third sanctuary, Jacj Cuisi (land of dreams), often has no volunteers at all, even though it's near Rurrenabaque, one of the most popular jungle tourist spots. We have no fewer animals to care for, only fewer people, tighter budgets and less land. It has been confirmed that the government will be expanding the road that goes through Machía, so busy now it often takes twenty minutes for Nena to cross it, going between her spider monkeys and her house on the other side of the road. There are just so many trucks. This new road will destroy a large portion of Machía's infrastructure, killing swathes of jungle and leaving countless animals without homes. We're trying to find a way to move the animals in our care to Jacj Cuisi, but it's a mammoth task.

Every year, it seems that Western science delves a little bit further into the different sentient intelligences that human beings share this planet with. Catching up, just a little bit, with what many Indigenous communities have known for a long time. It's been proven by scientists, for example, that birds can see Earth's magnetic fields, and this is how they migrate. Every single cow has its own unique moo. An octopus not only uses tools but stores them for future use. The nocturnal African dung beetle orientates itself by the Milky Way. And pumas are not solitary carnivores. As it turns out, in the wild they exist in complex social networks, spreading over great distances, which include such friendly social interactions as sharing food.

Despite this, though, the illegal wildlife trade just keeps on growing. It's a multibillion-dollar industry and has only increased with the advent of social media—where photos of a "cute" baby puma doing "cute" baby things will go viral instantaneously. In Bolivia—and of course, across the world—there are countless animals and humans who are homeless. Or homed in dire conditions. And there are the animals and humans that Nena and the parque struggle to care for every day, because we don't have the space, we don't have the staff, we don't have the volunteers, we don't have the support from the government, we don't have the money, or we simply are just too fucking tired.

I'm in my little house in the parque packing my bags to go back home. Wayra has been in her "new" enclosure for almost two years now and I've been lucky enough to be here again, spending several months with her and helping out where I can. I swallow the guilt about the flights because the alternative is that I do not see her. I try to rationalise it, try to make it sound better in my head. This is the only flight I'll take all year! I'll plant trees to make up for it! I'll balance it out, I swear . . . but really, the truth is, I'd just be heartbroken if I didn't come. If I couldn't see her again.

I'm not alone in how much I return. But there are many, of course, who don't return so much. Many who didn't return at all. This doesn't make the love they found here any less. Each one could write a book, and I wish I knew how many people have come to the parque, for two weeks or two years, and changed the trajectory of their lives because of it. I can name hundreds who, as a result, have become vets, nurses, environmental scientists, biologists, lawyers, social and environmental campaigners, activists and organisers. I, in turn, became an artist and a writer. I ran ONCA in Brighton for six years until I finally realised that after the parque, I'd never be happy in a city. I moved to a little Scottish island with my rescue dog, Nelo, who is quite a lot like Wayra, and who has found life on the island to be healing, although sometimes—like Wayra—he still finds it impossible to forget.

ONCA, at the time of writing, is thriving. It's run by a team who blows my mind every day and I love them with all my heart. They have taught me, when I'm sad, to remember that the boundaries of our worlds can stretch, as long as our imaginations are broad enough. That is the hope that I find in the parque too. It is a place that wouldn't have existed without the imagination of those first Bolivian volunteers, their bravery and force of will. It was built not with a pointy stick, a sword, a singular hero. But more as a bag, a carrier, a vessel. This is a thought taken from one of the writers who's helped me process this journey. Ursula K. Le Guin. In her visionary essay from 1986, "The Carrier Bag Theory of Fiction," she talks about how it might be possible to change the way stories are told—moving away, perhaps, from the violent power of singular heroes. Towards collaboration and compost, cooperation and connection. The parque, for me, is a place where these things come together. Where we "compost" side by side, and where not just people but creatures—whatever species, whatever their story, whichever way they are broken—find homes. Where we all just bob along together to make the connections that matter. Because it's the connections that make the difference, right?

My bag is packed, and it is half the size it was when I arrived. It contains the same things I bring every year. The leggings, the shirts, full of holes and stained, smelly no matter how many times I wash them, but soft. A few silly eighties jackets, great against the mozzies. My head net, an old friend, and my head torch. Some bras. Absent are the jars of peanut butter I've lived on over the past few months, the presents I brought for Doña Lucia, and all the pills, ointments, vet equipment. The turmeric for the cats, glucosamine, milk powder. I pick up my feather-light bag and before heading out the door, I take a last long look at my room. Hopefully I will be back by around this time next year. Hopefully I won't be too late for a bit of swamp. And hopefully, just hopefully, Wayra will still be here, waiting for me at the turn of the trail, where the jungle turns bottle-green.

ACKNOWLEDGMENTS

Ever since I first visited Ambue Ari, I've been writing this book in my head. It's a love letter to Wayra, to the jungle, and to the place and the people that changed my life.

I would never have gone to Bolivia, and I would never have met Wayra, if it hadn't been for my parents. I would never have continued to go without the support of my whole family, and my friends. You know who you are. There are not enough words to say thank you.

To all my first readers—my collaborators, listeners and my friends. My mum, first and last and a thousand times in the middle. Jo, my sister. Sarah, Karen, Persephone, Alex, Lucas and Jon. And to Nelo, always.

To Nena. It just isn't possible to express everything that you do, and all the love that you have in your heart. Thank you, Nena. Thank you more than I can say. Thank you for creating this home, for keeping it safe, and for never ever giving up.

To Oso, Germán, Jaime, Agrippina and Eugenia. Germáncito, we love you, and you will always be in our hearts.

To Doña Lourdes, for love given always and without question.

To todos los bomberos, the firefighters and protectors.

To every single one of Wayra's volunteers and friends.

To my wonderful agent, Samar, and editor Liza, for your unfailing patience and belief in me, and this book.

To Wayra, Coco and Faustino, Panchita, Lorenzo, Big Red, Flighty, Bitey, Bambi, Rudolfo, Herbie, Tony, Gordo, Sama, Lazy Cat, Leo, Sayan, Koru, Juan, Carlos, Rupi, Ru, Katie, Amira, Inti, Wara, Yassi, Engine, OB, Kevo, Luci, Marley, Elsa, Roy, Flashman, Capitán, Gato, Balu, Iskra, Matt Damon, Mundi, Bruce, Panapana, Panini, Teanji, Tess, Mimi, Angela, Beepers, Vlad, Biton, Romeo and Juliet. And to all the others I cannot and haven't named.

To Vanesso, who died of tumours in his heart while I was writing this ending.

And lastly, but never last, to the jungle.

Wild animals are not pets. They should live in their own habitat with their own species. Maybe there is a future where no animal is kept in a cage. Maybe somewhere, places like CIWY will not need to exist, and books like this won't need to be written. But for now, proceeds from this book are going to support CIWY's work fighting the illegal wildlife trade, supporting local communities and providing safe homes to those who need them. If you too would like to help, either by volunteering or making a donation, please visit CIWY's website: www.intiwarayassi.org.

ABOUT THE AUTHOR

Photo © 2020 Eva Coleman

Laura Coleman was born in Sussex, in the south of England. She studied English literature and art history at university and received a master's in art history. In 2007, she went to Bolivia and joined the NGO Comunidad Inti Wara Yassi (CIWY), which manages three wildlife sanctuaries and gives homes to animals rescued from illegal wildlife trafficking. It was this work, and the communities and the stories that she found there, that inspired her to start the Brighton-based organisation ONCA. (*Panthera onca* is the scientific name for *jaguar*.) Bridging social and environmental justice issues with creativity, ONCA promotes positive change by facilitating inclusive spaces for creative learning, artist support, story sharing, and community solidarity. In 2018, Laura moved to the Small Isles in Scotland with her friend, a dog called Nelo. She lives and writes by the sea, whilst still being on the board of ONCA and Friends of Inti Wara Yassi, the UK-based charity that supports CIWY's work.